Joel White

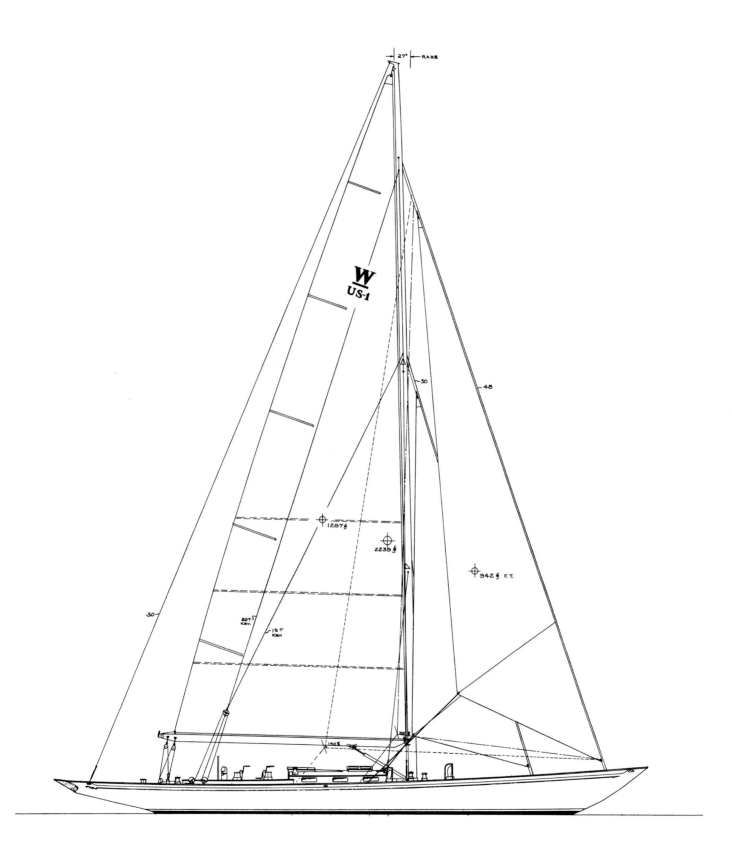

Joel White

Boatbuilder / Designer / Sailor

By Bill Mayher and Maynard Bray

Photographs by Benjamin Mendlowitz

NOAH PUBLICATIONS
BROOKLIN, MAINE

Book design by Faith Hague

Printed by Mondadori Printing, Italy

Published by NOAH Publications, Reach Road, Brooklin, ME 04616

www.noahpublications.com

Distributed by W.W. NORTON & COMPANY, INC

500 Fifth Avenue, New York, NY 10110

www.wwnorton.com

First Edition

ISBN 0-9608964-0-6

1 2 3 4 5 6 7 8 9 0

Illustration Credits

Color photography by Benjamin Mendlowitz

Color drawings by Kathy Bray

Black-and-white photography courtesy of Joel White's family and friends

Plans drawn by Joel White, except where otherwise noted

For Joel White

1930–1997

Contents

Foreword

Joel White would have strenuously resisted the notion of a book that focused such attention upon him. Not that he would have resisted publicizing his designs—at least those he was proud of—but he would focus much more on them than on him. Such was the unassuming style he brought to his days overlooking Center Harbor where, from his drafting table three stories above the Brooklin Boat Yard pier, he watched the actions and motions of water, wind, and all manner of boats. At once an artist and a scientist, he was a romantic with a realist's sense of discipline. He was not drawn to the spotlight, but to the perfecting of his art, and his toughest client was himself.

Yet he was far from all business. Those of us who treasured his friendship loved and appreciated his ability to respond to us as if we were the only persons in the world who mattered. He could focus intently on the needs of the moment, whatever they were. But I am sure he had no idea how many lives he touched with his quiet, unpretentious, and generous style. Indeed, an observer unfamiliar with his character might ask how he came to inspire such wide admiration and respect when he spoke so softly and with such economy; when he worked so hard to avoid the seductive glow of the limelight; when he protected so carefully his privacy, and the quiet and happy constancy of his days—at the boat yard, at his drafting table, at the helm of his *Ellisha*; at home in the evening with his wife, Allene.

Joel was a colleague, a mentor, and a friend, and he influenced my own life and work tremendously, in much the same way that he influenced the the lives and works of many others—mostly in ways unseen to him. He encouraged the kind of excellence and integrity that helped elevate the standards to which we at *WoodenBoat* continue to aspire. His legacy extends far beyond the boats he designed and built. He was a great listener, and there was very little that he didn't take in. He was also a great counselor. Especially in his ability to remain silent until he had something useful to say. When he spoke, others listened. His wisdom and experience were especially invaluable at Connecticut's Mystic Seaport Museum, where he was a devoted trustee and a member of the Yachting and Watercraft committees, and where he brought his firm but gentle style to much of the planning and thinking.

Joel's design style was very much in the tradition of the great genius Nathanael Herreshoff, and yet thoroughly original, as in the case of the little Nutshell pram, perhaps his best-known design, which we commissioned, and for which about 2000 sets of plans have been sold around the world. The response to this design surprised and delighted no one more than he, and I think he loved those modest royalty checks more than almost any other fees he received. But it's a design elegantly simple and practical, and it was no wonder that so many have thought so much of it. His astonishment only confirmed his lack of pretension. These days, many yacht designers work hard to complicate their creations; Joel worked hardest to simplify his, remaining committed to the concept of spare and unadorned elegance, and to the future of wooden boats. He was a man who worked and lived exactly according to his beliefs. There are people who saw in Joel's days a life perfectly lived, and he was the envy of many. He lived what he loved, and loved what he lived. I think he felt very lucky, but I also think he felt very ordinary—not special at all. He just did what he loved to do, and made no more of it than that.

Years ago, I wrote a profile of Joel for a magazine called *Mercedes*, published for the car owners. There is a point in the piece where I referred to his having listened to his father's early advice that the most important thing in life was to work at something you loved. When the story was published, I got a letter from his father, who had just received a copy of the magazine. He began by lamenting the fact that he knew about the story only because he had a Mercedes, not because Joel had mentioned it. But he found himself surprised to read that Joel had ever paid attention to anything he'd said to him. He was, he wrote, proud to know that his son had listened at the right moment, and that he'd accomplished so much with what he loved.

When Joel began his battle with cancer, it became much harder for him to travel, but in the summer of 1996, he decided to attend the WoodenBoat Show at Mystic. An occasion arose to salute him when Donald Tofias, the man who commissioned his design for the 76-foot W-Class, announced at the exhibitors' dinner that construction of two boats was soon to begin. The crowd of some two hundred began to clap, and we persuaded a reluctant Joel, who'd been quietly resting a tired leg weakened by a recent hip replacement, to stand and receive the applause. As he labored to his feet with his crutch to support him, the crowd rose quickly to a standing ovation, and there was hardly a dry eye in the place.

These days, the waters of Eggemoggin Reach and our nearby bays feel emptier without Joel White sailing upon them. But the wakes of his boats have crisscrossed these waters for decades, and we can still sense his trailing wakes. We can see where he's been, and feel what he's seen. The legacy he left in the boats he designed and built is a rich and inspiring one, and this book is a celebration of that legacy. He would, no doubt, be a little embarrassed at the ways in which Maynard Bray, Bill Mayher, and Benjamin Mendlowitz have made so much of him, but they would have done no less to esteem and honor his enduring contributions to the world of classic boats.

—JON WILSON, FOUNDER, *WOODENBOAT* MAGAZINE

Introduction

Joel White was a boat builder and naval architect who lived and worked in Brooklin, Maine. Joel was well known in wooden boat circles for the vessels built at his yard, for his designs, and for his writing in *WoodenBoat* Magazine. The impetus for this book came when Donald Tofias, the yachting entrepreneur for whom Joel White designed the W-Class 76', read the profile of White that Maynard, Benjamin and myself had put together for *Maritime Life and Traditions*, and suggested we expand it into a book.

Given our affection for Joel and our respect for him as a craftsman, the chance to write a more detailed account of his life around boats was both a daunting challenge and a treasured opportunity. Just as in the *Maritime* piece, one thing seemed clear: our primary goal must be to provide readers with access to the plans Joel drew, pictures of the boats he built, and as a bonus, share his unpublished writing about sailing. By doing this, we reasoned, people would come to understand that his mastery was based on a fusion of design, construction, and use. Here was a guy who never forgot his tool box; who couldn't walk through his boatyard on the way to his drafting board without those laser beam eyes of his scanning work in progress. If for Joel the drawn line and the sawn line weren't very different, then we should try to make it so in a book about him.

The other reason plans and pictures of boats must predominate is because that is what he would have wanted. For Joel, work was his life, and what he wanted to be remembered for was the boats. If readers could learn something from them or share in the happiness he felt every time he set out on the water, all the better.

Early on, readers are sure to note that there aren't any footnotes or much of anything in the way of attribution. This might raise questions about how we came to the conclusions we did. Our answer is simply that each of us spent a whole lot of time with Joel White. As designs took shape in his mind or on the drafting table, it wasn't long before Maynard was brought in as an integral part of the process. Their relationship (based so clearly on the respect Joel always held for Maynard's knowledge of and enthusiasm about boats) is the thing that makes the design commentaries in this book unique.

For Benjamin, Joel quickly recognized his talents as a marine photographer, encouraged him at every turn, and always welcomed him around the yard and around the boats. For a young photographer discovering the inklings of what he wanted to do with his life, such support made all the difference. Their relationship deepened as the two worked together on *Wood, Water & Light*, a striking collaboration that brought Joel to the front as a writer.

As for me, Joel and I were just chums sharing—for half a lifetime—afternoon sails down Eggemoggin Reach, weeks of cruising every summer, or (waiting for paint to dry) a quiet Saturday morning's talk in the shop. Over the years I learned pretty much all I know about boats from him, and it is no exaggeration to say that my new career as a cub reporter in the maritime trades developed because of the hours we spent together. Joel had a vivid way with language. When I wrote about our travels together for this book, it was easy to hear his voice. In fact, I hear it still.

This book would not have been possible without the enthusiastic involvement of Joel's family. His wife Allene and son Steve provided us unlimited access to his designs, family photographs, Joel's transatlantic diary, and to the recollections about his early life in boats that Joel was writing shortly before he died. Allene, Steve, Joel's daughter Martha and her husband Taylor Allen were also kind enough to read through the text of the book as we tried to get it down right. Their careful attention to detail and thoughtful suggestions are deeply appreciated. What errors remain, are ours alone.

In addition to the White family, Bob Stephens, Joel's design colleague at the Brooklin Boat Yard, read the commentaries and provided additional details concerning Joel's thinking on his later designs. The clarity and strength of Kathy Bray's renderings of boats from Joel's plans give us all a feel for them, especially those that were never built.

As mentioned, Donald Tofias played a crucial role. He not only had the idea for the book in the first place, but without his commitment and support of production quality, it would not exist in its present form. We are indebted as well to Jim Mairs at W.W. Norton & Co. for embracing the project, to Roger Duncan for giving us permission to quote from his *Cruising Guide to the New England Coast*, and to Kin Howland for providing photos of the schooner *Integrity*.

We are particularly grateful to Deborah Brewster for her patience, good humor, and sharp eye as the book's editor. Drafts are easier to write when one is confident they will be treated well. Julie Mattes and Anita Jacobssen of the NOAH Publications staff made myriad contributions to the production. Finally, we would like to thank our art director, Faith Hague, who quickly and skillfully grasped the concepts we were shooting for and then put them into practice on every page.

At last we come to our wives Anne, Caroline, and Deborah whose long friendships with Joel made them invaluable partners over the course of the project.

—BILL MAYHER, BROOKLIN, MAINE

PART I

The Making of a Designer

By Bill Mayher

A Life Full of Boats

Amid the clutter of modern yacht design, a Joel White boat stops us in our tracks. It is so straightforward, so clean. Yet for all its simplicity, our glance can't break away. White is hardly the most famous yacht designer of recent times, nor the most prolific, yet few others have brought forth a more consistently defined blending of gracefulness and performance in their work than he, especially in the last years of his life. Looking at one of his designs we find ourselves standing still, eyes gliding over its harmony of lines and surfaces—a harmony that makes us wonder what life-history around boats made this possible.

Joel began his career as a boatbuilder when, at the age of ten, he and his father found time together to build a little rowing scow from plans in the *American Boys Handy Book*. *Flounder* was launched in the pasture pond below their barn so that Joel could go about the serious business of catching frogs and learning to row. From that event—through a lifetime of building and designing at his own boatyard—the drawing, construction, and use of a boat would form for him a single, continuous arc of considerations. A state of mind. No lines, points or stations would go down on his drawing board without simultaneous thought about how these elements might actually be built; and nothing would be built without careful consideration of ultimate use. Before sharp tools were applied to wood, there would be practical choices: choices that he welcomed and seemed to make instinctively.

From Joel's point of view, a boat should contain no unnecessary components and—as far as possible—should avoid serving cross-purposes. Cruising sailboats should look good and deliver us in comfort and in good season. Daysailers should take us down the bay swiftly and in style. A scow with a crane on it should have the muscle to get the work done. Yet at the same time, boats were meant to be more than strictly utilitarian objects. Joel always left room for magic. Accordingly, he thought a rowboat should do more than bring us out to the mooring. Each time we set out, it should remind us of the fun and elegance of rowing. He despised waste. It made him snort, audibly. But things done in support of a boat's aesthetic, if successful, were in no way extraneous because boats, by his way of thinking,

Grace, *the first Center Harbor 31.*
Elegant, simple, and fast.

The Nutshell Pram—a perfect boat for learning to row.

were meant to delight us with their beauty. Why else would we own them? Why else would we let them take over that corner of our lives having to do with water and sky and a morning's breeze?

Besides *Flounder*, other skiffs and peapods would come along to carry him further afield under oar power, first around his home waters of Allen Cove and later out of Center Harbor on the other side of town. Joel was drawn by the independence an able skiff provided. These tiny voyages turned him into a lifelong rower and he never lost his knack for achieving an efficient, graceful stroke in different boats and in varying sea conditions. Later in his life one of the things he regretted most acutely about the contemporary boating scene was the arrival of the unrowable rubber ducky tender. For Joel their near universal acceptance as dinghies meant that most youngsters would never experience the thrill of learning to row a good rowboat and thus have no incentive to learn how to row at all. His convictions in this regard became so strong, in fact, that he designed and built the Nutshell Pram precisely so that Maynard Bray's daughter, Sarah, and my daughter, Jenny, would never lack for safe, small boats—boats that would, above all else, be fun to row. As for Joel, little boats never lost their fun. On many mornings over the course of a cruise, we would hear him awake early to take his peapod for a long row combining exploration, exercise, and meditation in equal measures.

Joel's Herreshoff 12½ footer Shadow *poised for yet another summer. Acquired when he was a boy, she taught him all he could learn from a small boat. He never sold her.*

Five years after the launch of *Flounder*, Joel's father helped him buy a used gaff-rigged Herreshoff 12½ footer. Joel named her *Shadow* and set out onto Eggemoggin Reach with his first command. As it turned out, *Shadow* and Joel were born in the same year. For people who witnessed their travels, day-after-summer's-day, such coincidental birth dates seemed like no accident. Soon he grew experienced enough so that his parents (both of whom shared considerable anxiety about boats themselves) allowed him to venture forth on solo camping trips aboard *Shadow*. The trip he remembered most vividly was a three-day circumnavigation of Deer Isle. Here is what he would write about the voyage in the last year of his life:

It took a great deal of coaxing before my mother could be talked into this desperate escapade, which seemed to be to her the height of folly, and it was only my father's quiet intervention which finally made it happen. I suspect he was a bit nervous about the idea, but remembering his own inexperienced youthful sailing days, felt the time had come for the fledgling to spread his wings. I loaded the boat with food, sleeping bag, tarp to go over the boom for shelter, water jug, a scary single-burner gasoline stove, and tied the dinghy astern before setting off towards the Deer Isle Bridge and East Penobscot Bay. The first night was spent in the outer reaches of Northwest Cove off the town of Deer Isle. After supper as night was falling, we were visited by a big thunder storm which filled the western sky with churning black clouds and a quite impressive lightning display. Just before the storm hit, a kindly man rowed out from shore and suggested I might prefer to weather it out on a pretty little cruising ketch rather than in the cramped cockpit of *Shadow* under a leaking tarpaulin. I gratefully accepted his offer, quickly rowed over, and spent the next hour aboard the ketch while thunder and lightning, wind and rain, swept the cove.

The next morning we (*Shadow* and I) sailed down the western side of Deer Isle, tearing along under double reefs in the strong northwester and sparkling sunshine which had filled in behind the previous night's storm. Jibing over to port at Mark Island lighthouse we entered Deer Isle Thoroughfare, zipping past Stonington with its large fishing fleet and granite quarry, and finally fetched up for the night in Webb Cove, providing good shelter from the northwester. The next day the regular southwester had returned and we made easy work of the passage home, through the Lazygut Islands, past Sunshine, back into the eastern end of Eggemoggin Reach. This was my first cruise as captain of my own ship, and I still remember it as a milestone in my nautical life. My mother seemed excessively happy to see me on my return to the house in North Brooklin—she was never really comfortable with things maritime, and had probably spent a bad three days worrying over the errant navigator. For me the trip only whetted my appetite for cruising to farther shores in larger boats.

Clearly those summers aboard *Shadow* taught Joel nearly all a boy could learn from a small boat and he remembered the lessons well. No matter how large the yachts he designed later in his life became, Joel believed that whenever he or anyone else took the helm of a sailing craft, they should feel the boat move through the skin of their fingers, just as he had done as a boy aboard *Shadow*. Each design of his—from the 7½ foot Nutshell Pram through the 76 footers *Wild Horses* and *White Wings*—surprises us with its lightness of touch.

Joel also had fond memories of sailing aboard his father's little cruising boat *Astrid*. He recalled his first experiences this way:

> I became interested in boats at an early age—my father was boat crazy and passed that rogue gene on to me. My earliest boating memory is of standing on a dock in City Island, New York, looking down onto the deck of a pretty double-ended cutter named *Astrid*. Her hull was white, her decks light green set off by darker green trim and guardrails. Her wooden spars were painted an orange buff color and her furled sails were of khaki canvas. Her massive tiller was varnished, of an unknown southern hardwood with a strong grain pattern. It was 1935 and my dad had just purchased *Astrid* for use around our home waters in Maine. She was a Larry Huntington design, thirty feet in length with a raised deck amidships to give headroom. (She

Mark Island Light—one of the landmarks that guided Joel on his first solo cruise.

actually provided headroom for my mother who was 5' tall, and for me, who was five. My dad, who was 5'10" had to stoop a little.) After the delivery trip to Maine, she was a summertime member of the family, hanging to her mooring in Allen Cove in Blue Hill Bay, and transporting us on many a day sail, short cruise, or perhaps most common of all, a mackerel fishing expedition. Mackereling was a big summer occupation in those days, and the schools were numerous and bountiful. They were caught by chumming, attracting the schools to the boat with chumbait made of ground-up clams, oatmeal, cornmeal, and vegetable or olive oil. The fish were caught on weighted jigs at the end of a light handline, baited with a clam. It was not uncommon to catch 200–300 in an afternoon, sharing the catch with friends and neighbors and putting up many of them in jars to eat next winter.

My most vivid recollection of *Astrid* is of her smells. She was built in Florida of southern cedar, and its strong aroma was always present aboard. In addition there was the slight presence of kerosene, from the running lights stored in the forepeak, tarred marlin in the brown ditty bag, and just a trace of mothballs, left over from last winter's storage of the bright red Hudson's Bay blankets on her main cabin bunks. Sometimes a whiff of gasoline from the Palmer auxiliary behind the companionway ladder, and traces of breakfast bacon.

I liked everything about the short cruises I took with my father— the preparations beforehand when we collected food, ice, clothing, and drinks on the shore which were rowed out to *Astrid* in her eight-foot dinghy. I liked casting off the home mooring and bearing away for new places, the ebb and flow of the strong Maine tides, the selection of the destination for the night, and the splash of the kedge going down in the late afternoon. I liked the warmth of the Shipmate stove fired with short pieces of wood or charcoal briquettes. I liked the boat meals cooked on the Shipmate, the washing up afterwards in the tiny sink. Most of all I liked the snug feeling of bedtime in the forward pipe berth, the gurgles and slap of water against the hull, the creak of the anchor rode on the bowsprit roller as a small puff swung her in some deserted, spruce-rimmed cove. Waking early in the low, strong morning light, I would creep on deck to examine the new day and imagine its pleasures yet to be.

This joy of cruising has never left me—it remains undiminished sixty years after those first early trips. The same simple pleasures still delight, just as they did when I was only eight or nine. The smell of

*Sunset on Eggemoggin Reach,
Joel's home waters for a lifetime.*

the wood smoke from the Charley Noble is the same smell, the afternoon sun glinting off the wave tops has the same sparkle. So much in life changes beyond repair or recall that there is a wonder in small changeless things. Crawling into the bunk at night after a day of great sailing, with the anchor down in a new cove, and the last light of day fading from the sky, the old thrill returns, as does the small boy.

Between those boyhood days aboard *Flounder*, *Astrid*, and *Shadow*, and full-time work as a boatbuilder, Joel attended Phillips Exeter Academy and Cornell University, took a degree in naval architecture at MIT, married Allene and started a family, worked six months as a naval architect at Newport News Shipbuilding and Dry Dock in Virginia, was drafted into

Joel and Allene back in Brooklin upon their return from his Army duty in Germany.

Before building boats, Joel went lobstering.

the Army, served as an enlisted man in Germany, and then headed home to Maine for good.

The first summer back home in Brooklin he bought a bare wooden hull built in Nova Scotia, had her towed to Brooklin, finished her off as a 30′ lobsterboat, and went to haul traps in Jericho and Blue Hill Bays. As a boy, Joel had often accompanied his neighbor Charlie Henderson out lobstering, and remembered those trips with great fondness:

Charlie liked to get underway early, to beat the afternoon breeze, and because the early mornings are so fine. The skiff is loaded with tubs of bait and two five-gallon cans of gasoline. The boy crawls in the stern, and the oars creak in the locks as the skiff moves out into the anchorage. Aboard the boat, Henderson goes through his start-up ritual. The ancient Palmer is fired by magneto, which is carefully swaddled in a bit of old sweater against the night damp. This is removed, the gasoline poured into the tank, the bait swung aboard and stowed beneath the washboards aft. The copper knifeswitch is carefully closed, several turns of pot warp wrapped about the flywheel, and Henderson grunts as he tugs hard on the warp. The engine sighs but does not start.

On the second try, to my great relief, the engine comes to life, running fitfully for a bit before settling down to an even pace. Henderson goes forward to attach the skiff and cast off the mooring. We head across the cove, round the point, and turn to the south heading down the bay towards the first traps of the day. Charlie sharpens his jackknife on a small round whetstone, carves a chunk of tobacco from the plug of George Washington, kneads it in the palm of his hand to break it up, and lights the first pipe of the day. The strong aroma seems to loosen his tongue, and he starts to joke about local events and amusing neighbors. He even bursts into occasional song, especially when a trap comes up with several lobsters in it. I help fill the bait bags, and throw the shorts overboard. Henderson plugs the keepers with wooden pegs, hand-whittled and kept in an old coffee can alongside the wheel. The big crate slowly fills with angry crustaceans, and Henderson, concerned with their well-being, moves the crate out of the sun, and throws wet kelp on top to cool them.

In late morning, we stop for lunch, sitting on the washboard as the boat drifts. Charlie's lunch pail contains a battered Thermos of coffee, and several biscuits split, buttered, and filled with chunks of meat. My own is tomato sandwiches, milk, and fresh-baked cookies.

After lunch we continue hauling in the rising breeze.

By early afternoon, we are at the end of the strings of traps, between Ship and Trumpet Islands. The bottom here is heavily overgrown with kelp, and the water looks brown instead of blue. Each trap that comes up is festooned with kelp leaves, and Henderson must lean over the side and clear them away before the trap can be lifted clear and onto the washboard. The traps are well-filled with lobster, and my friend sings again.

The sou'wester has sprung up with the afternoon and on the way home Henderson trims the canvas riding sail to catch the wind and help the Palmer with its work. The breeze is sending rollers up the bay, and we angle off before them, heading for the point around which lies the sheltered cove and the home mooring.

Joel always thought you couldn't do much better than haul traps for a living.

Not surprisingly, such experiences made Joel an enthusiastic lobsterman. Equally important (because Joel was at root such a pragmatist) was the fact that he had a real aptitude for catching lobsters. He was so good at it that in later years on those occasions when he became discouraged about the future of wooden boat building, he often remarked that if things continued to get worse, he'd just go fishing. When his youngest son, John, decided to become a full-time fisherman, Joel was tickled. He thought you couldn't do much better than haul traps for a living, and in John's first year as a fisherman Joel accompanied him to the fishing grounds several times to give advice and simply enjoy the pleasures of revisiting favorite spots around the bay.

His love for lobstering notwithstanding, in the fall following his return to Brooklin full-time, Joel went to work for Arno Day, a local boatbuilder well known for lobsterboat design and construction. First Joel just showed up to help out. Soon enough he was getting paid for a full week. These days were an important grounding experience. They allowed him to cross over from being the son of out-of-towners who made their living in mysterious ways involving the arrival and departure of a great deal of mail, to a man respected for work done day-to-day. In this crucial period, he got to know the men he worked with on common terms. Just as they did, every fall he "got his deer." Just as they did, every summer he went on codfishing expeditions in the yard workboat to offshore hotspots like Spirit Ledge and The Drunkard, afterwards camping out under army surplus tents and dining in bachelor splendor on fish chowder and quarts of Narragansett beer.

In these years Joel became his own man in his own eyes. Given his father's stature as a writer (not to mention his strong-minded mother's

After building Martha *for his dad, writer E.B. White, the two enjoy a sail together.*

stature as the fiction editor at *The New Yorker*), such self-definition was crucial to his emergence as a boatbuilder, designer, and man. Although there would always be undeniable similarities between father and son in matters of outlook and personal style, the fact is that Joel never thought of himself as shaped by either his father's vocation or his father's fame, let alone some line of poetry or a phrase in an essay. If someone sidled up to Joel hoping to shake loose a little vicarious E.B. White magic, he grew visibly uncomfortable and tried to change the subject.

After Joel had worked for him for a year or so, Arno walked in to work one morning, and like a bolt out of the blue, offered Joel a partnership stake in the business. Several years later (and just as unexpectedly) Arno opted to move on, leaving Joel the sole proprietor of Brooklin Boat Yard. Those first years on his own were a real test. The yard itself was an unprepossessing jumble of waterside buildings, several of which had originally been built to house a sardine cannery. Also, at that time, Maine was still isolated by both geographic circumstance and its historic poverty. Customers were few and snug with a dollar. In the old days, for example, when the phone at the yard rang at three minutes before seven, the guys huddling around the woodstove waiting to start work used to joke that it must be their particularly wealthy customer, the one with the mansion around the point, calling long distance from Boston—minutes before higher daytime toll rates took effect.

Back then the crew was small—local guys with backgrounds in house carpentry or fishing. Over the years this included: John Berry, Henry Lawson, Cecil Smith, Sonny Williams, Elmer Bent, Raymond Eaton, Ken Taintor, Belford Gray, Alvah Kane, Captain John Allen, and Timmy Horton. They learned the shipwright's craft working elbow-to-elbow with Joel. His skills with tools were amazing—God-given, one concludes, if only because he could never explain precisely how he came by them. Watching him work, one quickly realized that a plane or a chisel was an extension of his hands; a way of expressing design ideas by the most tangible means possible. Nobody worked faster than Joel. In *WoodenBoat Magazine*'s early days when a photographer was dispatched to the Brooklin Boat Yard shop to chronicle a "How to Build" piece featuring Joel at work, the photographer had to keep asking him to slow down or restage what he had just finished because the pieces he was working on were going together faster than the camera could, with any sort of graphic clarity, record for the magazine's readers.

Long before teaching at the WoodenBoat School, Arno Day had a hand in teaching Joel boatbuilding.

The choice of Beetle Cats by Brooklin's Center Harbor Yacht Club reflected the members' faith in Joel's skill and interest in caring for the fleet.

I got a taste of this speed each spring when the two of us painted the deck of his cruising cutter *Northern Crown*. On one of those limpid mid-June mornings so wistfully described as "State of Maine days," I could count on a call from Joel to join him down at the yard to help. Things would get underway methodically and at no great speed while we gathered the necessary supplies: a quart of Biloxi beige, a quart of semi-gloss white to mix in for the proper shade of off-white, brushes, rags, brushing thinner, a tiny can of nonskid compound to shake into the brew, two paint stirrers, a couple of paper pails—all laid out in a cardboard box of sufficient size to serve as a mixing station. After stirring our concoction to a consistency appropriate to given temperature and humidity conditions, we would commence at the bow and work our way aft. Working side-by-side we would talk about the weather, recent books, the cruise we planned to take later in the summer, how the paint seemed to be setting-up (always too quick, as I remember),

whether we should shake in a dite more nonskid, or natural history odd-
ments—like the guy attacked several times by an owl over in East Blue Hill.
I don't necessarily think of myself as a slow painter, but whatever the subject
under discussion, no matter what the temperature/humidity index, or how
many years we worked our way through the precise stations of the task, Joel
to starboard, me to port, he always finished sooner than I did, and (at least
by the lights of my own furtive once-over) he always did a better job.

In the earliest days of the yard, Joel and the crew took what work walked
through the door which, most often, turned out to be new lobsterboats for
guys from Brooklin, Deer Isle, or Stonington. Given his respect for local
fishermen and his conviction that traditions of local craftsmanship set a
proper standard for work at the yard, he never regarded these jobs as
beneath him. On the rare occasion a yacht design commission offered itself,
Joel would ascend the narrow steps to the chilly office on the second floor of
the cannery building, shove billing records and other paperwork aside on his
drawing board, and—working evenings and weekends, unwilling to lose a
day's work in the shop—get the job done.

To say these early days taught him to value his customers would be an
understatement. When anyone came to speak with him about either the
care of an older yacht or the construction of a new boat of any kind, they
received such thoughtful attention from Joel and the men at the yard that
they went away feeling not so much like potential bill payers, but partners
in a mutual undertaking of great importance.

When it came to older boats in need of work he was clear-eyed, often
ruthless about those he believed were not worth saving. For those that were,
however, he turned over the full wealth of his skill. In the years before 1985
when most of the yachting world dismissed wooden boats as impractical
eccentricities, he was one of the rare ones, defending Brooklin's brave little
collection of Herreshoffs and Aldens and Concordias from the ravages of
modern life.

In later years, no matter what one had in mind to discuss with Joel,
upon arrival a visitor invariably found him leaning over a surprisingly fresh-
looking piece of vellum drawing paper. Unlike many creative people, Joel's
work surface didn't look like a battlefield of indecision and revision. No pall
of molten eraser dust hung over the scene. In fact Joel drew so clean and
fast, some conclude he had the power to see the shape of a boat whole in
his mind's eye before he struck the first line—much like one of those com-
puter-graphics programs that has the power to render objects in three
dimensions and then can rotate them before our eyes. His ability to see and

*It was love at first sight between
Joel and his Nielsen-designed
cruising cutter* Northern Crown.

Good boats flocked to Brooklin Boat Yard, among them the Concordia Yawl Porpoise.

think spatially made Joel an invaluable resource to customers struggling in their own minds to visualize their perfect boat. Joel was a gifted listener who helped people refine their ideas as they spoke with him, especially because he was so interested in thinking through the opportunities a new design offered. As a matter of principle Joel thought boats were fun and interesting. He loved their variety. This enthusiasm for possibilities was an intoxicating invitation, and for the boat-minded dreamer who happened to climb the stairs to discuss designs with him, it was always an unforgettable experience. After his death a remarkable number of people wrote or spoke about special talks they had had with him about boats.

When Joel was diagnosed with cancer in the fall of 1995, a fruitful collaboration began with yard employee Bob Stephens, a collaboration that

Designed by Joel's young protégé Bob Stephens, the sloop Lena *carries on traditions of speed and classic good looks.*

allowed Joel to keep working on new designs through the last stages of his illness and ultimately provided a remarkable posthumous continuity— a drawing out, so to speak—of his final design conceptions.

Ever since Bob was ten years old he had wanted to design boats for a living. Although he majored in history at Bowdoin College, he had taken a semester at Mystic Seaport, had studied at the Landing School, done a rookie stint at Brooklin Boat Yard, hung out his own shingle as a builder and designer of small wooden boats, and then returned to the yard full-time to work first as a carpenter, then a project manager, and finally as a designer.

Bob says, "I started learning from Joel before I even met him because I had been reading *WoodenBoat* since 1975 when I was thirteen." He continues, "One of the things the magazine and Joel's writing pulled together for me was the idea that modern boat design could also encompass traditional elegance. That the modern world could include that kind of boat design was encouraging for a traditionalist like me who, at the same time, is drawn to modern construction methods. Another thing he and I shared in terms of a philosophy of construction was an appreciation of elegance as an expression of minimalism. We both thought, if you can make something simpler, then you should do so."

Bob Stephens' ability to understand that "elegance could be an expression of minimalism" is striking. We expect such counterintuitive insights to be hard won over a lifetime of designing, not the ideas of a young man who had never drawn up anything much bigger than a rowboat. Yet, it was this very ability to quickly grasp such a concept that helps us understand how White and Stephens were able to work together smoothly enough so that, toward the end of his life, Joel was heard to say he was having trouble knowing exactly where one of his drawings stopped and one of Bob's began.

Another notable collaboration was between Joel and his son-in-law, Taylor Allen. They first got to know each other back in 1981, when Taylor attended the WoodenBoat School's class in boat repair taught by Joel. At the time, the boat school was a new undertaking and nobody knew exactly what to expect. Compounding these uncertainties was the fact that Joel had never formally taught anybody anything and was naturally rather nervous about the way things would go. He feared, for instance, that his class would be filled with obsessive restorationists who would hover over projects without actually getting anything done. He had seen too much of this at various maritime museums he had visited. He wanted to show students of boat repair that time was important too, that triage was part of the deal, and that sometimes you had to dig pretty deep into the structure of things to get a boat really fixed. When Taylor showed up on the first day of class it was a big relief for Joel. Not only did Taylor bring considerable experience with tools from years of work at his family's boatyard in Rockport, he brought his own patented blend of cheerful "Oh! What the hell, let's just do it!" spirit to the group. Without ever being sloppy or careless, Joel had much the same kick-start approach to getting a job up and moving. He and Taylor became fast friends over the two weeks of the course and later in the summer when Taylor dropped back to visit, Joel offered him a job at Brooklin Boat Yard to help build the 50-foot powerboat *Maine Idea* that Joel had just designed for a couple in Blue Hill.

His twelve-month sojourn in Brooklin was a life-changing event for Taylor. He had been pondering whether or not he should commit to the management of his family's boatyard. Sometimes the idea of taking over the yard seemed fine to him, at other times he felt like moving way Down East and doing something different. Working at the Brooklin Boat Yard made two things clear to him. The first was that, instead of being part of a crew, he really liked being his own boss. The second was the realization, from the way Joel ran things, that running a boatyard specializing in the care and construction of wooden boats could be interesting, reasonably profitable, and fun.

After his year in Brooklin, Taylor went back fully settled on the idea of running the family business. Since his return, Rockport Marine has grown into one of the premiere boatyards on the East Coast. An important component of this growth has been an ongoing relationship with Brooklin. Not only did Taylor build the W-76 sloop *White Wings*, he has built all three of the W-46s, as well as a powerboat Joel designed for Taylor's father, Luke, and a fast picnic boat designed by Bob Stephens. When Taylor married Joel's daughter Martha, everyone felt he had been part of the family all along.

In the early years at the yard, Joel's time away from the shop was necessarily limited. For his own sailing pleasure in those years he had to be content with the occasional use of a friend's boat for short family cruises. This situation changed in the summer of 1972 when he purchased *Northern Crown*, a double-ended Aage Nielsen cutter built by the Walsted yard in Thurø, Denmark in 1956. Joel had long admired Nielsen designs, especially *Northern Crown*, so much so he had clipped out her sail plan and design

Before becoming Joel's son-in-law and going on to build the W-76 White Wings, *a young Taylor Allen proves himself with a varnish brush.*

White Wings *on launching day at Taylor Allen's Rockport Marine yard, September 1998.*

review from the issue of *Yachting* in which it had been published. As he was to write many years later, "She never fails to satisfy my aesthetic needs—her ample North Sea double-ended stern a delight of curves, the high blue-painted bulwarks rising above her white topsides, the tall varnished spar hinting of good sailing qualities."

Commencing in 1972 and for the next twenty years, my wife Caroline and I (often with Anne and Maynard Bray aboard as well) cruised aboard *Northern Crown* with Joel, along the coast as far east as Cape Breton Island on the tip of Nova Scotia to as far south as Bermuda.

These were golden years. *Northern Crown*, although only 35′ in overall length, always seemed like enough boat for us. Her motion in a seaway was easy, particularly off the wind as she lifted smoothly over the yanks and tumbles of following seas. Summer after summer we journeyed Down East into the fog mulls of the Bay of Fundy and Nova Scotia. When the anchor went down—with her iron cookstove and snug, old-world joinerwork—*Northern Crown* was chowder heaven; a perfect boat in which to sit out a day or two of impenetrable weather amid the comfort of good books, a pot or two simmering on the stove, good talk, and even readings aloud (when the fog was really thick) from various cruising narratives or (only slightly tongue-in-cheek) from that compleatest of cruisers, L. Francis Herreshoff himself, our spiritual guide.

Joel was totally at home aboard, his mind and heart tuned to the moment. Curious about what lay around the next bend in the creek, he was always ready to up-sail at the first sign of wind, but if conditions dictated, equally content to stay put. One August, for instance, we spent a sparkling blue-sky day weaving through the islands of Passamaquoddy Bay, ending up in the late afternoon anchored off Bliss Island on the New Brunswick shore. When at dusk it looked like the northwesterly breeze was freshening and we could ride a strong ebb tide down the Bay of Fundy to Cutler, forty miles to the westward, we ate our stew and set sail again on a moon-drenched close reach none of us would forget.

Until the late 1970s, life for Joel and the crew at the Brooklin Boat Yard flowed steadily along. Besides the regular stable of yachts under his direct care, Joel made it his business to support local fishermen by offering them ready access to his marine railway and reduced labor rates (he would think of it as professional courtesy) for work done by his crew. As for new work,

*Lady Jeanne's building crew, 1980:
Left to right: Sonny Williams, Belford Gray, Henry Lawson, Joel, and Tim Horton.*

Northern Crown *racing in an
early Eggemoggin Reach Regatta.
She's beefy but fast.*

about every winter he either built a wooden boat or finished off a fiberglass
hull into a fishing boat. By then Joel was very much part of everyday
Brooklin, a three-pairs-of-pants guy (two for work, one for good) who ate
lunch with the crew of four or five (each sitting on his own particular nail
keg), talking about the new fire truck in town, the most recent indignities
suffered by the Red Sox at the hands of the Yankees, or in the fall of the year,
deer hunting. Around mud season when things became particularly desperate
in the fresh conversation department, someone like Belford Gray might glue
a quarter to the shop floor to fool an unwary visitor. At home after work Joel
and Allene shared early suppers, news of their three children, the lousy TV
reception of rural Maine, and a love of reading. Books and magazines flowed
never-ending through those evenings, as essential to the life of the household
as red blood corpuscles, and no matter what time of year one dropped by, no

*Messing around with a peapod's rig.
Early collaboration between Joel,
Jon Wilson, and Maynard Bray.*

Joel and WoodenBoat *founder Jon Wilson
enjoy a sail aboard* Northern Crown.

matter how early it got dark, a visitor could count on a warm reception in their well-lit kitchen, and join in a conversation that spanned the globe.

While life at home remained constant, life at work was about to change. Joel and his boatyard were about to become famous. Several factors combined to make this happen. *WoodenBoat* founder Jon Wilson moved his magazine to Brooklin. Within a year, Jon hired Maynard Bray as *WoodenBoat's* Technical Editor. With the yard already well established as a haven for wooden boats, an era of notable collaboration between Wilson, Bray, and White quite naturally occurred. Each of the men brought his own strengths. Jon provided idealism, a publishing vehicle for their shared ideas, and an unquenchable belief that all things were possible. Maynard was fresh from his job as the head of Mystic Seaport's shipyard in which he had (among other things) supervised the construction of a large lift dock and the refloating of the whaleship *Charles W. Morgan*. He brought an encyclopedic knowledge of specific boats and their life histories, as well as a dogged faith that the long slide in the health of traditional boats of all kinds on the East Coast could be turned around. Joel brought his pragmatist's touch, hands-on experience, a willingness to share what he had learned, and his ability to draw boats.

When, for example, either Jon or Maynard had an idea about a project, the next day (or sooner) Joel would hand over a drawing. He was their sounding board, except he answered back in pictures. Together, these three gave vision and substance to what was becoming known as "the wooden boat revival." No longer would boats made from wood be regarded as either outlandishly pampered baubles largely out of reach of the common man, or punky remnants of another time. The synergy between Jon and Joel and Maynard meant that wooden boats could be relevant: craft that, with wit and skill (and it was hoped, a subscription to the magazine), a boat lover could actually do something about with his or her own hands. Suddenly Joel had a voice as a designer and design critic. His plans for the Catspaw Dinghy, the Nutshell Pram, the Marsh Cat, the Haven 12½, the Shellback, the Pooduck Skiff, and the Flatfish—all developed in some measure out of conversations between Jon and Maynard and Joel, all published in *WoodenBoat* and offered for sale as how-to-build plans—speak to the vitality of their collaboration.

Beyond this, several other factors led to Joel's emergence from relative obscurity. The first of these was the decision by his oldest son, Steve, to return to Brooklin and work at the yard full-time with an eye toward taking over its day-to-day operations. As anyone with even a nodding acquaintance of the dynamics inherent in a family business well knows, father-to-son transitions can be painful, even incendiary. At Brooklin Boat Yard all the elements necessary for combustion were present, especially because Joel and Steve came together with such different visions for the yard. For his part, Joel liked things pretty much the way they were: small, traditional, predictable (and accordingly not so profitable); a yard isolated from the hurly-burly of both the yachting press and the international yachting scene; a yard that year-in-year-out had the same guys sitting on the same nail kegs. In an era that was about to open up onto the technological wonders of the personal computer, the maniacal cycling of dot com wunderkind, and end up with a 250-million-dollar shortstop—an era in which the process of creation would be relegated to faded photographs or "living" museums—Joel wanted the yard to be a place free of distractions, a place focused on the here-and-now of putting wood against wood, economically and well.

Judging by the way things worked out for the future at the yard—now a forty-man crew working on three different floors in three new shops, building multiple large, cold-molded yachts simultaneously—Steve seems to have had something else in mind all along. But more notable than the differences between them was the degree of harmony they achieved throughout the changes. First of all, they liked each other enormously. Then there was Joel's remarkable willingness to trust that someone from the next generation could have an idea different from his own yet still be right. One can't discount the fact that his own father had all along urged Joel to listen to his inner voice and do, for work, the thing he loved to do. On a more practical level, Joel found Steve's ability to grow cash flow at the same pace he grew his "vision" for the yard reassuring. Beyond these things, Joel was not only struck that Steve didn't have to hover over every detail going on in the shop as he had always done, he was amazed by the quality of the work he saw being done. Over and over he spoke of Steve's hiring hunches, his ability to bring out the best in the men. Invaluable additions to the building crew over the years were—Rick Clifton, Peter Chase, Frank Hull, Brion Rieff, Brian Larkin, Mark Littlehales, Keith Dibble, Bob Bosse, Fred Pollard, Norman Whyte, and Paul Waring. While Joel never aimed to run a bigger and bigger company, he loved seeing Steve do it. So much so that instead of fighting the changes Steve was bringing forth (or feeling left out, or worse yet, obsolete), he became one of their biggest proponents.

In 1982 Steve married Laurie and Allene quickly introduced her to the world of boatyard bookkeeping. Changes in the yard called for the addition of a winterized office over the machine shop, and with it, under Laurie's direction, much-needed equipment was purchased—a new phone system, computers, fax machine and copier. More help was hired for the growing paperwork.

Joel's son Steve takes a maiden row in the first 9½' Nutshell Pram.

Brooklin Boat Yard stepping the scow schooner Vintage's *mast, hewn from a Brooklin spruce tree, back when Joel was running the shop.*

A continuous source of inspiration for Joel was the collection of fine wooden boats moored in Center Harbor.

A design office was also built overhead, helping the smooth transition from father to son. Finally Joel would have the proverbial clean, warm, well-lighted place in which to expand his ideas and begin to practice his talents as a designer. That his office also offered a panoramic view of Center Harbor and the boats that he had nurtured with such care over the previous two decades iced the cake. Health was also a factor in his move toward full-time design. Beginning in 1981, Joel had become increasingly vulnerable to the dusty conditions in the shop. Nearly three decades of non-stop exposure to sawdust and the fumes of adhesives, resins, and paints had taken their toll on his sinuses and lungs. With Steve willing and able to take command of yard operations, Joel could give himself a break and hit the drawing board full-time.

In 1984 Joel was asked to join the Board of Trustees of Mystic Seaport. Concordia Company founder Waldo Howland, a Mystic trustee who had long served as the chairman of the Seaport's Ships Committee and was seeking to cut back his responsibilities, recommended that Joel, because of his long experience in running a boatyard specializing in traditional craft, would be an ideal successor. Joel was honored to have been asked to join the Seaport's board. He had long admired the museum and its fine collection of watercraft, and he looked forward to direct involvement in decisions regarding their care.

Joel's neighbors Maynard Bray and Jon Wilson were trustees as well, and the three enjoyed the opportunity afforded by the 14-hour round-trip from Eastern Maine to Connecticut to talk boats non-stop. Needless to say, the time they had to refine their ideas about museum policies before they arrived made them a potent force at trustee meetings, and soon they were good-naturedly referred to as the "Brooklin Mafia" by other members. Over the years, Joel not only made a considerable contribution to the well-being of the Seaport, the Seaport in turn provided him with an invaluable opportunity to expand his knowledge through the study of its collection of vessels and archives of ships plans. Visits to Mystic also gave him a chance to sail aboard significant yachts like *Neith* and *Brilliant*, and to meet naval architects and maritime scholars from all over the world. His Mystic trusteeship contributed to making Joel a respected member of the yachting establishment.

In 1987 Joel altered his sailing patterns when he decided to finish off one of the fiberglass hulls built to his Bridges Point 24 design, for use as his personal sailboat. *Northern Crown* was a great boat, but she was no daysailer. This new sloop, to be named after his granddaughter, was a boat he could get underway easily by himself after work, and this put him out on the water more frequently. Although her underbody was traditional, *Ellisha*'s generous sail plan provided plenty of horsepower. She also featured both an adjustable backstay and mainsheet traveler. Joel had always been a meticulous helmsman and lively trimmer of sheets aboard *Northern Crown*, but *Ellisha* allowed him to tweak pretty much full-time as he single-handed up and down Eggemoggin Reach, often tearing by modern-looking sailboats half again her size. From this point onward, the lure of performance sailing aboard *Ellisha* (rather than destination sailing aboard *Northern Crown*) would sweetly beckon.

In Joel's first year with *Ellisha*, Steve began building for himself *Vortex*, a narrow and speedy sloop based on Knud Reimers' Swede 55 design. For the past couple of years he had been experimenting with various cold-molded hulls of which the rowing wherry *Bangor Packet* is an example. Believing cold-molding to be the wave of the future as far as new construction at the yard was concerned, Steve thought the successful completion of a major project like *Vortex* would put him in a position to credibly bid on large cold-molded projects. It proved a prescient decision. Following *Vortex*, the yard built *Aurora*, a flat-out racer designed by Bill Tripp, Jr. and *Lucayo*, a modern cruising sloop by Roger Marshall. The publicity surrounding these well-executed projects presented Brooklin Boat Yard with the chance to build the large, fast, ocean-going ketch *Dragonera*, and gave Joel White the chance to design it. It was, to this point, his biggest design project by far.

By this time he was well aware of the positive strength-to-weight ratios made possible by cold-molded construction. In addition, for several years, he had been working with a computer software program that provided hydrostatic analysis, and allowed him to conveniently determine the relationship between sail area and stability. Up through the design of the Bridges Point 24, his stability projections although accurate were time-consuming and had been to some degree a seat-of-the-pants endeavor. Now he could get hard numbers very quickly. Access to this software gave him the tool to begin designing boats with high-performance underbodies and still remain confident the boats would have the necessary stiffness in a strong breeze. Joel loved what this software could do for him, and in subsequent years he became so enamored of the power of computers to work through complex design computations that, as soon he had developed a set of preliminary lines for a boat, he made it a point to visit John Letcher's AeroHydro offices in nearby Southwest Harbor for the chance to massage his hull shapes on screen with Letcher's "Hydro 1 C" program. Over the last few years a lot of us have let computers march in and take over our work spaces. Joel never allowed this. A pencil and a piece of paper on a flat surface was still his way. That Joel clung to such an anachronistic modus operandi when more

Joel sailing his Bridges Point 24 Ellisha. *This small and handy boat got him out on the water frequently.*

Steve and Laurie White's Vortex, *Brooklin Boat Yard's first large cold-molded project, established the yard's credentials in this modern technique.*

efficient means were easily available to him puzzled someone like John Letcher who says, "The way he embraced the creation of lines on the screen, it always amazed me he wouldn't take on one of our [drafting] programs."

On the surface, this is quite an inconsistency, especially given the fact that Joel was willing to have Letcher's firm provide specific design services like computerized lofting and the computer modeling of bulb keels for his last designs, the Center Harbor 31-footers and the W-Class sloops. Yet, it is in understanding this apparent inconsistency that we can come to understand the design genius of Joel White. On the one hand, here was a man sufficiently grounded as an engineer to comfortably travel into the new world of computer-enhanced design, yet on the other, remain a man resolutely rooted in the most basic of traditions. Arguably it is this very duality (rather than inconsistency) that explains why his final boats look so good above the waterline and go so fast below it. To put it differently, this explains how he was able to render a boat in two dimensions of time: the beginning and the end of the last century. Without such a fusion of understandings and techniques, boats like *Lala*, the double-ended 23-footer, the Center Harbor 31s, and *Wild Horses* and *White Wings*, the W-Class 76-footers, which most eloquently express his monumental blending of old and new, might never have been created.

The development of the W-Class represents a defining moment in Joel's career as a designer. In the fall of 1995, Donald Tofias, a Boston real estate developer, approached Joel and asked him to do preliminary designs for a new class of boats. What Tofias had in mind was a big, swift, handsome sloop that would recapture those glories of yachting's golden past when identical large sailing yachts went head-to-head on the race course, without the inequities of handicapping that prevail when boats of varying size and type race together.

Like many of us, Tofias believed that we have become too accustomed to big boat races determined to the third decimal place on a scratch sheet instead of boat for boat on the water; that approaching some bulletin board to check posted results two hours after the event can be a more puzzling and adrenaline-producing event than approaching the starting line of the race in the first place. He sought to change this and told Joel he was prepared to sponsor the design, construction, and operation of a 76′ sloop to campaign in 1999. It was to be a staggeringly ambitious undertaking which he hoped would inspire others to order identical boats to compete in fleet and match

At 74 feet, the ketch Dragonera *was Joel's biggest design and construction project as of 1993.*

races. Beyond the one-design aspect, Tofias' vision demanded that these "W-Class" boats would look good. He wanted graceful overhangs and a sheerline as sweet as anything Joel White could draw, which (as anyone familiar with White's designs surely knows) would be sweet indeed. Without a rating rule to dictate design parameters, aesthetics would be in the driver's seat: aesthetics combined with out-and-out sailing performance.

I had lunch with Joel a day or so after Tofias had broached his W-Class idea. Drawing upon a well-stocked supply of Yankee skepticism, Joel supposed the scheme wouldn't ever amount to very much. But he loved the idea of designing a yacht to the scale Donald had laid out for him, especially a Grace Kelly sort of boat with pure speed as its principle objective. With this in mind, Joel said, if it never came to more than a set of drawings, it would be worth his efforts.

Yet for all Joel's doubts, the idea kept hanging around. Tofias—the proverbial dog with a bone—wouldn't leave it alone. He loved the drawings Joel produced, and as soon as he saw them he commissioned Kathy Bray to do a color portrait of a W-Class boat and used it to promote his idea in full-page advertisements in the yachting press and at boat shows. Next he asked Rockport Marine to build a one-inch-to-the-foot, radio-controlled sailing model complete with a 94-inch mast. Then with characteristic flourish, in June of 1997, he announced at the exhibitors' dinner at WoodenBoat's annual show held that year at Mystic Seaport that he wanted Brooklin Boat Yard and Rockport Marine to each build a W-Class boat.

Sooner than anyone (aside from Tofias himself) had hoped, the dream of head-to-head racing between W-Class boats became a reality. Sailors would soon have the chance to catch a glimpse of two great boats flashing by in unison. Crew members aboard the sloops, feeling the motion of one boat beneath their feet, would see that same motion mirrored in the other. And as the breeze piped up on a race course—plunging the boats into smothers of white water—this mirroring effect would, by some exponential magic, multiply the pleasures of sailing into something far exceeding the sum of two boats.

When *Wild Horses* was launched in the spring of 1998 to begin her racing career that summer, the boating press lauded her design, construction, and performance. The knowledgeable Allesandro Vitelli, writing for *Boat International USA*, commented after a day aboard, "Once the sails are set, she simply takes off. She is stiff, her high ballast-to-weight ratio ensuring that puffs are converted into acceleration, exhilarating on any point of sail, tracks well and has a sweet, light touch to the helm. The impressive rigidity

Launched after Joel's death, the 76' W-Class sloop Wild Horses *was Joel's final design.*

and strength of her structure can be felt when strapping down sheets for windward work in a breeze, a procedure that usually elicits 'complaints' from inferior boats. Sitting at the helm working her to windward, I started fantasizing about sailing in a fleet to the weather mark."

Commenting on her design after a day's sail, *Classic Boat* editor Nic Compton wrote, "One major benefit of keeping the ends light is that it keeps the motion easy. And with massively hollowed-out cheeks giving a certain amount of flair forward, most of the spray is deflected off the hull before it reaches the cockpit. The great beauty of long ends is that the hull naturally adopts the best shape for the conditions. In light winds it sits upright, giving shorter waterline and less wetted surface area, while as the wind increases the hull heels over, lengthening the waterline to maximize speed."

Joel's success is clearly reflected in these critiques. From the broadest brush strokes down to the tiniest detail, a remarkable harmony prevails. The following letter from White to Tofias as the project evolved shows the care taken.

W-Class visionary Donald Tofias enjoys the first sail aboard Wild Horses.

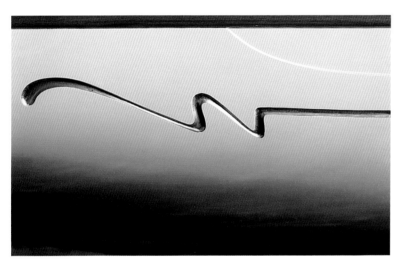

The W-76's covestripe ends with the subtle W sketched by Maynard Bray.

Dear Don,

I have been wrestling with the covestripe problem off and on for two days. We have tried a number of versions using the basic sail logo W, but to my eye, at least, they have all been failures. The thing about covestripes is they have to be very subtle, subdued, and in keeping with the type of yacht on which they are carried. With the modern type of racing yacht, which [is] basically dirt-ugly, and covered with graphics of all sorts, it doesn't much matter what you do. But with these yachts, which are designed to have great aesthetic appeal, and to follow a fairly restrictive traditional look, I think that we could really spoil the whole effect if we don't get this right.

After a lot of different tries, I am back to Maynard's original calligraphy-style W on each end of the stripe. Both Bob Stephens and I think this works well, is aesthetically pleasing, and doesn't leap out at you like a tiger. The fact that it is different from the sail logo seems immaterial to me—when the sail is up, the large, black W on the mainsail will dominate. When the sail is down, and someone looks at the hull and covestripe, they will gradually recognize that the endings are indeed subtle W's and say to themselves, "Hey, that's pretty clever".

If this doesn't make sense to you, then I think we should go back to square one, and develop a couple of very traditional vine-and-leaf endings, as shown on the sail plan drawing. These have the full weight of tradition behind them, and no one can fault us for bad taste.

Sister Ws, Wild Horses *and* White Wings *under sail together at last.*

Sorry to be pig-headed about this, but I feel pretty strongly about it. We should all keep thinking about this, but I am not happy with any other W's that I have seen yet.

Best regards, Joel

With the launch of *Wild Horses'* sister ship, *White Wings,* Tofias has been off and running on the classic yacht racing circuit. From the Eggemoggin Reach Regatta in Maine to races in Nantucket, Newport, St. Tropez, Antigua, and a dozen more besides, the W's are the gold standard of the neoclassic yacht revival.

Without Joel White's lifetime of work as a builder, designer, and sailor, the act of going fast in a sailboat might never have become an option for boats that are also beautiful enough to stop us in our tracks.

Cruising Man

In the summer of 1972 Joel decided it was finally time to buy a cruising sailboat of his own. Over the past years he had borrowed boats, willingly offered by customers, for short family cruises, but these moments had been catch-as-catch-can. Furthermore, as a father of young children and the proprietor of a fledgling boatbuilding and repair business that kept him busy at least six days a week, *not* owning a boat had made sense. By 1972 however, the kids were bigger, and for the first time he could foresee the possibility of taking well-planned chunks of time off from work, so he began to sniff out the used boat market.

He would be, needless to say, a discriminating consumer. Here was a man who could take in a week's worth of details in the sweep of an eye, from the way a boat would go to windward to how your back would feel if you took the helm for a couple of hours. He knew how long keel bolts would last; he knew how to check the swage on turnbuckles for signs of premature fatigue; he could pull out a fastening and give you its life story. Yet for all his fascination with analyzing boats, Joel had never been a reckless boat shopper coveting any old boat he saw along a dock. In later years, in fact, he was so circumspect in this regard, he was one of the few *WoodenBoat* readers who didn't turn to the classifieds first when a fresh copy of the magazine arrived in the mail. When *Northern Crown* came his way he fell in love with her and bought her, and as far as a personal cruising boat was concerned, that was it.

Designed by K. Aage Nielsen (an all-time favorite of Joel's), she was a 35′ x 11′9″ double-ended cutter showcasing Nielsen's familiarity with and affinity for the classic North Sea workboats of his native Denmark. *Northern Crown* was built in 1956 by the Walsted yard in Thurø, Denmark, planked with mahogany that was copper riveted to laminated white oak frames. As a boatbuilder, Joel appreciated the details of her structure so much that often when he awoke aboard, he would spend several delicious minutes looking over the way she was built. He would write years later,

Much of the charm of small wooden boats is that the structure itself becomes an integral part of the interior decor. On *Northern Crown*

The Barred Islands on a hazy summer morning—a favored destination for the cutter Northern Crown.

Northern Crown—*beautiful above deck and beautiful below.*

the first thing visible from one's bunk is the cabintop, with its beaded narrow planks laid over closely-spaced cabin beams. Because of her heavily rounded corners where cabintop meets the cabin sides, these beams are not simple arcs of circles, but rather have a more elliptical shape. The clever Danes who built her took the time to ovalize the bottom edges of these beams—perhaps to lessen the damage to one's head in a close encounter—but, I suspect, simply because it brings a hint of elegance to the work, and signifies that care is being taken with all the elements of the job. After inspecting the cabin top from the depths of my sleeping bag, and noting that the area over the galley needs to be scrubbed to get rid of the smoke stains from the galley stove, my eyes move to the deck structure just above me in the port quarter berth. Heavy oak beams support the deck, and are dovetailed into the fore and aft carlin which lies underneath the cabin sides. The outboard ends of these beams are notched into the clamp where deck meets topsides. Again, the Danes have seen fit to dress up this joint by the addition of facia pieces covering the deck edge structure, which tends to be a bit gnarly with its many bolts and fastenings. There are occasional ⅜″ diameter galvanized steel tie-rods from carlin to clamp, one of which is strategically placed to aid in levering me out of the quarter berth and into an upright position. Below the clamp, varnished walnut ceiling covers *Northern Crown*'s laminated frames—the strips of ceiling have just enough space between them to promote good ventilation, and to allow the observer to follow the run of each frame behind the ceiling's facade. Above the quarter berth, against the side of the hull, a deep shelf holds my clean clothes for a week's cruise—underwear aft, shirts and jeans next, socks forward, as well as the current book being read. I like the compactness of cruising—what few necessities are required take up but little space— space that is at a premium, and must be carefully rationed. There simply isn't room for non-essential items.

When Joel bought *Northern Crown* he was tickled to have a cruising sailboat of his own and eager to get underway. At the same time he proceeded deliberately in getting to know her. Generally this was the way he went about things, but his new boat also had several problems. While the latter meant her asking price was low and her selling price even lower, it also meant he must move ahead cautiously. Problem number one was a balky engine. When he first slid down into her ample engine compartment for a look around, what he saw was evidence of ceaseless mechanical strife: a couple of extra 12-volt batteries, jumper cables all too handy, a jumble of used or soon-to-be used cans of starting fluid. As he recalled later, you could almost hear the ghostly mutterings of one mechanic after another struggling to get her to go.

Besides starting problems, *Northern Crown* had a mysterious leak in the vicinity of her laminated horntimber; a leak that had outwitted several repair yards. There was also ample evidence of bunk-soaking drips coming through the deck. Finally, an overall level of grunge and dishevelment hung over the outfit. Clearly this pall of diminished resolve explains why her owners at the time were willing to put a boat like *Northern Crown* up for sale in the first place.

Seeing these things, a less experienced buyer might have shied away from putting down good money. Several maybe had already done just that. But Joel had the skill, he had a boatyard's worth of tools, and he had a Buddhist's patience. On occasion he also had a sporting outlook that invited risk. Luckily, on the day he saw the ad his devil-may-care inclinations were up on top. This made the leap into a fixer-upper boat seem spicy to him; the challenges involved almost essential to a satisfying life. Later on he might have foundered on the all-too-evident complications of such an enterprise and let the whole thing slip by with the tide. But at forty-two, eager to take charge of a new project, the complications and risks caught his imagination. Yet for all the iffyness involved, Joel was no plunger. On his first day of ownership, for instance, he invited me to help him and his son Steve and daughter Martha sail *Northern Crown* home to Brooklin, but when the day dawned thick-o-fog, having no desire to weave through the islands of Penobscot Bay on his way to Center Harbor in zero visibility, directed by several compasses he knew nothing about, he postponed the trip.

Center Harbor's Brooklin Boat Yard in the fog.

When he and the kids did get her home several days later, he began, in that quiet way of his, to ponder her condition. Moving step-by-step and taking nothing for granted, he started in on the engine. Compression good, fuel good; he went to the wiring. Once there, it didn't take long to discover faulty glowplugs. The pre-ignition indicator wire glowed cheerfully enough, but the actual plugs weren't hooked up correctly so no heat made its way to the cylinders. In a minute he set things right and the engine fired off. From this point onward Joel knew he and this rattling chunk of Mercedes iron would be friends. Over the years a familiar sight aboard when under power would be Joel lifting *Northern Crown*'s engine hatch a crack every half-hour or so to check her vital signs, put an ear to her thumpings, and otherwise sniff about like a curious physician. If it turned out that a trip down the hatch to tend something or other was called for, he would carefully wipe his hands afterward with a paper towel from the roll he had installed handy-by above the engine. Performing these rituals, day or night, made sense as preventive maintenance. Equally important, it was Joel's way of proving that all was right with that part of the world under his direct control; a simple pleasure that stayed fresh throughout his stewardship of the boat.

Northern Crown's horntimber leak would have to wait until the following spring. Like others who had assessed the problem, he couldn't discover either fastenings in need of renewal or some obvious void in need of caulking. He concluded, therefore, it must be an invisible problem lurking deep in the laminated timber itself. That spring, after her winter's haulout, when

Northern Crown's hull was at its driest, he drilled a series of holes into the horntimber, tapped fittings into the laminations, and with a grease gun, pumped her full of marine goop. His cure was pragmatic, cheap, slightly mysterious, and above all it was effective. After that first summer of pumping the bilge and wondering, he finally had himself a boat that didn't take in water. In the years he owned *Northern Crown*, a second pleasure he took was slipping off the bronze cover of her deck-mounted bilge pump after a day's sail to give her a couple of strokes, just to hear the pump suck air.

Before launching *Northern Crown* that spring, he also sheathed her decks with Dynel and painstakingly laid an artful bead of 5200 caulking compound around each top timber where it penetrated the covering board, thus ending that most irritating of all boat problems: decks that drip down your neck when you're trying to get some sleep. With the completion of these three jobs, two of them simple, he could work to make her go. But first, he had to make her stay put. Surprisingly, that took a little doing.

It wasn't until mid-July of the first summer before Joel took his wife Allene out for her first day on the boat. Well aware of her skepticism concerning floating objects, he opted for a short jog down through the islands south of Deer Isle and anchored in the little bight along the east side of Coombs Island. He and Allene rowed ashore in the peapod, had a picnic on the broad ledges, and walked around the island. When they returned he noticed that *Northern Crown* had moved. Worse yet, she was moving still—quite swiftly in fact—and heading straight toward a half-tide ledge. Quick as a flash (and Joel could be very fast in these situations) he dragged the peapod down the beach and rowed full steam until he could jump aboard, start the engine (no need for starting fluid these days), and return her to safe water.

After reviewing this near debacle in his mind, Joel concluded the culprit must be the plow anchor *Northern Crown* had come equipped with. Even before the event, his ground tackle of choice was a yachtsman anchor. After *Northern Crown*'s little holiday, his doubts about other anchors intensified. He never set the plow again. In fact he pulled it right off the boat and rigged the only sort of ground tackle he knew could handle the rock-strewn and kelp-infested bottoms he would frequent along the Maine Coast: a fifty pound yachtsman anchor spliced directly into a two-hundred foot, $\frac{7}{8}$ inch nylon rode, eschewing chain entirely under the belief that the weight of a short length allowed the rode to all-too-easily loop around the projecting fluke as the boat swung with wind and tide. As usual, his thinking proved itself out. No matter how much *Northern Crown* jogged and circled through a night, rarely did we haul in the rode and find the anchor fouled in the morning.

The schooner Grace Bailey *off Deer Isle. The companionship of schooners always enlivened a cruise.*

With *Northern Crown* drier and safer, Joel lengthened her bowsprit two feet to carry the anchor and to give the yankee jib a wider slot to tack through. He then ordered new sails. Until that point none of us knew how fast she would sail. Even though Joel would always modestly maintain that her apparent speed was a matter of deception—that nobody expected much from a chunky boat like her—she actually was quite swift. In fact, with her powerful sail plan, long waterline, and a little of that Nielsen magic through her aft sections, *Northern Crown* had so delighted her second owner, John Wilson of Marblehead, Massachusetts, that he commissioned Nielsen to expand her lines into a larger version. This new ketch, *Holger Danske*, managed the remarkable feat of winning the 1980 Newport to Bermuda Race, 16 years after she was built.

One change that Joel looked forward to making to *Northern Crown*, one that he thought would definitely improve her performance, was to replace her original iron keel with a heavier one of cast lead, thus allowing him to remove all her considerable inside ballast and put it outside where it belonged. Joel never found time to make this change, but when he sold *Northern Crown* to his daughter Martha and son-in-law Taylor Allen, Taylor made the alteration at his Rockport Marine boatyard. Without question, Joel had been right. The first time we raced the boat with her new keel it was a particularly breezy close reach during the Camden Feeder Race leading up to the Eggemoggin Reach Regatta. *Northern Crown* was a far stiffer, more weatherly boat with all her ballast on the outside, and that day she showed her heels to a number of boats she might not have beaten in the past.

Just as Joel wasn't a boat shopper, he wasn't a gear guy either. While others appear to own boats as much for the expanded arena of consumption they provide as for the actual sailing, Joel got no thrill from gizmos. If a taffrail log provided the most accurate measure of distance covered, why fiddle with mechanical or electronic devices subject to seaweed, atmospheric vagaries, corrosion, the whim of repairmen, and certain obsolescence? If you only need to know how deep it is occasionally, why isn't an old paper recording fathometer that swings out into the companionway preferable to the distraction of perpetually flashing digits? For all her ample functionality, *Northern Crown* maintained (and still maintains) a Shaker-like simplicity.

This simplicity represents one skirmish in Joel's lifelong war to make the world less complicated. As a builder and designer, even though it would be

Rocky shorelines, however beautiful, demand accurate piloting.

profitable for him and the yard to tack on extras, he regularly found himself in the position of trying to talk his clients out of stuffing extraneous apparatus into their boats. He just couldn't seem to help himself. When he heard about some new piece of equipment, his first thought was, "When's this thingamabob going to break down, anyway?"

The case of Loran pretty well summed up his thinking on this matter. Early in our cruising days when Loran was just becoming affordable for small boats, we would often meet up with a befuddled yachtsman marooned in some foggy outport by a malfeasance in his new Loran receiver—vacation days sliding recklessly by, his wife mumbling below in the grip of near-miss-induced catatonia. What this skipper needed was either improved visibility or the arrival of technical help and, most likely, neither of these things was about to happen any time soon. For Joel, such moments seemed like Old Testament retribution. What we have here, he would later suggest, was a man lured beyond the range of his navigational capability on the slender thread of some sort of electronic fiddle-faddle. No such thing would happen to us. We would stick to the tried-and-true: our dividers, our parallel rules, our taffrail log, and our compass. Furthermore, we would keep our navigational skills honed by welcoming the challenges of fog at every opportunity.

In this state of mind, we sailed eastward summer after summer into fog so thick you could spread it on an English muffin. Fog defined our cruising. Day after day we stared into an impenetrable gray wall with nose adrip and ears ringing from a lack of bell buoys, monitoring depth contours minute-to-minute on the old paper recorder, and recalculating current flow estimates with each passing pot buoy. But after such days when at last we battened down in some snug anchorage, it must also be said that we shared levels of contentment and satisfaction unknown to today's mariners guided by the wizardry of the latest electronic devices.

Of course to make navigation work the old-fashioned way, Joel had to be a patient fundamentalist never discombobulated by either carelessness or a crumbling faith in his own reckonings. In the fog we never aimed for an area rife with prickly hazards. Instead we sought bell buoys or bold shores to shoot for, even if these took us out of our way. Joel also thought everyone aboard should be familiar with where we were headed. This meant several of us reviewed his calculations before setting out in the navigational equivalent of the "measure twice and cut once" axiom used by carpenters. In the pell-mell conditions when breeze combined with fog, Joel knew just how easy it was to get factors turned around 180 degrees or to figure a course using "true" compass readings instead of "magnetic."

Shipmates found his fundamentalism comforting. Sailing in fog can be a spooky business. Your eyeballs feel as if they will explode in your head as you grope for the loom of an approaching shore. Your ears play tricks as sounds are distorted by layers of fog. In such conditions, confidence in one's figuring combined with a faith that everyone aboard understands the full picture makes for a happy crew. Accordingly, a staple feature of sailing with Joel was the morning meeting in which the day's plans were discussed. Of course it was never referred to as such and a meeting was never formally convened. Rather, a gathering of those aboard materialized sometime after breakfast cleanup. By that time we had a feel for outside conditions and had listened to the NOAA weather forecasts. In these meetings Joel showed his leadership skills by such indirection that it didn't seem like a decision had

The sudden appearance of lobsterboats in the fog kept crew members on their toes.

even been made. Somehow we just arrived at a plan—an offshore passage perhaps, gunkholing up the bay, island walks, searching out interesting boats, laundry, cod fishing, or just hanging around the woodstove with a book and a cup of tea. On most days that's how many choices there seemed to be and that's, ultimately, why cruising together was (in spite of all the fog) such fun.

Navigation and planning was also helped by the fact that, as addicted chart junkies, we had already spent plenty of time gazing at the area's charts and thinking through potential routes and anchorages before we even set out. In fact chart study and visualization of what things might be like on a cruise had often commenced the previous winter when a basic itinerary had been sketched. I well remember (for example) the time Joel received a shipment of charts and cruising guides for the Nova Scotia coast after we had decided to sail there in 1976. Up in the old cannery office at the boatyard we rolled them out, sheet after sheet of exotic territory to explore: Ecum Secum, Necum Teuch, Port Matoon (an outport named, as I recall, for a long past event in which an explorer's sheep, supposedly tethered on the foredeck, managed to jump overboard and swim ashore).

At the time, Canadian charts had an antiquarian quality to them, featuring steel engravings of shoreline profiles from a seaward point of view, as well as an archaic smattering of pre-electronic soundings so widely spaced along the chart that one could almost visualize the progress of the original survey vessel as the leadline was cast. The Nova Scotia charts showed enticing anchorages free from tourist clutter, several year-round island communities, and the siren call of crescent beaches. All this infused the place with a sense of authentic old-fashionedness; a quality we feared had all but disappeared from the Maine Coast.

By day's end none doubted the pleasures of a Down East cruise.

By July 24, 1976, *Northern Crown*'s log shows we were underway to Nova Scotia with a crew made up of Joel, my wife Caroline and myself, and also Maynard Bray who had moved to Brooklin the previous summer. After delaying our departure the first day in a fuzzle of rain and fog, we sailed to Burnt Coat Harbor on Swans Island that afternoon under clearing skies. The next morning we hoisted the anchor at four-thirty. An expected cold front had broken through and a northwest breeze scuffed the surface of the harbor. Overhead a sliver of moon darted among scudding clouds. By full daylight the sky was deep blue with the northwest breeze hooting along at a steady twenty-

Hockamock Head Light at Swans Island was the jumping off point for the first Nova Scotia cruise.

five knots and gusting higher. Nothing gets an offshore cruise off to a better start than a breeze blowing straight off the Canadian prairies. It makes the wave tops jump and the shearwaters swoop the hollows from crest to crest.

Even though the wind gradually diminished through the night, over the next twenty-four hours we would cover more than 140 miles. By mid-morning of the second day we thought we had cleared the hazardous waters around Cape Sable Island off the southwest corner of Nova Scotia and were free to close gently with the coast. Because the visibility was about as good as it ever gets at this fog-choked crossroads, instead of turning in toward an anchorage, we decided to run through the following night all the way to Lunenburg. Without Loran, GPS, or radar to provide precise fixes offshore, good visibility was no small blessing and the decision to carry on allowed us to cover a maximum distance with a minimum of fumbling.

Lunenburg, Nova Scotia:
still doing things the old way.

Furthermore it gave us a day ahead to savor the antiquarian delights strung out along Lunenburg's waterfront. Principle of these was a dory shop still pounding together pine-planked dories that look straight out of a Winslow Homer painting, Vernon Walters' blacksmith shop forging its own line of galvanized fisherman anchors and other gear, and the Lunenburg Foundry, manufacturer of a half-dozen models of seagoing cast-iron cookstoves. There was also a handful of ship chandleries serving, as they had for close to a century, the Banks fishery. But most intriguing of all was Dauphinee's—perhaps the most recklessly old-time manufacturing facility still operating in North America.

At Dauphinee's every machine drew power off a central overhead pulley and line shaft system. As pulleys hummed and whirred, as each leather belt slapped out its own signature cadence, a throbbing industrial symphony swelled across the shop floor to carry us back into the world of Arkwright and Slater. At one mesmerizing station an old-timer turned one oar after another on a lathe that could be stretched out to make fourteen footers. At another, lignumvitae was milled into blocks and deadeyes for the yacht trade. At another, steel sheaves received a final finishing before galvanization. We didn't know it then, but the Dauphinee family was about to shut down this facility and relocate to a smaller, more modern plant on the next peninsula. If we had been aware such a move was afoot, we would have surely lingered even longer soaking in the sights and sounds of a whickety-whackety-thumpety-clickity world we felt lucky to glimpse.

After touring Lunenburg's ancient delights, we repaired to *Northern Crown* for refreshments. But before a bottle cap was popped, a dory rowed by two husky gentlemen pulls off from shore. Rather than going on any particular errand, the oarsmen seem to row a set course as if they are practicing or working out. Because the cult of physical fitness had hardly hit Maine, not to mention Nova Scotia, this routine makes us curious. It also awakens a competitive itch in the otherwise mild-mannered Maynard Bray. So rather than just sit there sipping drinks while these guys rowed around us, Maynard and I hunt up the second pair of oars in the forepeak and jump into the peapod to have a go. As the big dory passes close by we skitter out on an obliquely intersecting course. No words are spoken, but our actions are clear. Quickly the boats establish a parallel track and as we even-up, Maynard and I pickup the stroke. In an instant, they follow suit.

At first the lighter, sprightlier pod dances to a precocious lead. Maynard establishes an audacious (some might say reckless) pace. Oars dip and flash as we approach hull speed. Although we have never rowed together in this manner before, we manage a surprising degree of unison and for a few moments think to ourselves that maybe we can hold these guys. Soon enough, however, such thoughts prove to be wishful thinking in the extreme. (The word hubris might even be applied.) Our lead of twenty feet or so melts as the dory gathers way. Waterline length, stove-pipe-sized forearms, and precise oarsmanship born of daily workouts will have their day. We push on gamely for a bit, laughing out loud as we bend the oars, and then break off just before their lead becomes embarrassing. When it is clear who is still champ of Lunenburg Harbor, they let us draw alongside. One of them allows that these "short sprints get 'em winded" and we choose to take the remark as a compliment.

Asked about their workout, they tell us they are practicing for the International Dory Races held each year between fishermen from Gloucester and fishermen from Lunenburg. When they join us later on *Northern Crown*, it turns out that Sonny Heisler, the older of the two, has won twenty-one of his last twenty-three starts over the past seventeen years. Furthermore, his father, who raced until he was forty-six, retired undefeated. Clearly our challenge had been on the puny side; until Sonny tells his story, we didn't know exactly how puny.

As the beer drinking and talk goes on aboard *Northern Crown*, we hear about Sonny's involvement with another sport: amassing returnable beer bottles. Like his and his dad's record against the men of Gloucester, the statistics are impressive. The previous year, for example, he put together some 1,200 dozen in his basement—an amount that we figure works out to be something in excess of $500 worth of empties at the current rate of return. Even to the hardened crew of *Northern Crown*, accustomed as we were to reckoning bottled stores in reasonably high numbers, 14,400 beer bottles seems like an impressive number. We suggest that a brewery might be interested in some sort of sponsorship deal. Maybe several breweries.

Without question Joel enjoyed these antics as much as the rest of us. Although it was not his style to reach out to strangers, when he found himself among new people he often loved the experience and made lifelong friends. Nowhere was this more true than on the Island of Grand Manan in the Bay of Fundy.

I remember the first day we sailed to Grand Manan as if it were yesterday. For the week preceding, Joel, his daughter Martha and a friend, Caroline and myself had sailed eastward in *Northern Crown*. Our original goal had been the Roque Island archipelago, with its melancholy offshore islands named The Brothers standing sentinel over its several anchorages and crescent beach. At Roque we had sat out a hurricane in Lakeman Harbor along with Mt. Desert boatbuilder Farnum Butler and his wife Gladys. We then joined them on their Controversy Yawl *Constellation* for an afternoon sail out between the barrier islands to experience the vast swell caused by the storm passing by to the south.

At Farnum's urging we continued east through thick fog to the secure but tiny harbor at Cutler. Once in Cutler, we read what Roger Duncan, in his *Cruising Guide to the New England Coast*, had to say about points of interest beyond. He not only introduced us to Grand Manan, but when his chapter on the island concluded with the sentence, "The amateur sailor with a staunch and well equipped boat and a competent navigator would add

Grand Manan's Swallowtail Light welcomed us on all our cruises to the island.

great interest to his cruise by spending a few days at Grand Manan," the words "staunch" and "competent" lead us seaward again.

Duncan's advice for finding Grand Manan in thick fog (and we certainly had plenty of that) was simple. "An ideal plan," he wrote, "is to leave Cutler in the morning on the first of the flood and steer for the bold west shore of Grand Manan south of Dark Harbor. This course runs about 17 miles and, as almost every possible wind in summer will be fair for it, a sailing vessel should reach the island in about three hours. Don't worry about fog, as one cannot miss the island on this course. . . . When the time has run out, keep a sharp watch for the cliffs. They appear in the fog as a great dark mass above the gray water, divided from it by a light line of surf and light-colored rocks. In daylight you'll probably see the land before you strike, as the shore is very bold."

As usual, Duncan's "plan" (based as it was on a lifetime of summer cruises in these waters), proved perfect. At the very moment we began to nervously anticipate their appearance through the shimmering fog, the mighty cliffs of Grand Manan loomed overhead, the light line of surf came clear. At that point, all we had to do was take a left and follow the cliffs to Long Eddy Point, make a couple of right turns marked by noisy buoys and fog signals, before slipping into the "made" Harbor at North Head.

By the time we arrived at Long Eddy Point, however, these navigational aids were rendered moot. The morning's fog had burned off. With unlimited visibility and warm sunshine we were free to experience a miraculous upwelling of marine and avian life drawn to the plankton-rich waters of the Long Eddy. Porpoise and dolphin tumbled through the bright waters. Finback and minke whales rolled and sounded. Red-throated phalaropes, tiny pelagic shorebirds often found in the speeding waters of the bay, stirred up copepods on the surface with a patented spinning move—their continuous snatching and dibbling at unseen zooplankton, suggesting the richness of these waters. In addition to phalaropes, Leach's petrels danced their butterfly dances across the surface in search of food; gannets and terns peppered the waters whenever a school of herring pushed to the surface; while overhead for miles, gulls and kittiwakes by the thousand shrieked and dipped for scraps along the tide rips.

Mesmerized by this symphony of water and fish, this confetti of birds, Joel shut down the engine and we drifted through a sweet prelude to the life of Grand Manan. Before we had taken time for its soaring geology—a geology more reminiscent of the Montana wilderness than the Atlantic Coast—before we had visited the island's sturdy harbors stocked with some of the handsomest wooden fishing boats in North America, we had already tasted Grand Manan's magic.

Slowly the flood tide eased, and with the slack water, the hubbub dispersed. A strong southerly breeze made up, and sailing a series of long and short tacks, we worked our way around the Swallow Tail toward North Head. In preparation to slipping inside the arms of the big government dock, we lowered sail and started the engine. A minute or two later, a rare look of panic on his face, Joel shut it back down again. The engine's temperature gauge was jammed to the top and was sticking right there. Because our position put us too close to the lee shore of the ferry dock to make sail and claw out of trouble against an afternoon seabreeze blowing straight in at a steady twenty-five knots, there was nothing for us to do but anchor in fifty feet of water. Lucky for us we had that big yachtsman anchor with plenty of rode ready to go off the bowsprit. But even with the anchor down and

The government dock, social hub of Grand Manan's fishing community, provided refuge for Northern Crown.

appearing to hold, as Joel rowed into the dock to hunt up assistance, we took the extra precaution of assembling the three-piece Herreshoff storm anchor on deck, just in case.

At that precise moment—wouldn't you know it?—we got a panicky blast of fog horn as the ferry from Black's Harbor, New Brunswick, swept around the point to find us anchored in her path. With worried looks all around on both vessels, the ferry shuddered into reverse, backed down full astern, reconnoitered the situation, and then managed to wriggle into her berth behind us just as Joel returned aboard a herring "pumper" called the *Lady Streaker*, manned by a full compliment of competent and amused fishermen, curious to find out just why a sailboat would come all the way to Grand Manan and then anchor in the mouth of the ferry slip.

By this time we were pretty famous ashore. The government docks of the island serve as far more than structures to tie up fishing boats. They are equipment service facilities, refueling stations, net mending lofts, lookout points, and above all, places to keep up with the news on an island where everyone knows everyone and what they've been fishing for, and what they've been catching, and what they just sold it for. Needless to say, our "rescue" was occurring in front of plenty of eyewitnesses.

As the *Streaker* boiled toward us, her crew flipped a couple of rubber tires over the rail. She slid alongside to catch lines, ferried us inside of the dock, and deftly deposited us outboard of a couple of fishing boats already made fast. Over the next hour, other boats of varying shapes and sizes tied up outboard of us. Suddenly we found ourselves part of a cheerful community of fishermen coming and going across our decks. Joel jumped down into the engine compartment to check over the cooling system while we bought a round of beers for our rescuers and anyone else who happened along.

Within a few minutes he discovered a shredded impeller on the saltwater pump, located another in the spares box, and had it installed and pumping. Without question his mechanical skills struck an appreciative chord with the beer-drinking assemblage of onlooker fishermen accustomed to repairing their own engines, and before we knew it, several had offered their pickup trucks to us the following day so we could explore the island.

After our lively entrance, we settled into supper and then decided to take a walk ashore. It was there we got to know an old-timer eager to share the history of the island with us. At his urging we piled into his commodious sedan and headed out to see whatever sights there were to see. Our tour guide turned out to be Gleason Green—high-line lobster fisherman; sales agent for Nova Scotia-built fishing vessels on Grand Manan and the

Grand Manan's working waterfront.

A highlight of any cruise Down East—a sardine carrier, loaded with fish and running full throttle for the cannery.

Maine Coast; and tireless representative of the energy, integrity, and intelligence we found to be qualities on the island.

Over the next six years we were to return to Grand Manan every summer. In those years we became close friends with several of Gleason's sons and grandsons as well as a couple of the fishermen who had participated in our original rescue. Back then herring (the fish that when canned we know as sardines) was a major cash crop. Along the shore of the island, they caught herring in fish traps called weirs. The idea behind a weir is that as a school of herring swims along shore in the evening—feeding on plankton—it is diverted seaward by a wall of net (the Indians used to use brush for this purpose) into a heart-shaped containment area. Thus confined, a school tends to swim in circles without noticing that the way it came in might also be a way out. When each evening a weir keeper checks things out and discovers fish in sufficient quantity going round and round, he simply drops a net across the entrance and he's made his catch.

Thanks to our new friends on the island, we were invited to tend weir with them many times. Often this involved steaming around at sunset checking for fish (an altogether agreeable occupation, taking place as it did along one of the Atlantic's most beautiful coastlines). When there was a major catch, we also helped get the fish out of the weir. This task was accomplished by purse seining the fish trapped inside the weir. First a purse seine was rowed around to encircle the fish. Next its bottom was "pursed-up." At that point several of us would jump into a dory to help gather in as much net as possible, thus "drying out" the fish in a space small enough so that a "pumper" (remember the *Lady Streaker*?) could come alongside, insert a ten inch suction hose into the mass of silvery fish, and pump them from the purse seine into the hold of a sardine "carrier" that had drawn alongside the pumper.

All this activity called for a choreography of boat handling, economic interrelationship, ancient know-how, and brute strength—the whole job lubricated by a steady flow of humor. Everybody in the boats seemed to be related by blood as well as by some kind of "share" in the deal. The guys drying up the net in the dory got a share of the take. The pumper and its crew filtered off the herring scales as they pumped fish into the carrier and these they sold to a plant in Eastport, Maine, that used the scales' "pearl essence" to bring out a sparkle in cosmetic products like nail polish and lipstick. The carrier (whose captain appeared to be everybody's cousin or brother-in-law), was employed to transport the fish to the cannery.

We felt privileged to share the work and to watch such a wide variety of traditional wooden fishing vessels doing the jobs they were designed to do. The seine boats and dories held great appeal of course, but to us the real queens were the double-ended sardine carriers. Highly maneuverable in the confines of a weir, seaworthy when fully laden (a carrier was said to be "floating on her fish"), and fast enough to deliver fish fresh to a distant cannery—the sight of these lovely vessels steaming homeward at full throttle never lost its thrill.

Not surprisingly given his boat smarts, Joel was sharply attentive to the way these vessels went about their business. Here was his chance to soak in at close range elements of both design and construction, to watch them maneuver (first empty then loaded) inside the weir. Finally, he could talk over the various histories of boats with men who took the enterprise as seriously as he did—men whose livelihoods revolved around (indeed depended upon) commercial vessels combining natural grace and sturdy functionality with such ease.

Inside a herring weir at Grand Manan.

Working the weirs and then later snugged down in *Northern Crown*'s cabin with a splash of rum and a bit of cheddar close at hand, Joel mulled through what became for him a crucial design synthesis; a building of contexts connecting form, function, and tradition. One could see him, as he talked about the boats, laying down a set of imperatives as to what worked right and looked right. Because these Down East trips immediately preceeded Joel's most generative years as a designer, one can only conclude these imperatives were critical to what he became as a naval architect. Banished from his designs after these trips would be that smattering of 1950s-style portlights—or something extraneous like a clipper bow grafted to a basic lobsterboat hull—that seemed to occasionally infiltrate his early work. Purged forever would be what he later referred to as his "youthful embarrassments." From that point onwards, there would be a firm and recognizable conciseness to the boats he drew. No lines just for the hell of it.

Furthermore, as his experience on the Maine and Maritime coasts deepened, as he talked through the evenings with fishermen and yachtsmen about boats and their uses, it became increasingly clear to him that very little in the way of inspired design just happened. Everything worthwhile had a precursor. Nothing came out of the blue. Perhaps this explains why he became increasingly comfortable in seeking evolution rather than revolution in the boats he drew. The situation could have evolved differently. He could have taken a very different approach. With his M.I.T. education, his ample curiosity, and his eclectic reading habits by which he seemed to process in whole gulps most everything the modern yachting press had to offer, he certainly had the tools and the training to be at the cutting edge of technology and design.

Lobsterboats like this were a common sight off Grand Manan.

Yet, counter to any impulse he might have had to go "modern" stood most of the other components in Joel's life. The make-do fun of a boyhood spent whittling out elements of play in the shops and barns and fields of his parents' farm in North Brooklin was one of these components. Then there was a young manhood spent working in close quarters to Arno Day, a boatbuilder who had learned the trade from his father and grandfather. Finally, there was the influence of his father, E.B. White, the writer whose traditionalist inclinations are so eloquently summed up in his essay, "Farewell My Lovely," about the passing of the model T. But whatever his reasons, without becoming either a reactionary or an antiquarian, Joel remained most comfortable doing things (and designing things) the way they had been done and designed before he came along.

The upshot of this was that in the last decade-and-a-half of his life

Returning to Eggemoggin Reach—always a sweet moment.

when he finally found the time and space to put pencil to paper in earnest full-time, instead of spinning off to chase originality for its own sake, Joel became a synthesizer—using his knowledge of maritime traditions and aesthetics, in combination with hard-won skills as a boatbuilder, to elaborate and expand context and performance in the modern, old-time beauties he was to design and build.

Considered in this light, cruising for Joel was more than setting sail down the bay, more than just a chance to step down off the treadmill of work at the yard. Cruising, it seems, helped define his art.

Ocean Passages

Integrity

In the late fall of 1969 Joel was invited by Alan Bemis to sail with him and several others from Portugal to the Caribbean aboard the schooner *Integrity*. Bemis was a well-known summer resident of Brooklin whose forty-four foot, 1930 Herreshoff Fishers Island class yawl, *Cirrus*, remains to this day a jewel of the Brooklin Boat Yard's storage fleet. Joel had been a regular crew member aboard *Cirrus* in local races and had won Alan's respect both as a seaman and for the work of his boatyard, which

Bemis described for the *1968 Cruising Guide to the New England Coast* as "the best yard anywhere, bar none."

An invitation to sail aboard *Integrity* held special appeal for Joel. Launched in December of 1962, *Integrity*'s design and construction were the culmination of Waldo Howland's seagoing dreams. Howland, whose Concordia Company of South Dartmouth, Massachusetts, was best known for the creation of the Concordia yawl, intended to build a vessel that— with as much "integrity" as possible—would recapitulate the finest traditions of the 19th-century New England schooner. When work commenced on the vessel in the fall of 1961, wooden boat building had descended to a new low point. Fiberglass stock boats were on the march and seemed to be the future of boatbuilding. Against this industrial juggernaut stood Howland and his trusty sidekick: boatbuilder, designer, and fearless advocate for pine tar, linseed oil, and red lead—Pete Culler. With the construction of *Integrity*, Howland and Culler would not only build a beautiful boat, they would demonstrate that a vessel built in traditional ways could be viable. The white oak of her double-sawn frames and bottom planking as well as the white pine for her decks were harvested from local trees, just as in former times. Her topside planking was remilled longleaf yellow pine salvaged from a turn-of-the-century school scheduled for demolition. *Integrity*'s spars came from trees hauled out of the woods near the yard, and her standing rigging was traditionally wormed, parcelled, and served. Even though synthetic line had been available for years and had proved its superiority in handling and durability, her cordage would be traditional manila. She was launched with flax sails.

Integrity became a familiar sight along the New England coast, a stunning reminder of past glories, a harbinger perhaps (and this was Waldo's fondest dream) of a wooden boat revival to come. After a trip to the Caribbean under his son Kin's command, in the spring of 1969, Waldo chartered her to an old friend, a Colonel Herrington, who sailed her to Europe to join the bicentenary of the Royal Cork Yacht Club and other nautical events in Britain. For Joel, the opportunity to join *Integrity* on her return voyage from Lisbon to the Caribbean was the chance of a lifetime. Thanks to Allene's willingness to tend the home fires as well as the yard's bookkeeping and daily business, and his confidence in yard foreman Henry Lawson and lead carpenter Elmer Bent to keep things running smoothly (the 35′ sloop *Cachalot* was being planked for an early summer launching), he flew to Portugal at the end of October, 1969. Fortunately Joel kept a diary of the passage.

The schooner Integrity.

Joel White's Transatlantic Diary aboard *Integrity* (Lisbon, Portugal)

Arrived 10:30 A.M. October 31. We were met at the airport by Col. Herrington and Count Caria. We were driven into the city by Count Caria, who is a Lisbon businessman and yachting big-wig. The city is beautiful—modern, much new construction, cobblestone streets (not all). It is built on hills rising from the banks of the Tagus River, which widens out to form a really large commercial harbor. There is a lot of shipping passing up and down the river—everything from giant tankers and freighters down to small fishing vessels, and a fleet of sailing barges.

Integrity is at one of the yacht basins alongside the river. The basin is nearly full of boats of every description, some beautiful, some awful, including a Chinese junk!

The crew consists of Rex Yates, captain; Jill Parkers, cook (both English); and Mark Priva, deckhand, from New Bedford. They are very nice and will be good shipmates. Rex has a beard that would be the envy of King Neptune.

We were taken to the apartment of Count Caria for dinner—very nice time, good buffet supper. The whole *Integrity* crew was there, plus Mr. and Mrs. Waldo Howland, their son Charles and wife who are about to leave for the Azores for six months to teach English, I believe. Home at midnight to catch up on sleep I missed on jet.

Saturday, November 1

Late breakfast, stowed stores, took walk along river, did a little photography, came back and started this log.

Monday, November 3

Still beautiful Indian Summer weather, warm hazy days. Shoving off tomorrow, I hope. Fresh stores are due today; Bemis, the Colonel, and Charles Thompson will be moving aboard, and a lot of last minute details. Got the fresh water hose aboard this morning and washed off the grime which settles out of the air in Lisbon. The Sour Kraut, our neighbor on a large motorsailer, is having his topsides patched by a Portuguese workman. He has a lot of visiting friends, but never seems to go out. Still, I don't wonder. The mooring system here in the basin, with lines and chains fore and aft, and boats on all sides, makes it a major production to get in and out. Some of the maneuvers are as good as a circus, with people hanging over the sides of nearby boats fending off.

Tuesday, November 4

We're off! Got our big anchor up, plus two belonging to neighbors in the basin. Luckily, we got clear quite easily. Powered down the Tagus—beautiful day, no wind. The sights are quite impressive as you leave Lisbon, with towns climbing the hills on the north side of the river, a big fortress with walls dropping into the water, and lots of shipping. When we got clear of the river, we continued powering as the wind was very light NW. Slight swell from NW. About 3 o'clock we made sail as the wind had picked up to about 12–15 knots NW—about the minimum needed to keep *Integrity*'s heavy gear asleep in a seaway. Making sail is quite a production, with Mark, me, and Rex providing most of the muscle. After tea, added fisherman staysail, which helped her speed as well as steadying her motion. Making perhaps 5–6 knots. Course 235° for Madeira. The plan is to head for Madeira unless the wind is unfavorable.

The watches have been chosen with Rex and Charlie taking the first, Mark and Alan next, and

Jill and I scheduled to go on the 8 to 12 tonight. Colonel Herrington stands watch pretty much as he feels like it.

MONDAY, NOVEMBER 10

Sorry about this gap in log, but I haven't felt much like literary efforts until today. Had a three or four-day spell with some kind of bug which made me feel miserable, but am back on top now. We are now about 100 miles from Lanzarote, the most easterly of the Canary Islands, only 80 miles off the African coast. Calms, light head winds, and a heavy swell from the west have all conspired to keep us from Madeira, and we have made most of our progress by diesel propulsion until today, when we got a nice sailing breeze from the west. We are now stepping along nicely under four lowers plus fisherman staysail. *Integrity*'s range under diesel is considerable—moving slowly at 1,300 RPM, she does about 5 kn. and only uses 1½ gals. per hour. With 240 gals. of fuel, this works out to 160 hours of running time and a range of 800 sea miles. Pretty good. She needs it, however, as she simply will go nowhere to windward or in light airs. It takes a 15-knot breeze to even get her underway. We ran one night under power into a nasty sort of head sea and she reminded me of a snowplow—she would smash into a sea until it stopped her, then back off and smash it again!

Had a fine swimming party yesterday. We stopped the engine for a check up, and all hands except the Colonel and Charlie went swimming. Water really warm, crystal clear, and a deep indigo blue. Felt good to soap up with detergent and rinse off some of the dirt. Yesterday afternoon we began to see small Portuguese men-of-war, sailing in lazy circles in the flat calm. At sea in a flat calm, one begins to get the impression that the boat is smack in the center of a bowl-shaped depression in the water, which slopes upwards in all directions to the horizon. The more you think about it, the deeper the bowl gets.

Alan and Mark saw a spectacular meteorite on their watch—it left a luminous trail in the sky, then exploded with a great deal of light into two pieces, which continued on. They said the cloud formed by its passage through the atmosphere lasted for more than half an hour.

A curious porpoise leapt high above deck yesterday at cocktail hour, but not liking the looks of the hors d'oeuvres, refused to reappear. Outside of porpoises, petrel, and shearwater, life in the sea is not too plentiful in these waters. The shearwaters are great glider pilots—they skim the contours of the large swells very closely, and seem to go for miles without a stroke of the wings. I suppose that the speed of advance of a large swell creates an uplift on the forward side of the wave, which the shearwaters use to their advantage.

Rex, and particularly Jill, have been helping me learn a little about celestial navigation. The mathematics is not too complicated, consisting mostly of entering tables and making corrections to observed angles. But the physical aspects of taking sights—which I haven't had much chance to practice yet—are interesting. Sun sights can be taken any time old sol is at a reasonable height above the horizon—20° or more—and the noon sight for latitude is taken when the sun reaches its highest altitude for the day at local apparent noon. But the star sights, which Rex really counts on for fixes, have to be taken just at sunrise or sunset, when both the body and the horizon can be seen well. It is quite a trial to bring a star down to the horizon with a sextant, especially if the boat is bucketing about. But three or four accu-

Joel takes a sun sight from Integrity.

rate star sights will give a tight little triangle of lines of position, and you can be sure that your ship is somewhere inside it.

THURSDAY, NOVEMBER 13

On Tuesday morning, on awakening at 6:30 A.M., land was close aboard to starboard. And what land! Great volcanic peaks, many with cones partially blasted away on one side, and great dark lava flows running towards the sea—the island of Lanzarote, Canary Islands. It is a barren looking landscape with small villages of white stucco houses, some at the water's edge, others high among the peaks and valleys. Still no wind, so we motored SW along the eastern side of the island to the city of Arrecife, the principal port of the island. Entered the southerly of the two harbors which are formed by building breakwaters. Found several yachts there, among them *Easter*, Royal Cruising Club, *Maggie May*, also English,

and *Rose Rambler*, with Humphrey Barton aboard. All these yachts are also bound across the Atlantic. The inside of the breakwater is lined with Spanish fishing vessels, some of them quite large tuna fishermen. Yesterday we went in alongside one of them to refuel from 55-gallon drums brought down to dockside, and while awaiting the fuel, made friends with a couple of fishermen who took us aboard a couple of the boats. The method of fishing is interesting—they first set seines to catch millions of sardines for bait. These are kept in bait tanks across the stern of the ship aft of the engine room, which have water continuously pumped through them to keep the bait alive. The bait is used to attract tuna to the ship, where they are caught on bamboo poles with short lines and hooks, just as is done on the West Coast, USA. We saw several of these boats unloading tuna, many of them 400–600 pounders. Our tour included crew's quarters forward, very nicely fitted out with triple-deck rows of bunks, officers quarters aft under the pilot house, and engine room, which is kept like a surgical operating room. The chief engineer proudly showed us the 8-cylinder Deutz 490-hp diesel, a smaller diesel generating plant and bait pump, refrigeration for the holds, electrical switch panel, and complete workbench, all in apple-pie order and gleaming with polished brass and copper. With a smile he swung open a manhole cover in the aft bulkhead and there, behind a plate of glass, were the bait, millions of them, swimming in slow clockwise circles in their tanks, illuminated by sunlight shining down through the hatches on the after deck. A startling sight! After our tour, conducted mostly in sign language and much incomprehensible Spanish, back to *Integrity*. The fuel had arrived and we siphoned it into the tanks (and all over the decks) with borrowed hoses, helped by our fishermen friends. One, the cook on the tuna boat, also produced a fish, which we had for supper, and after an hour's absence, a bottle of cognac which he brought aboard and polished off with the help of the crew of *Integrity*. Cognac made his tongue move more swiftly, and by the end of the bottle, he was absolutely loquacious. Thank God Jill can speak a little Spanish, but she had to slow him down in order to get the gist. A busy afternoon, and most instructive. Alan and Charlie had gone on a tour of the volcanoes, and arrived back at the end of all this.

The town of Arrecife, into which Mark and I walked one afternoon, is not particularly attractive—the streets are lined with blank house fronts, and much of it seems to be in the process of rebuilding. Along the waterfront, they are building a high-rise hotel, there is a new yacht club where water is available, and they seem to be making an effort to attract tourists and yachts. Their best feature at the moment is the harbor, which is still reasonably clean, with wonderful clear blue water, showing every detail of bottom 20 feet down. Great swimming and snorkeling, which I tried yesterday for the first time.

We are all topped off on fuel and water, resupplied with food and drinks, the wind has shifted northerly, which is perfect for us, and we plan to leave today about noon.

SUNDAY, NOVEMBER 16

We sailed from Lanzarote about 2:30 Thursday afternoon, having a beautiful broad reach SW along the lee shore of the island. Saw our first flying fish of the voyage, several quite large ones bursting from the water and making flights of 20–50 yards, mostly downwind. About sunset passed between Lanzarote and the island of Fuerte-

ventura and as we reached more open water, the wind and sea picked up. It was a rather uncomfortable night, and mal de mer struck down some of the crew. By dawn next morning, we were passing Las Palmas, on the island of Gran Canaria, wind still NE, on a broad reach. All day Friday, WNW, towards Tenerife, the highest island in the Canaries, with a conical peak which reaches to 12,000 feet! Our course would just let us stand into the city of Santa Cruz, and we decided in the late afternoon to put in, partly to give Alan more rest, as he has reinjured an old hernia, and partly to enable us to tighten up the mainmast rigging, which is just loose enough so that the topmast bends quite a lot with the fisherman up. Santa Cruz turns out to be a very busy commercial port, with lots of shipping inside the two breakwaters, the most northerly of which is under construction day and night. We powered in just at dusk, and after finding quite a swell at the anchorage off the yacht club, went up to the north and anchored in 30 feet off the stone quarry where blocks for the breakwater are being cut.

Had a quiet night, and next morning, turned to setting up lanyards on main rigging. A five-part tackle is hooked up to the lanyard, the throat tackle made up to that, grease the lanyard, and haul away. Got everything humming tight, and the mast sits much better now. Left about noon, moderate NE trades, sailed SSW down eastern side of Tenerife. Peaks hidden in cloud until just before sunset, they suddenly appeared—a great sight. The wind picked up some at night and shifted more E, so had fine sail all night, averaging about SW, and making 22 miles a watch. By dawn Tenerife no longer visible, though I think if the atmosphere had been really clear, it would certainly have been well within sight.

Breeze picked up more at dawn, and the sea

with it until now it is blowing about 30 mph and we had taken in the fisherman. The old girl is moving along as though she really wanted to get home.

My thoughts turn to home often, and wonder how all is going. It is hard to realize that Christmas and cold weather are hard by—here we are lounging on deck in shorts, with the temperature in the 70s, I would guess. Well, at this rate we should be there in time to open our stockings.

TUESDAY, NOVEMBER 18

The wind dropped Sunday afternoon, and all day Monday was in light northeasters. Day's run noon to noon 66 miles. Wind is a little better this morning and we hope to do better today. Made breakfast this morning, bacon and fried eggs, and it wasn't too bad if I do say so. Aired out bedding after breakfast—getting to be a regular little housewife. Beautiful trade wind day, with bright sun, puffy clouds, and moderate NE winds. The nights are getting warmer, and more humid, and just a sheet is all one needs for bedclothes.

Had a busy watch last night, as we had to jibe over to port tack. This means taking down fisherman staysail, then resetting it on the other side. It takes about 30–45 minutes at night to jibe. Then the wind went very light, and Jill and I took down the mainsail to stop the slatting. We have found fisherman staysail and all other forward sails, but no mainsail, the best rig in very light air, and with a vang each way on the foresail gaff we can keep that sail from banging about. The mainsail is impossible unless there is at least 10 mph of wind to keep it steady.

I am going to try working out some sun sights today, to see if my navigation reading is doing any good.

I have been reading Robin Knox-Johnson's book about his single-handed non-stop voyage around the world. Fascinating, the motives which send people out for feats of derring-do.

I find a sea voyage the perfect place to read such a book as one can more easily identify with the problems and pleasures he experienced.

It looks like we might easily be out 30 days on this passage from Tenerife to Grenada, as it is about 3,000 miles, and with light wind such as we are having at present, we will do well to average 100 miles a day. This is fine with me, but has caused unhappiness amongst some of the crew, namely Charlie and Alan, who seem to be all-concerned with the deadline of Dec. 15, the day on which we have our tickets home. Their discontent makes Rex uneasy, as they try to pressure him for more speed, but there isn't much he can do, poor guy. *Integrity*, traditional in all things, is, as all schooners, traditionally slow downwind. Oh well.

SATURDAY, NOVEMBER 22

This log has been neglected for several days, mainly because life has been pretty uneventful. We have had practically no wind all week, and have been making poor progress except for a few hours under power. We are powering now, with a very light SW wind—no sign of a real trade wind. We are heading for the Cape Verde Islands, and apparently Alan and Charlie are planning to fly home from there. This is going to cause a major rescheduling of the voyage, as we will be short-handed after they leave. Rex is going to try to get his friend Elmer to come down from England to join us, and perhaps Waldo Howland. I plan to stay on, unless there is some pressing reason at home why I shouldn't. But it looks like it may well be Christmas or after before we reach Grenada. Alan's hernia is not good, and also he seems to be worried about Chapie [his wife], which is prompting him to leave, and I think Charlie is glad of an excuse to go home, as he doesn't really seem to be enjoying the trip.

I had the mid-watch last night, and as I didn't get much sleep before midnight I slept right through breakfast this morning until 10:30 A.M. I find time passes very fast at sea, as one settles down to the routine of watches, and reading, sleeping, eating, housekeeping occupy the off hours. I am practicing navigation, checking my fixes against Rex's, and they are working out pretty well in general.

Every day or two, a bath with salt water drawn in a bucket over the side keeps us clean, though salty. I am going to have to get Jill to give me a haircut pretty soon, though.

Yesterday we were followed by a school of dolphins, beautiful silvery fish with a deeply forked yellowish tail and fins. Mark managed to catch four on a hook he made from a coat hanger, using tinfoil and bubble-gum for bait. Fish for supper tonight. In the moonlight last night, the school could be seen trailing astern and alongside, with the moonlight glinting off their silver sides. About 2 A.M. a school of porpoises came by, filling the night with sounds of sighing, and an occasional splash.

This afternoon, just at tea time, we ran up to a pod of small blackfish on the surface. We got really close before they sounded.

TUESDAY, NOVEMBER 25

Yesterday had a good southerly breeze, 25–30 mph, but of little use to us as it makes our course dead to windward. After tacking back and forth for some hours, laying about 65° off the wind, and probably making about 1 knot to windward, we gave it up as a bad job, took everything off but the foresail, and hove her to, making about 1 knot to leeward. This eased the motion considerably, and she behaved very well. The wind eased at sunset, and the sea began to go down, so at 9 P.M. started diesel and plodded on towards Cape Verde, about 250 miles off. Powered all night, light SW wind, same this morning.

Took a detergent and salt-water bath this morning, including shampoo. The detergent is very difficult to wash out, and the result to my hair was about like pouring fiberglass [resin] over my head and letting it harden! Mark calls me Simon Smooth.

I have just finished reading Ernest Gann's book *Song of the Sirens*. It is very good, and quite funny. I remember reading about his square-rigger *Albatross*, which he sold for a school ship, capsizing in a squall in the Gulf of Mexico, with the loss of several lives.

I image that Allene and John are leaving today for Thanksgiving in New Hampshire—wish I were going to be there. It worries me that we may be so late getting to Grenada that I may not see too much of Steve and Martha at Christmastime. Perhaps our luck will change and we'll get good wind for the ocean passage and make a quick trip. The last few days have been frustrating, with nothing but calm and head winds. The pilot charts, which give the possibilities of these conditions as practically nil, have come in for some heavy abuse and coarse humor. Ernest Gann has very similar remarks in his book.

THURSDAY, NOVEMBER 27

THANKSGIVING—Jill and I had the 0400–0800 watch this morning, and when we came on deck, Rex was looking for the light on Santa Antao Island, which should have been visible. It was another hour, and the light nearly abeam, before we saw it. The sailing directions say these islands are often shrouded in mist, and this seems to have been the case this morning. Shortly after sighting the light, which has an elevation of 531 feet, we could see the peak of the island above the mist. It is a high island, over 6,000 feet, and lies about 7 miles NW of Sao Vicente Island, where we are headed. We hove to until after sunrise, and then made sail in our first good NE trade wind. The CCA (Cruising Club of America whose burgee flies from the mast) sails in triumph into the Cape Verdes!

The large alternator, which charges the 32-volt system batteries, quit day before yesterday, and our batteries are getting very low. We have had several attempts at fixing it, but to no avail. As I write this, Rex is getting ready to try a new alternator. This boat has a spare for almost every piece of equipment aboard.

Later—no joy on the alternator yet. Made Porto Grande about 2 P.M., in the first good sailing breeze of the trip, strong NE trades. The harbor is in a big cove, with breakwater to protect it from W and NW winds. Terrific screaming squalls came down off the high volcanic mountains surrounding the town. The population seems to be mostly poverty-stricken blacks, with a few Portugeuse and English. It is a transshipment center for all the Cape Verde Islands, as it has the only decent harbor.

Alan and Charlie are leaving the ship here, and I expect we will be here a week or so awaiting crew replacements. They are taking a boat tomorrow for Lisbon, and then flying home from there.

PORTO GRANDE—We stayed at Porto Grande from Nov. 27 to Dec. 5. Waldo Howland, owner of *Integrity*, and Elmer Storey, an Irish friend of Rex and Jill's, joined us for the crossing. Both are delightful, gentle people, and we are a happy ship

again. They each had to fly to the Isla de Sal, and we were going to sail over and pick them up, but when we came to go, the trades blew so hard that we gave up and came back. Sal is 125 miles dead to windward of Sao Vicente, and we decided it might well take us three days of hard powering to get there. So Waldo and Elmer managed to get to Sao Vicente on their own, by the little local airline.

By the time we left Porto Grande, the decks were covered with volcanic sand despite repeated washdowns. A virulent sort of stomach disorder was loose (!) among the crew, and we were all thoroughly glad to get away. We sailed on Dec. 5th at 10:00 A.M. in what amounted to a minor sand storm, with visibility cut to about 2 miles. We never saw Santa Antao Island, 5 miles to the west, but took our departure from Punta Marlado Lt. on the SW corner of Sao Vicente. Wind light NE.

DECEMBER 8

The past three days have been pleasant, if somewhat frustrating due to light air from E and NE. Distance made good in these days, about 220 miles, including 12 miles a day free ride from the current. The stomach bug has run its course and everyone is feeling better. We have settled into sea routine, and time passes quickly.

Last night the wind held up enough (just barely) so that we could keep the mainsail set all night, and progress was a little better (34 miles from 8 P.M. to 8 A.M.). Maybe this trade is getting ready to settle down and blow. We had nocturnal visits from porpoises last night, great soughing masses and fast streaks of phosphorescence, punctuated by an occasional entrechat as they leaped high above the rail to examine us.

Jill is making bread this morning—as a matter of fact, the galley is fairly running over with great high loaves and biscuits, as she used double the amount of flour by mistake. It smells delicious, and seems to attract admirers as honey attracts bears.

DECEMBER 10

The trade is doing better all the time. Noon 9th to noon 10th, 101 miles by the log, plus 12 miles current—113 miles for our best day's run so far. The sea is building somewhat as the wind increases, and the fetch from Africa gets longer, but it is not unpleasant. We jibed this morning from starboard tack to port, as Rex wanted to make some distance good to the south as well as west. The latitude of the Cape Verde's was about 17°, Grenada about 12°, so we must go about 300 miles south. The direction, as well as velocity, of the trades varies, going from about NE to ESE.

Waldo and the Colonel started betting a dollar each day on the length of the day's run— the Colonel picked a very conservative figure and Waldo a larger one—and the Colonel won for the first two or three days. But now the trend is reversed, as the days' runs are increasing. We also have a pool as to the day and hour of arrival in Grenada. I took the most optimistic view, picking Dec. 27, and they ranged all the way to 40 days by Rex. However, if we can keep up today's average, I can win.

I am beginning to long for home, as birthdays and the Christmas holiday near. I can't bear the thought of a desperately slow passage and missing the kids' vacation. Still, this is a poor attitude for the ocean voyager to take, as he is completely at the whim of the sea and its weather.

The weather is getting warmer, and it is uncomfortably hot lying in my bunk as I write this. I think I'll pour a few buckets of salt water over myself to cool off, and revive my wilting spirits.

DECEMBER 15

We are moving at last—our last two days' runs were about 150 miles each noon to noon, and I think we will do nearly as well today. I felt so optimistic yesterday I bet Mark a dollar we would have the anchor down in Grenada on Christmas Day, and if we can keep this up, I will win it. At noon today we will have about 1100 miles to go and ten days to do it, for an average of 110 miles a day.

The trades have settled into a real pattern. It blows up in the morning and the sea increases, then in the afternoon the wind dies a little, and later the sea diminishes somewhat. During the night, the wind is moderate, penetrated by rain squalls, some with quite a bit of wind for a few minutes. You can see the cloud approaching, with sheets of rain hanging down, and in about 15 minutes it is all over.

I have been fighting some sort of intestinal

Integrity—*tradition expressed in every detail.*

bug all the way from the Cape Verdes. Jill quickly put me on an antibiotic pill for three days and I think that has finally squashed it, although I am still going very easy on the eats. Yesterday I managed to pull a stomach muscle while steering—the boat gave a lurch and tried to throw me off the helmsman's seat—but it doesn't seem to bother me much today. Now if I can only kick my Cape Verde diaper rash!

My mood for the last five days has alternated between depression and optimism—I suppose due to feeling rotten, but this morning, with the thought that we are halfway there, from the time point of view, has buoyed me up. My daydreams are full of jet flights to New York and Bangor, family reunions, beautiful Maine winter, and SKIING! How I look forward to home—I think the trip has lasted a little too long. In point of fact, today is the day that I should have been on that plane back home.

However, we are having a great sail, averaging six knots, and land will be over the bow before we know it.

DECEMBER 18

Martha's Birthday! Fifteen years today, and halfway through teenhood. How time flies.

Time is flying on board *Integrity* too. We are on the downhill slant now, and I think everyone is looking forward to port. At noon today we have about 720 miles to go—not bad at all. We have been averaging about 135 miles a day for several days now. Day before yesterday, we had a vicious squall in the afternoon, and had to take down the main in the middle of it. The seas were really big and it was blowing hard, so we double reefed the mainsail and reset it, thus making *Integrity* in effect into a ketch, as her double-reefed main is about half normal size. This rig

works very well, as cutting down sail area aft makes her steer easier. We have left it up ever since. Yesterday the wind came from ENE to ESE, and as we were getting north of the rhumb line, we jibed to the port tack and are now able to head almost directly for Grenada. The wind has picked up again this morning, and we are making good progress.

I had another spell with my stomach complaint yesterday, but feel better today.

I must say something about flying fish. The water is full of them, and every night several come aboard. I got hit twice on one watch! During the day, it is fascinating to watch their flight. They swim right out of the water at a high rate of speed, usually headed to windward, and then take off on a curving flight which usually ends up heading down wind. They evidently can see out of water, as their path conforms to the contours of the waves. The distance they can cover is remarkable—almost 200 to 300 yards, although crashes are common. They often take off immediately after a crash, as though trying to accomplish a certain distance. I can't see that they use their tails or fins for thrust when in the air, but some of the flights they achieve dead to windward make me think they must.

DECEMBER 24TH

Christmas Eve will be our last day at sea. We expect to get into St. Georges, Grenada, late this afternoon or this evening. The last few days have been pleasant, and we have been averaging about 120 miles a day. Jill managed to produce a birthday cake without my seeing it on the 21st, and we had a fine birthday celebration. I even received gifts—a bottle opener, a steel tape measure, and a jackknife, which must have been purchased at either Lanzarote or Porto Grande. Even

Sunrise approaching Grenada.

a bottle of champagne (Brazilian and very flat) with supper.

Yesterday, we passed about 35 miles south of Barbados, and began to see evidence of land. A fishing boat in the distance, a large turtle on the surface, and two jets headed for the big airport on Barbados. We should sight the island of Grenada around noon today, 20 to 30 miles off.

It sounds as though everything in Grenada will be closed down for about 2 days (Christmas and Boxing Day). I hope to be able to get on the first available plane for Barbados and home, but anticipate it may be a bit of a problem over the holidays. We shall wait and see. I also hope that the ticket money for this airline reservation I sent home with Alan will be waiting in Grenada, as otherwise I will be pinched for cash.

We have made a good passage—19 days from the Cape Verdes and the weather has been great. All hands are looking forward to the land.

Upon reaching port, Joel found his money waiting for him. He booked a flight for New York the following day. When his plane arrived, the city was falling into the grip of a northeast blizzard. With La Guardia closed to outgoing flights, he boarded a train for Boston. He and the storm arrived simultaneously. Instead of waiting for things to clear, he opted for a cab ride to Maine—and to hell with the cost. Naturally he assumed he would have to shop the line of parked cabs for a driver willing to set off on a 500 mile round-trip in such conditions. Stepping outside South Station, he approached the first cab.

"How'd you like to go to Bucksport, Maine?" he inquired in that amused, matter-of-fact way of his.

"Sure," the guy said, "I come from there."

Without further ado or anything in the way of negotiation about the price of the trip, the cabbie called in and announced to the dispatcher, with laconic ease, that he was heading for Bucksport. He then proceeded to unscrew a prosthetic left foot and set it on the seat beside him, adding, "I always do this on a long trip. More comfortable." So off they went, Down East, for home.

Joel always remembered the trip with a chuckle, marveling at the spontaneity of the cab driver's life. No special preparations. No call home. Not even a full tank. Just head out into a blizzard for a 12 or 14 hour round-trip with your foot riding shotgun. Joel never got over how a man could manage such a thing.

The *Integrity* voyage had an enduring influence on Joel. In the years immediately following, he spoke often about his experience at sea as well as the pros and cons of sailing traditional vessels—often joking about *Integrity*'s doziness in light air and her legendary stubbornness about going to windward in virtually any conditions whatsoever. In this regard, the trip made such an impression on Joel that when he went boat shopping for himself a couple of years later, no schooner made his list of boats for serious consideration. Yet at the same time, he admired the schooner rig and its proud past, and yachts like Mystic Seaport's Sparkman & Stephens-designed *Brilliant*, as well as the Alden Schooners, were among his all-time favorite boats.

Years ago I remember sitting aboard *Northern Crown* with Joel watching Jim and Ginny Lobdell bring their schooner *Malabar II* to anchor after an Eggemoggin Reach Regatta. As usual the anchorage was jammed with boats, but *Malabar* rounded-up smartly into a particularly tight space and then—head-to-wind with Jim pushing her foresail boom forward—backed down smartly to set her anchor under sail alone. "Wow!" we remarked to each other at the time, the right schooner in the right hands certainly had a lot to recommend it.

Bermuda

In June of 1982, *Northern Crown*, with her regular crew aboard (Joel, the Brays, the Mayhers), sailed to Bermuda. We went because we enjoyed trips in this good boat. We were interested in the planning that was called for in an offshore passage, wanted the taste of a Gulf Stream crossing; and after a long, white winter, we wanted to get warm, anchor in the lee of a coral reef, and swim with tropical fish.

In this state of mind we started planning. First we talked about sextants and chronometers. It was Joel's thinking that a $16 plastic Davis sextant and an $8 quartz alarm clock would suffice for the short trip we had in mind.

Northern Crown, *weather cloths in place for her offshore passage to Bermuda, one of the few times she would be separated from her Jim Steele–built peapod.*

Joel aboard Northern Crown.

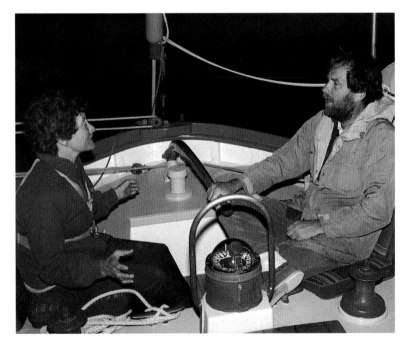

Bill and Anne—plenty of time
to talk on the dog watch.

Although he was always sensitive to other opinions, his logic in such matters was so clear he invariably carried the day. So a $16 sextant it was; that and a spare one, just in case the original fell overboard. After making the sextant decision, we read through Capt. Joe Thompson's "cookbook method" of celestial navigation as a prelude to standing in an open field on the shore of Jericho Bay practicing sun sights. As soon as we assured ourselves that a person could plot a relationship between a given celestial body and a hay-field in Brooklin, Maine, Joel figured we could find Bermuda.

With navigation settled, we turned to the question of a life raft. The options all seemed bad—expensive, chancy, cramped. Or as Maynard said while looking over a brochure for a reasonably deluxe unit, "If you think I'm going to get off *Northern Crown* and into that thing . . . ." We finally decided to borrow a friend's for the price of a certified repacking job. Cost: $280. State of mind: relaxed fatalism. To make sure we'd never have "to get in that thing," Joel and Maynard replaced a questionable plank below *Northern Crown*'s waterline before she was launched in the spring. Needless to say, setting off in a vessel that had received this sort of skillful attention was deeply reassuring—especially when the wind and sea began to pipe up all around us in the Gulf Stream.

After reading up on seagoing medicine, assembling provisions for what might turn out to be as many as ten days at sea, and purchasing enough flashlight batteries to jump-start the engine if we could have managed to get them end-to-end, we set out from Brooklin at 0900 hours on June 10th. The morning was clear and warm enough. A large low pressure system had passed offshore leaving a gathering northwest wind in its wake to hurry us down through the islands south of Deer Isle and into the Gulf of Maine. Except for spanking-new deck shoes all around and a few well-wishers at the dock, our departure didn't seem much different from any other cruise.

The first days were uneventful, although going to sea always involves relearning the various Houdini postures called for in putting on oilskins, and trying to get accustomed to the noisiness of a small boat banging about in big water. By our fourth day out, the Gulf Stream introduces herself with a smattering of sargassum weed. Little squall centers dot the horizon. Clouds hang curtains of rain down to the water. We pick our way through most of the showers, but with sea water up to 74 degrees, even if we get stuck in one, the rain doesn't hurt much.

At 1700 hours a more concentrated group of squalls ranges ahead of us. A lumpy band of dark water bunches up under a knotted skein of clouds. This riot of waves and wind and current—everything colliding from different directions and punching the sea into sloppy pyramids—we figure has to be the Gulf Stream. A wise sailor once said, "Never go to sea in a boat with a waterline length less than your age." As we bobble and slug and tumble off one shifting pyramid after another, we're understanding what he meant by that.

Sailing closehauled east of the course, we slog on for 24 hours. At dusk Maynard notes a new regiment of stratocumulus blocking our course. This is a cold front, he says, our troubles will soon be over. After a shower or two we'll have air from the north to put us back on the rhumb line. With advancing darkness the pace quickens. The breeze flicks menacingly, clouds have a green tint. Needing no further prompting, Joel and I take in the mainsail and the forestaysail, set the storm jib on the forestay, and then, as the wind tumbles down upon us, make the decision to heave to for the night.

You learn quite a lot hove to through a night. As *Northern Crown* crouches and battles in the river of the sea, you learn to trust the boat you are in. You go below and son-of-a-gun, things are pretty snug down there after all. You tidy up as best you can and crawl into your bunk to catch some rest even though your sleeping bag is soaked and twisted. Although the storm that night is not one of those fateful (occasionally fatal) microbursts, what we go through certainly qualifies as your garden-variety (50 or 60 knot) Gulf Stream humdinger. Shrieking wind. Rain like needles against your face. Dull orange and yellow detonations of lightning alternating with classic blue-green bolts.

With first light, the fair-weather side of the front glints astern along the northern horizon. By full daylight we set sail once again, ease sheets and take a ride, free for the first time to swoop down foaming crests. A tropic-bird crisscrosses our wake, its long tail and flashing black and white wings a perfect evocation of the wind itself.

We feel grateful to have weathered the night. As coastal sailors we were accustomed to controlling the events of a cruise. Alongshore, the luxury of a safe anchorage remains a given. Each day is always a separate entity. If conditions change, one just changes plans. In the open sea there is none of that. You deal with what comes your way. This lesson isn't lost on any of us, least of all Joel. Although never cavalier about the risks inherent in ocean passages, to experience the fury of the ocean in a 35-foot boat reinforces his conservative nature and guarantees that the boats he will design from that point on will have an extra layer of strength built into them for good measure.

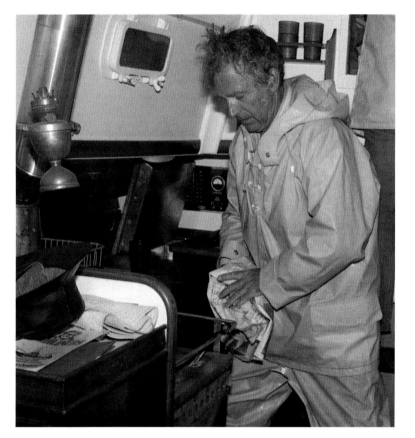

Stove lighting on a wet night.

*The sturdy W-Class sloops benefited
from Joel's ocean sailing experiences.*

As if to prove this point, twenty years after our Bermuda trip, the ketch *Dragonera* that he designed and built gets caught in an even stronger blow on her maiden offshore passage across the same patch of Gulf Stream. At the storm's height, a huge sea crashes across her afterdeck. It not only explodes the Shellback Dinghy set in chocks there, but slamming into a horseshoe life ring, mangles the $1\frac{1}{4}''$ stainless-steel stern pulpit: a stunning example of the force of crashing water. No other damage is sustained aboard *Dragonera*.

The same impressive durability has been displayed by the two 76-foot W-Class sloops. Although not initially conceived as offshore passage-makers, both *Wild Horses* and *White Wings* have shown remarkable resilience as they crisscross between New England, the Caribbean, and even on a transatlantic run from Europe to Antigua. For all the gracefulness and speed of his boats, Joel would never design one that wasn't also strong. After the Bermuda trip, it became clear from the way he talked through designs with clients and the men in the shop that he would never design or build a boat that wasn't double tough.

PART II

The Designs

SELECTED BOATS AND PLANS

Commentary by Maynard Bray

Martha's Tender

DESIGN NO. 2 (1963)

LOA	*9'6"*
Beam	*4'4"*
Draft	*6"*
Weight	*105 lbs. (approx.)*

J oel designed this V-bottomed tender back in the 1960s and he and his crew built several, including one for his dad to go with his 20′ Crocker-designed sloop *Martha* that Joel built in 1967. Some, including E.B. White's, were kept tied up to the boatyard float in the summertime. Through this exposure, many of us came to know and admire these fine little boats, so it came as no surprise that the WoodenBoat School incorporated "Building *Martha*'s Tender" as one of its early course offerings. Belford Gray, who had built a number of these boats while working for Joel at Brooklin Boat Yard, agreed to teach the course and he and his students turned out a record twelve boats in two weeks. Joel's shop drawings by this time had long since served their purpose and vanished, so he and I measured his dad's tender and from that information *WoodenBoat* had Dave Dillion draw up detailed plans suitable for publication. *Martha*'s Tender then became a three-part how-to-build article for the magazine. And, of course, *WoodenBoat* began offering plans for sale to back up those articles.

Joel designed *Martha*'s Tender to be simple to build, easy to row, reasonably stable, and above all, to tow well behind whatever craft she was tender to. You can also fit a small outboard motor to her transom. Compared with Joel's later designs for lapstrake plywood, *Martha*'s Tender is more conventionally built. She is planked with single side and bottom panels of ¼″ plywood that meet at the chines and are backed up by an oak chine stringer.

Sometime after the initial design, Joel drew up a sailing rig along with a centerboard trunk and rudder, so those who planned on building *Martha*'s Tender could sail as well as row or motor.

Martha

LINES & OFFSETS

When WoodenBoat first became sales agent for his designs, Joel was busy managing Brooklin Boat Yard. Drawing plans was a sideline, and he simply didn't have time to prepare plans in sufficient detail for the magazine's readers to build from. (He didn't feel in those early days that his drafting, especially his lettering, was quite up to publishable standards.) That's why this plan and the construction plan (facing page) were drafted by Dave Dillion.

OUTBOARD PROFILE

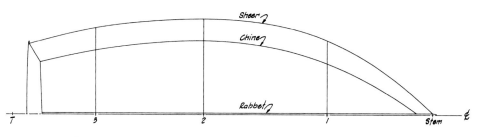

PLAN of HALF BREADTHS

TABLE of OFFSETS						
	Station	Transom	3	2	1	Stem
Heights above base	Sheer	1·6·5	1·7·7	1·8·3+	1·5·6	1·0·6
	Chine	2·6·7	2·8·2	2·9·4+	2·7·0	2·1·7
	Rabbet	2·8·6	2·10·1+	3·0·3+	3·0·3	-
	Keel	2·11·7	3·0·5+	3·1·7	3·1·3	-
Half breadths from ℄	Sheer	1·7·1	1·11·3	2·1·7	1·8·0	0·0·3+
	Chine	1·2·1	1·5·3	1·7·7	1·1·6+	0·0·3+
	Rabbet	0·0·3+	0·0·3+	0·0·3+	0·0·3+	0·0·3+

Offsets given in Feet·inches·eighths to outside of planking.
Stem is moulded 1" to Sta. 1, then increases.

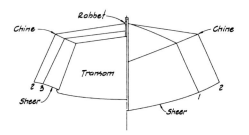

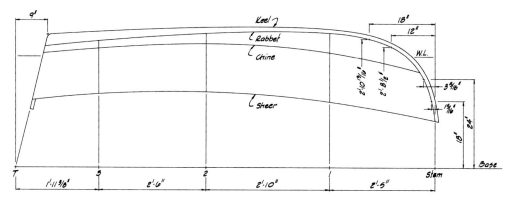

PROFILE

SAIL PLAN

When she first came out, *Martha*'s Tender was for rowing only—or possibly for a small outboard hung over the transom, although that option is nowhere on the drawings because Joel so hated outboard motors. Later, requests for sailing rigs became so numerous that Joel drew up this sail plan along with the necessary information to build spars, rudder, centerboard, and trunk, and it became a part of WoodenBoat's plan package.

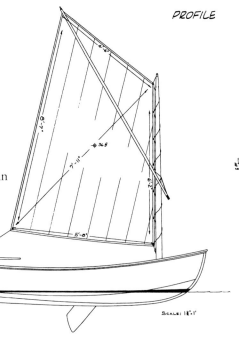

SCALE: 1½"·1'

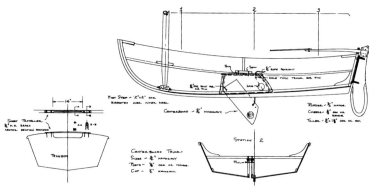

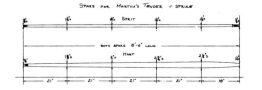

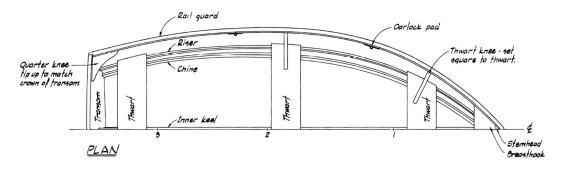

PLAN

Rail guard
Riser
Chine
Quarter knee tip up to match crown of transom.
Transom
Thwart
Inner keel
Thwart
Oarlock pad
Thwart knee - set square to thwart.
Thwart
Stemhead
Breasthook

MATERIALS

Inner keel · 2 layers ½" × 1⅛" oak steamed to shape and beveled for landing of plank.
Chine · ½" × 1 9/16" oak · steamed.
Seat riser · ½" × 13/16" oak.
Rail cap/rub rail · oak · see detail.
Transom · 1⅛" cedar or pine.
Planking · ¼" marine plywood · fiberglass outside to rail.
Keel/stem · oak · sided ⅞". Molded 1" from stemhead to Sta. 1 then increasing. See offsets. Face tapered to ⅝" from painted W.L. to stemhead. Forward part (stem) steamed & bent.
Thwarts · 1 11/16" pine or cedar.
Knees & breasthook · ⅞" oak.
Oarlocks · 9½" aft of thwart edge.

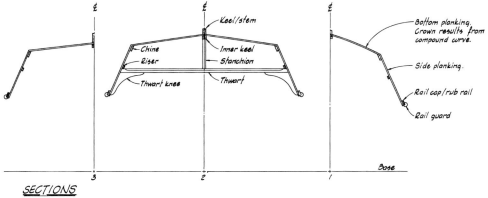

SECTIONS

Keel/stem
Chine
Riser
Thwart knees
Inner keel
Stanchion
Thwart
Bottom planking. Crown results from compound curve.
Side planking.
Rail cap/rub rail
Rail guard
Base

FASTENINGS

Inner keel · 1"-#12 ring nails. To fasten layers together.
Planking · ¾"-#12 or #13 ring nails to keel, chine & riser. 1¼"-#8 screws to transom.
Chine & riser · to stem with 1¼"-#8 screws.
Stern knee · 2½" or 3"-#14 as shown. 2" or 2½"-#12 from outboard thru transom and from inboard down into keel.
Quarter knees · from outboard thru transom 2" or 2½"-#12. from outboard thru plank 1"-#12.
Thwarts · to riser with 1½"-#12. 3 per end.
Thwart knees · 1"-#12 thru plank. 5/16" carriage bolt at inner end.
Stanchion · 2"-#12 screws. 1 at each end into keel. 2 down thru thwart.
Breasthook · 3½"-#12 or #14 thru stemhead. 1¼"-#12, 2 thru plank each side.
Keel · ¼" carriage bolt thru inner keel as shown.

All fastenings bronze; screws & bolts · flat head.

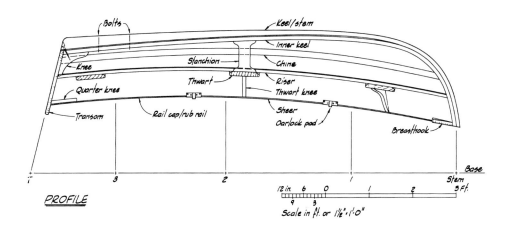

PROFILE

Bolts
Knee
Quarter knee
Transom
Rail cap/rub rail
Keel/stem
Inner keel
Stanchion
Thwart
Chine
Riser
Thwart knee
Sheer
Oarlock pad
Breasthook
Base
Stem

12 in. 6 0 1 2 3 ft.
9 3
Scale in ft. or 1½"=1'-0"

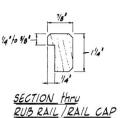

SECTION thru RUB RAIL/RAIL CAP

⅞"
¼" to ⅜"
1¼"
¼"

CONSTRUCTION PLAN

Unlike the shop drawings that Joel normally prepared, the drawings for publication had to include additional information like the materials list and the fastening list that are part of this sheet.

Cachalot

DESIGN NO. 3 (1969)

LOA	35'3"
LWL	29'0"
Beam	11'4"
Draft	3'6"
Displ.	19,500 lbs. (approx.)
Sail Area	615 sq. ft.

The story goes that when Joel's longtime friend and Brooklin summer resident Peter Sturtevant commissioned this design and asked Joel to build it, he had but two requirements: 6'6" headroom (Peter's a big guy), and a cost not to exceed $25,000 ready to sail.

Joel had built *Martha* for his dad a couple of years earlier to one of S.S. Crocker's designs. She was a handsome 20' sloop that sailed well, so it was logical for Joel to develop Peter's new boat from *Martha*, only enlarged. Thus *Cachalot* has a clipper bow with bowsprit, round-fronted trunk cabin, centerboard and outboard rudder, and a raking mast with a low aspect ratio mainsail and self-tending jib. Her hull was of glued strip construction instead of conventional carvel planking. Not surprisingly, below deck there's no resemblance to *Martha*. Here you'll find Concordia-type fold-down berths, a cast-iron woodstove, an enclosed toilet room to port, and V-berths forward.

Joel's wife Allene jokes that she and lead carpenter Elmer Bent built *Cachalot* while Joel was at sea on a transatlantic passage aboard the schooner *Integrity*. (It was a slow trip and Joel didn't make it back home until after Christmas.) Meanwhile, Allene and Elmer and the boatyard crew were doing just fine: Allene keeping up with the office work and payroll and Elmer running the shop. They were at a loss, however, when it came to building the rudder, as they couldn't find a drawing among any of those Joel had drawn and left behind. In any event, upon Joel's return, the rudder drawing surfaced (having been sketched out on the backside of another drawing) and the boat was finished in plenty of time for the 1970 sailing season.

Cachalot proved to be surprisingly fast under sail in spite of her short rig. With Joel at the helm, she won the 1971 two-day Round the Island Race that was sailed in blustery, post-Hurricane Doria winds.

When launched, *Cachalot* (named for a white whale, a carving of which hangs in her cabin) was appropriately painted white with a Persian red sheerstrake and green bottom—a color scheme that remained for some 20 years—after which she sported blue topsides with the sheerstrake done in white. Peter still owns *Cachalot* and has repowered her with a diesel, and last year commissioned a new ketch rig which was drawn up by Paul Waring, a boatbuilder/designer who works at Brooklin Boat Yard.

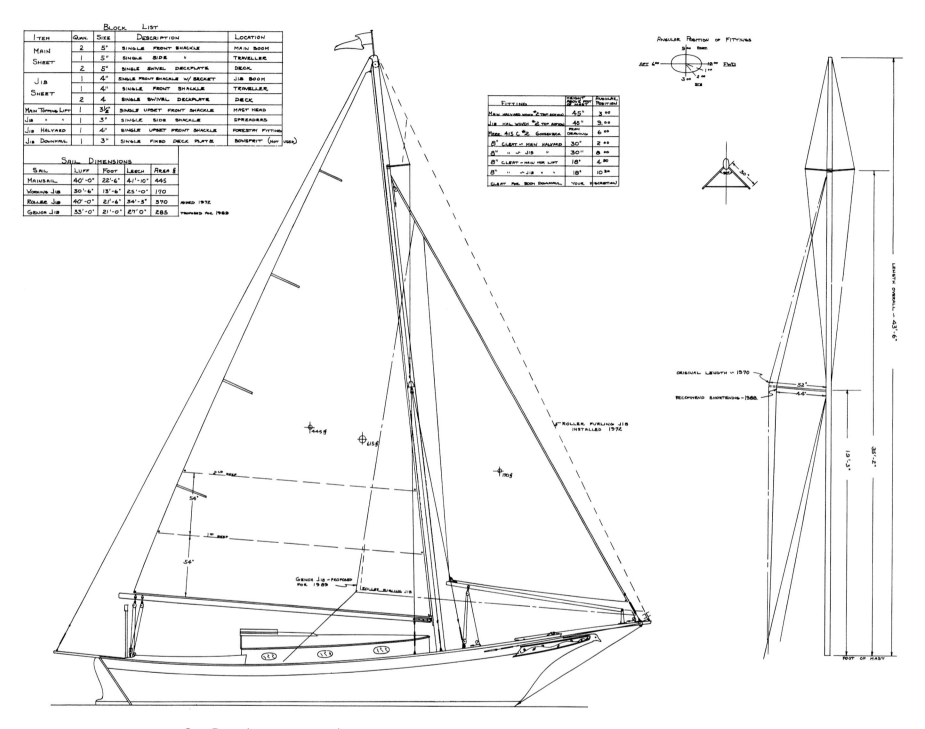

			BLOCK LIST	
ITEM	QUAN.	SIZE	DESCRIPTION	LOCATION
MAIN SHEET	2	5"	SINGLE FRONT SHACKLE	MAIN BOOM
	1	5"	SINGLE SIDE "	TRAVELLER
	2	5"	SINGLE SWIVEL DECKPLATE	DECK
JIB SHEET	1	4"	SINGLE FRONT SHACKLE W/ BECKET	JIB BOOM
	1	4"	SINGLE FRONT SHACKLE	TRAVELLER
	2	4	SINGLE SWIVEL DECKPLATE	DECK
MAIN TOPPING LIFT	1	3½"	SINGLE UPSET FRONT SHACKLE	MAST HEAD
JIB " "	1	3"	SINGLE SIDE SHACKLE	SPREADERS
JIB HALYARD	1	4"	SINGLE UPSET FRONT SHACKLE	FORESTAY FITTING
JIB DOWNHAUL	1	3"	SINGLE FIXED DECK PLATE	BOWSPRIT (NOT USED)

		SAIL DIMENSIONS		
SAIL	LUFF	FOOT	LEECH	AREA ☐
MAINSAIL	40'-0"	22'-6"	41'-10"	445
WORKING JIB	30'-6"	13'-6"	25'-0"	170
ROLLER JIB	40'-0"	21'-6"	34'-3"	370	ADDED 1972
GENOA JIB	33'-0"	21'-0"	27'-0"	285	PROPOSED FOR 1988

FITTING	HEIGHT ABOVE FOOT OF MAST	ANGULAR POSITION
MAIN HALYARD WINCH #2 TOP ACTION	45"	3.00
JIB HAL WINCH #2 TOP ACTION	45"	9.00
MERR. 415 C #2 GOOSENECK	6.00	FROM DRAWING
8" CLEAT ~ MAIN HALYARD	30"	2.00
8" " ~ JIB "	30"	8.00
8" CLEAT ~ MAIN TOP LIFT	18"	4.30
8" " ~ JIB " "	18"	10.30
CLEAT FOR BOOM DOWNHAUL	YOUR	DISCRETION

ANGULAR POSITION OF FITTINGS

ROLLER FURLING JIB
INSTALLED 1972

2ND REEF

54"

1ST REEF

54"

GENOA JIB ~ PROPOSED FOR 1988

ROLLER FURLING JIB

LENGTH OVERALL ~ 43'-6"

35'-2"

19'-3"

ORIGINAL LENGTH ~ 1970

RECOMMEND SHORTENING ~ 1988

52"

4.4"

FOOT OF MAST

SAIL PLAN (ORIGINAL SLOOP)

Joel added a light-weather, roller-furling jib a few years after *Cachalot* was built, and called for a slight shortening of the spreaders so they'd be in the clear when sailing closehauled. Joel's original drawing had so faded that decent copies could no longer be made from it, so he redrew it in 1988 as shown here.

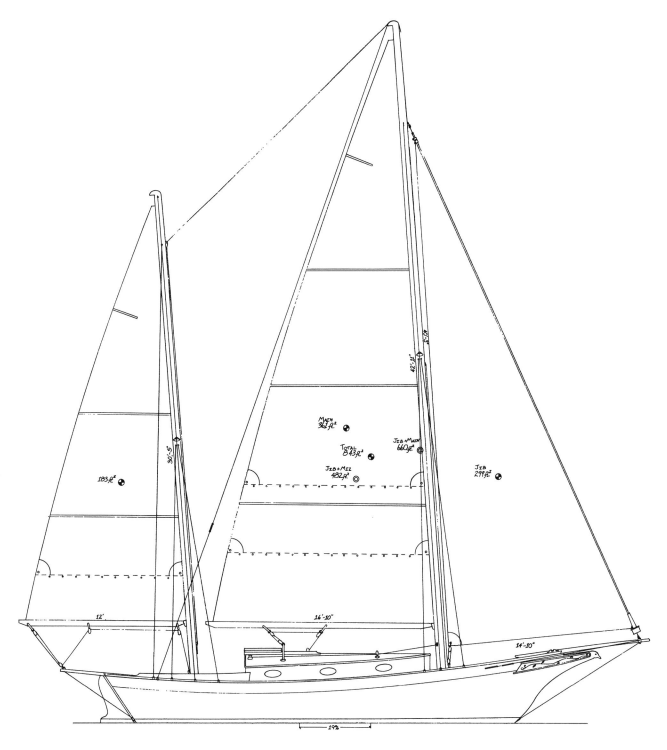

SAIL PLAN (SUBSEQUENT KETCH)

For the 2000 season *Cachalot* sported a new ketch rig making her easier to handle.
Paul Waring of Brooklin Boat Yard drew the conversion plans which called for a new
mainmast, a mizzenmast made from the original mainmast, and two new booms,
all of aluminum, as well as a new fully-battened mainsail and mizzen.

High Time

DESIGN NO. 5 (1975)

LOA	34'0"
LWL	31'11"
Beam	11'2"
Draft	3'6"
Displ.	13,250 lbs.
Power	210 hp Caterpillar diesel

Joel designed and built *High Time* for Brooklin summer residents Peg and Al Hunt who had decided upon getting a smaller boat than their 42-foot power cruiser *Harbinger*. Eldredge-McInnis had designed *Harbinger* and Newbert & Wallace had built her in Thomaston, so the Hunts considered it was indeed high time they commissioned a boat from Joel.

High Time is a picnic boat designed along the lines of a Maine lobster-boat with only minimal cruising accommodations. Knowing that his own yard would do the building, Joel drew only a lines plan to establish the hull shape and an abbreviated construction drawing just for yard use.

Joel learned boatbuilding from Arno Day, first as an employee and later as Arno's business partner. Together they turned out several lobsterboats of Arno's design, so when Joel designed *High Time*, well after Arno had departed, he was intimately familiar with lobsterboat hull shape and construction. Both *High Time* and *Lady Jeanne* benefitted from this kind of knowledge and experience.

The Hunts seldom used *High Time*, although they hired a captain who tended out on the boat daily as she lay on her mooring at the mouth of Brooklin's Center Harbor. *High Time* remained in the Hunt family for a couple of decades, even after Peg Hunt and Capt. Tyler died. Nowadays, with a change in ownership, she graces the harbor of Rockport on the other side of Penobscot Bay.

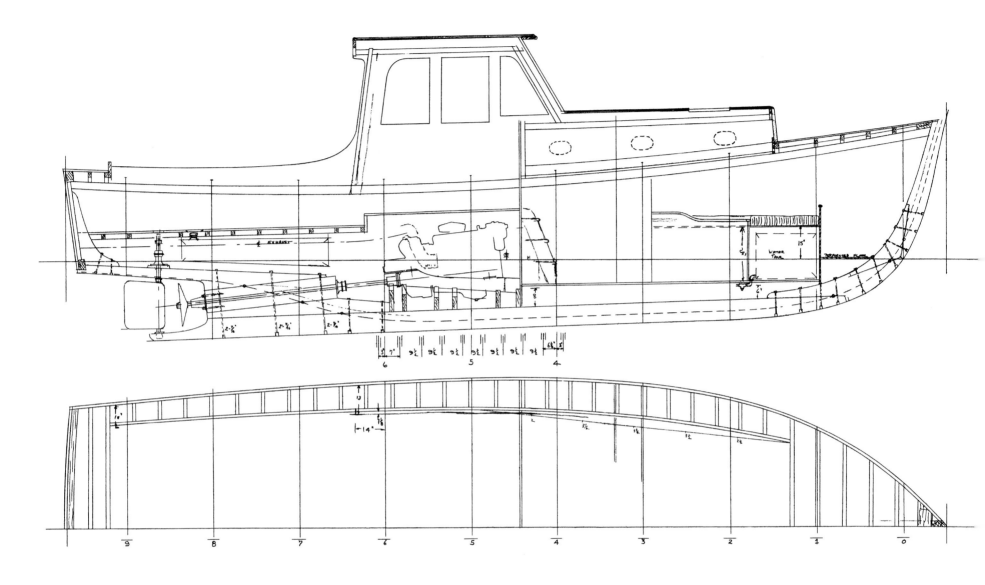

CONSTRUCTION PLAN

Because *High Time* was basically a lobsterboat only with more freeboard and Joel had built or helped build this type of craft, he didn't need much in the way of drawings. This is all that survives on paper of her construction. It indicates how the backbone is to be fabricated, how the deck frame is to be laid out, where the engine is to go, and gives an idea of the trunk cabin and wheelhouse.

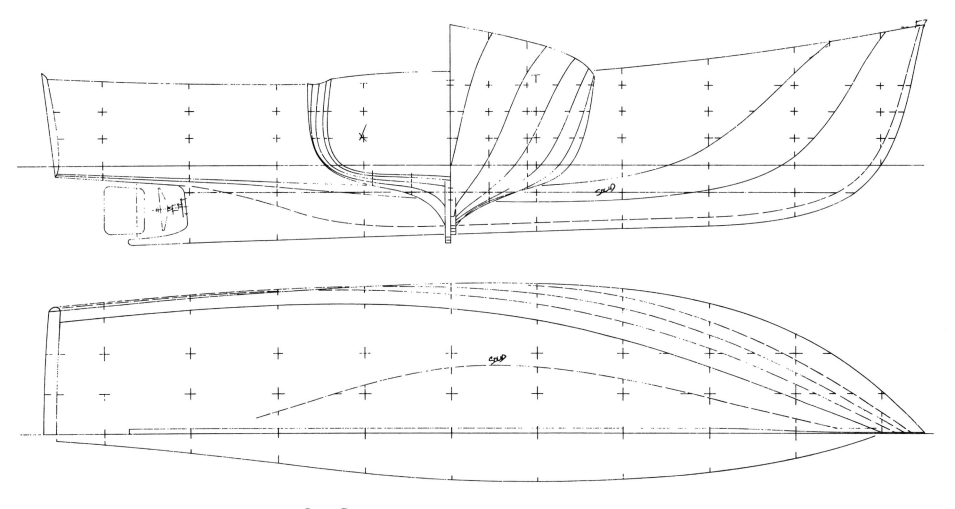

LINES PLAN

As I recall, WoodenBoat commissioned Spencer Lincoln to redraw this plan of
Joel's for publication. Before the magazine scheduled an article about *High Time*,
Lady Jeanne (Design No. 10) came along and seemed like a better subject. Their hulls
are similar, differing mostly in size, and Joel gave them both the semi-built-down
underbody favored by his mentor Arno Day.

Sailing Dinghy

DESIGN NO. 6 (1976)

LOA   9'0"
Beam   4'1"
Sail Area   37 sq. ft.

Yacht tenders sometimes have to be limited in overall length so they can be stowed aboard the yacht they serve, but there's usually no such limitation on beam. A short, fat little craft like this one is the result. To avoid tippiness, Joel made her wide at the waterline as well as at the sheer, giving her a quick turn at the bilge. To enhance her appearance, he rolled in the upper part of the transom in a trace of tumblehome.

For rowing any boat, fore and aft trim has to be considered. If there's too much weight aft the immersed transom will drag water and make rowing difficult, and if she's down by the head there'll be a tendency to sheer off to one side or the other. In this boat, as in most yacht tenders, two rowing stations allow seating options for getting the best trim.

For a sailing rig, Joel used a single spritsail with the mast partner consisting of a hole bored through the forward thwart. There are only two spars—the mast and a sprit—both of which will fit within the length of the boat.

Because of the twist in the forward end of the garboard planks and the quick turn of the bilge, this is not a particularly easy boat to build. For planking, there's an option of using either cedar or Brunzeel plywood. About nine planks each side are required, and 19 steam-bent oak frames—so there are a lot of pieces to cut out and fit. Joel designed and built this lovely little boat before he began to exploit lapstrake plywood and nearly frameless construction in later designs such as the Nutshell Prams and the Shellback Dinghy. The dinghy shown here has a more sophisticated shape, but building her is more of a challenge.

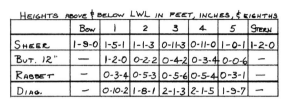

	Bow	1	2	3	4	5	Stern
SHEER	1-9-0	1-5-1	1-1-3	0-11-3	0-11-0	1-0-1	1-2-0
BUT. 12"	—	1-2-0	0-2-2	0-4-2	0-3-4	0-0-6	—
RABBET	—	0-3-4	0-5-3	0-5-6	0-5-4	0-3-1	—
DIAG.	—	0-10-2	1-8-1	2-1-3	2-1-5	1-9-7	—

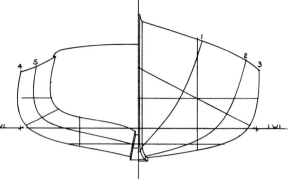

HALF BREADTHS FROM ℄ IN FEET, INCHES, & EIGHTHS

	Bow	1	2	3	4	5	Stern
SHEER	0-0-6	1-1-0	1-10-0	2-0-4	1-11-7	1-8-6	1-5-0
WL 6"A	—	0-8-3	1-7-5	2-0-3	2-0-5	1-9-3	—
LWL	—	0-4-1	1-3-5	1-10-1	1-10-4	1-2-7	—
WL 3"B	—	0-1-2	0-10-0	1-4-7	1-2-4	0-1-3	—
RABBET	0-0-6	0-0-6	0-1-3	0-1-7	0-1-6	0-1-1	—

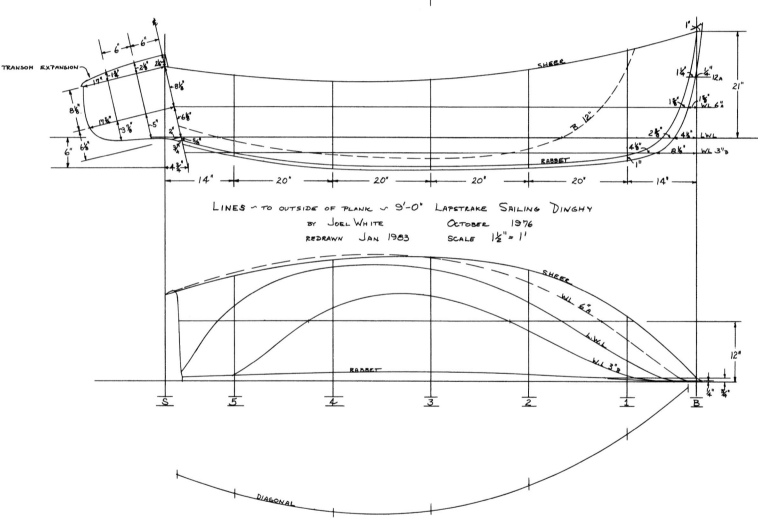

LINES ~ TO OUTSIDE OF PLANK ~ 9'-0" LAPSTRAKE SAILING DINGHY
BY JOEL WHITE   OCTOBER 1976
REDRAWN JAN 1983   SCALE 1½" = 1'

LINES PLAN

I suspect Joel placed the stations where he expected the molds to be located so as to avoid a full-blown lofting. Five molds may seem excessive in so small a craft, but she changes shape so quickly along her length, especially near the bow and stern, that fewer molds might not reproduce the desired hull.

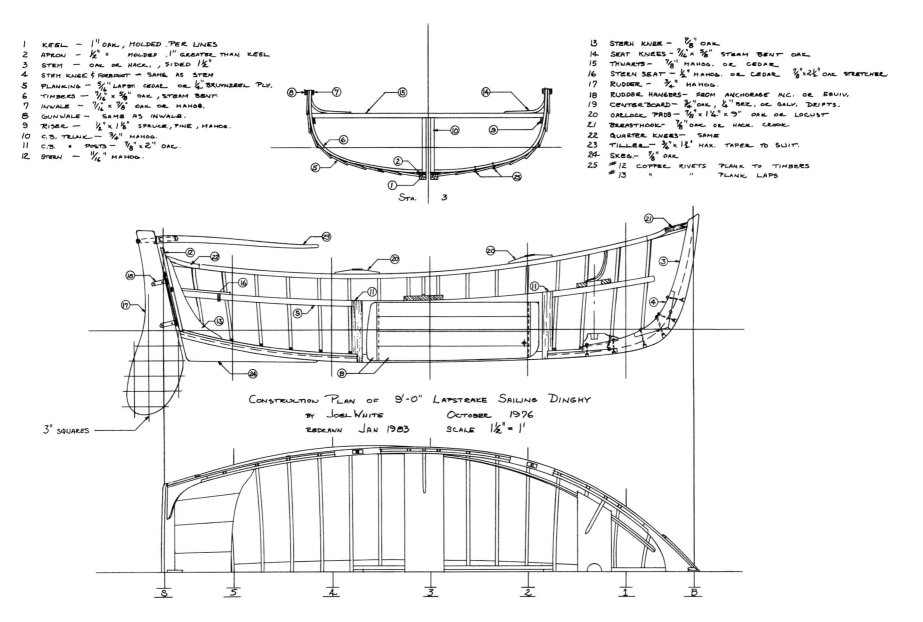

1. KEEL — 1" OAK, MOLDED PER LINES
2. APRON — 1/2" MOLDED 1" GREATER THAN KEEL
3. STEM — OAK OR HACK, SIDED 1 1/2"
4. STEM KNEE & FOREFOOT — SAME AS STEM
5. PLANKING — 5/16" LAPST. CEDAR OR 1/2" BRUYNZEEL PLY.
6. TIMBERS — 7/16" x 5/8" OAK, STEAM BENT
7. INWALE — 7/16" x 7/8" OAK OR MAHOG.
8. GUNWALE — SAME AS INWALE.
9. RISER — 1/2" x 1 1/8" SPRUCE, PINE, MAHOG.
10. C.B. TRUNK — 3/4" MAHOG.
11. C.B. POSTS — 7/8" x 2" OAK.
12. STERN — 11/16" MAHOG.

13. STERN KNEE — 7/8" OAK
14. SEAT KNEES — 7/16" x 3/8" STEAM BENT OAK
15. THWARTS — 7/8" MAHOG. OR CEDAR
16. STERN SEAT — 1/2" MAHOG. OR CEDAR   7/8" x 2 1/2" OAK STRETCHER
17. RUDDER — 3/4" MAHOG.
18. RUDDER HANGERS — FROM ANCHORAGE INC. OR EQUIV.
19. CENTERBOARD — 3/4" OAK, 1/4" BRZ. OR GALV. DRIFTS.
20. OARLOCK PADS — 7/8" x 1 1/4" x 9" OAK OR LOCUST
21. BREASTHOOK — 7/8" OAK OR HACK. CROOK.
22. QUARTER KNEES — SAME
23. TILLER — 3/4" x 1 1/2" MAX. TAPER TO SUIT.
24. SKEG. — 7/8" OAK
25. #12 COPPER RIVETS PLANK TO TIMBERS
    #13 " " PLANK LAPS

STA. 3

CONSTRUCTION PLAN OF 9'-0" LAPSTRAKE SAILING DINGHY
BY JOEL WHITE   OCTOBER 1976
REDRAWN JAN 1983   SCALE 1 1/2" = 1'

3" SQUARES

CONSTRUCTION PLAN

Unlike many dinghies, this boat's beam at the forward oarlocks is nearly as great as
at the aft ones, so rowing from that station is not at all pinched, and cross-handing
the oars is unnecessary.

Nicole

DESIGN NO. 8 (1977)

LOA	60'0"
LWL	56'5"
Beam	19'8"
Draft	7'1"
Displ.	111,560 lbs.
Power	GM 12V71

Nicole is the largest powerboat that Joel ever designed. She's also one of his few commercial boats. By 1977 when Joel drew these plans, the vast majority of workboats *Nicole*'s size were being built of steel or fiberglass—so the wooden-hulled *Nicole* was a bit of an anachronism. Had he lived a few decades earlier when wood was the material of choice, I believe Joel could have made an entire career of designing practical and handsome workboats such as *Nicole*. Steel construction didn't much interest him, and he grew to dislike working with fiberglass.

Joel was a demon designer who could turn out a set of plans within only a few days and with only a few erasures—especially if all he had to draw were the lines and arrangement drawings as he did for *Nicole*'s owner John Jones. Fast with a pencil also meant a reasonable design fee (Joel worked to an hourly rate) and that helped bring Joel his commercial design jobs. In *Nicole*'s case, both Joel and the owner knew that the Thomaston, Maine, yard of Newbert and Wallace that would be building this boat had long experience and would not need much in the way of construction drawings. Joel did stretch out the basic construction on a plan and ran it by master builder Roy Wallace for his comment. Roy approved it all, but suggested that *Nicole*'s sternpost be extended and bolted to the deck structure. Joel agreed and made this alteration to the drawing.

Nicole is a handsome craft with a springy sheer and an overall robust appearance. The crew quarters are forward of the fish hold and directly under the pilothouse, while the engine is located aft with access through a companionway back above the propeller. Draggers so arranged are known as western-rigged vessels and are popular in the smaller sizes. Joel shaped *Nicole*'s hull somewhat like a Maine lobsterboat, but with proportionally more displacement and a narrower waterplane aft. Viewed head on, *Nicole*'s lines show a slight knuckle at deck level from amidships forward where the lower guardrail runs. This gives the desired flare low down where it will keep the bow from plunging too deeply in a seaway, and also, because of the more vertical waist, prevents the forward deckline from becoming excessively full.

Owner John Jones praises *Nicole* as performing wonderfully well. With her he dragged for scallops off Cape Cod and landed them mostly at Hyannis, so we in Maine never saw much of *Nicole* after her launching.

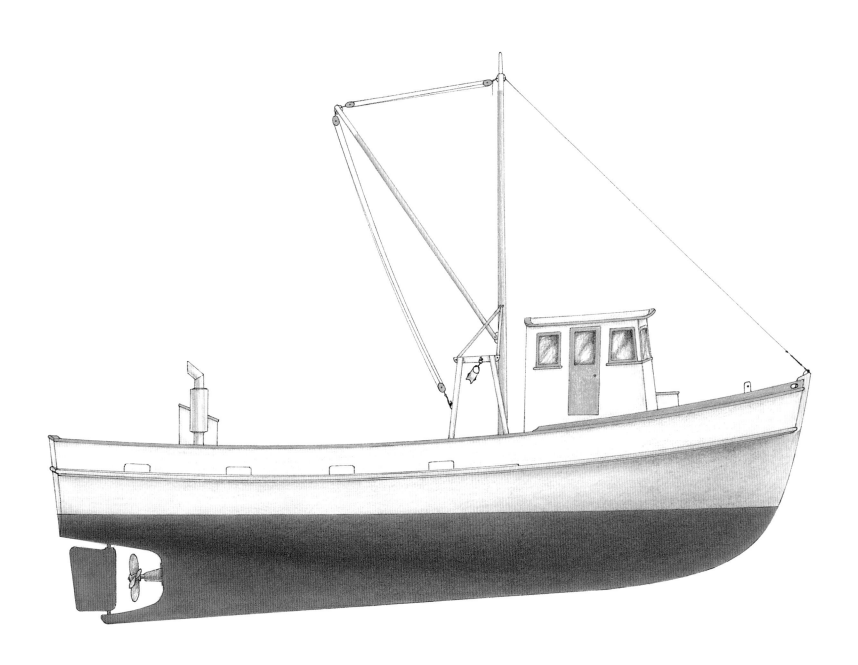

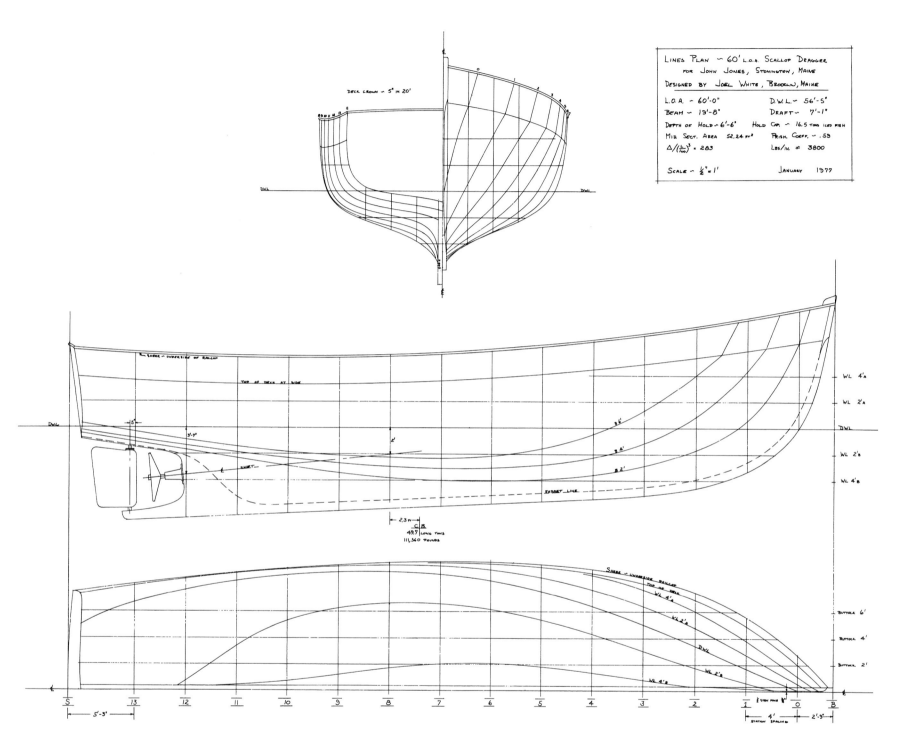

LINES PLAN

This plan shows a perfectly lovely, yet husky working scallop dragger, and one that performed beautifully in everyday use. Her shape is quite like a lobsterboat that's been enlarged and given a deeper body and proportionally more freeboard.

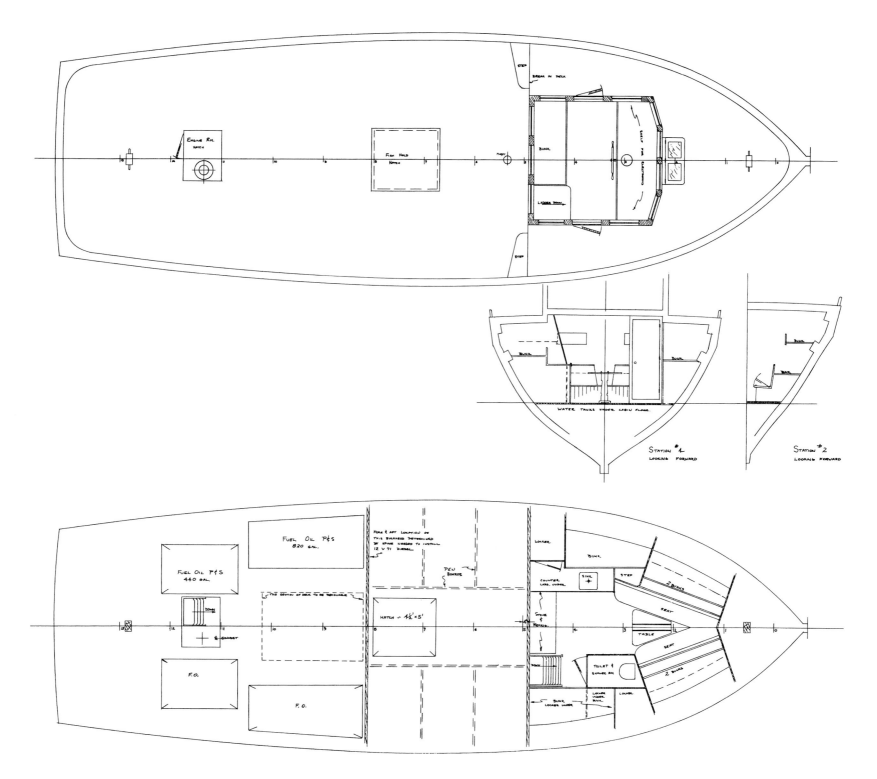

ARRANGEMENT PLAN

This drawing shows *Nicole*'s basic arrangement on deck and below. Crew quarters for six persons are forward with the fish hold amidships and the engineroom just aft of it. Plans drawn for experienced owners and builders don't require much detail.

Lady Jeanne

DESIGN NO. 10 (1979)

LOA	42'0"
LWL	39'11"
Beam	13'8"
Draft	3'11"
Displ.	26,512 lbs.
Power	GM 6-71 diesel

Jeanne and Joe Merkel had owned eight powerboats of widely varying description before they approached Joel about their ninth, so there was no shortage of experience on the part of the client. Likewise, Joel had designed and built several wooden power cruisers and lobsterboats, so ample experience also rested with the designer/builder. The result became the lovely *Lady Jeanne*, now named *Woody* in the hands of her most recent owner.

The Merkels wanted a more-or-less conventional cruiser, a type of craft known these days as a lobster yacht. She'd be laid out with the forward half of her 42' length devoted to below-deck accommodations, and with a larger than usual fully-enclosed pilothouse having its sole sufficiently high so there'd be no need for an engine box. But the Merkels insisted on a dry-type exhaust (with its exposed muffler and upwards-discharging stack), and *two* dinettes—both features being somewhat unconventional. A bathtub was also a requirement. Other client ideas included open storage lockers without doors, and shelving with high fiddles that acted as retainers.

Of course the boat would see lots of cruising, but she'd also be a year-round retirement home for the Merkels. There's a big and airy windowed pilothouse that contains the galley, the steering station, and one of the dinettes where one can enjoy seeing the outside world while taking meals, navigating, or just sitting.

Sleeping takes place below deck where the enclosed toilet room (complete with tub) is located. A second and more private dinette also shows on the drawings and was originally installed below deck—although a subsequent owner has replaced it with a double berth.

WoodenBoat featured an article by this boat's namesake and co-owner, and later Jeanne Merkel wrote a book entitled *Nine Boats and Nine Kids* in which this design plays a prominent role.

As has happened more often than not with Joel's boats, *Woody* (ex-*Lady Jeanne*) returns to the yard that built her each fall for winter storage.

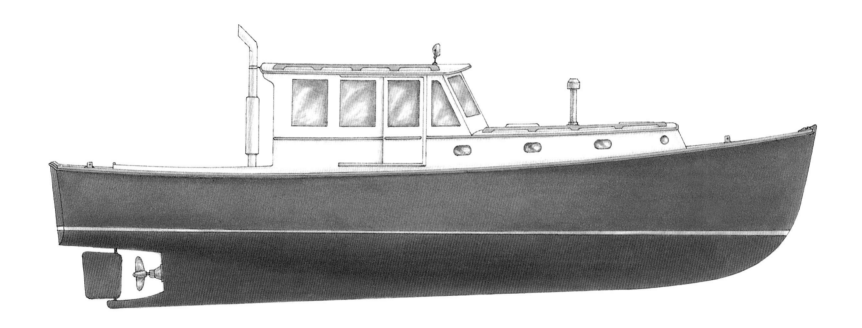

LINES PLAN

As with *High Time*'s lines, WoodenBoat arranged for Spencer Lincoln to redraw Joel's lines of *Lady Jeanne* in ink so they would reproduce more clearly. They were published in issue #37 as part of an article written by Jeanne Merkel who owned the boat with her husband Joe. Shown here is Joel's original lines plan.

ARRANGEMENT PLAN

Spencer Lincoln also traced this plan in ink from Joel's original for better contrast. But Joel's pencil drawing, computer enhanced and shown below, has been made perfectly legible.

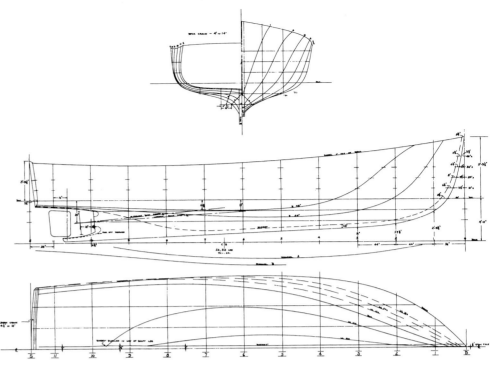

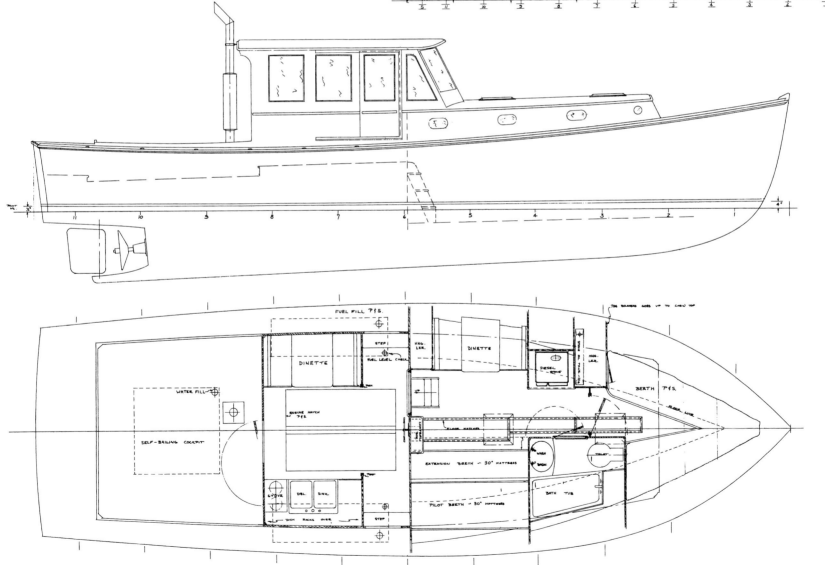

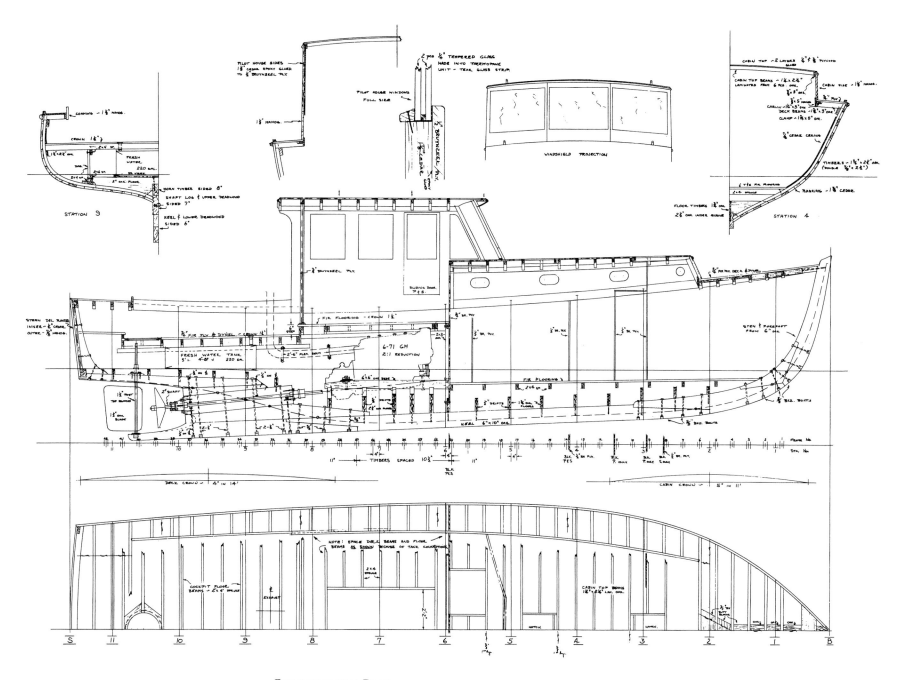

CONSTRUCTION PLAN

Joel always figured out the bolting of the backbone on paper before he began working the wood. He planned each piece of the stem assembly to not exceed the width of the live-edge oak that was commonly available. If the grain swept with the curve that was a bonus, but Joel always figured things based on straight grain.

Alisande

DESIGN NO. 11 (1980)

LOA	36'0"
LWL	31'0"
Beam	10'2"
Draft	5'2"
Displ.	18,127 lbs.
Sail Area	643 sq. ft.

Joel based *Alisande* on a design of the late William H. Hand, Jr. That boat, named *Fundulus*, started it all. Her key drawings, along with an inspiring essay, showed up in the first of Roger Taylor's *Good Boats* series of books and struck a chord with Kim Faulkner as a boat he'd like to own. Kim approached Joel about building her as well as developing the necessary drawings since the originals had not survived.

Joel dove right in, first drawing a new lines plan based on what had been published in miniature. (I think the length of the drawing as published measured only 6 inches from bow to stern.) He refined the transom by giving it a slight radius, established the shape and weight of the cast-lead ballast keel, and generally tweaked Hand's lines into a ¾" to the foot drawing that was fair and eye sweet—and from which Joel could measure the offsets and figure the boat's displacement, center of buoyancy, and other performance-oriented numbers.

An arrangement drawing followed, again generally along the lines of what Hand had shown, but with more detail. The long bridge deck that separates the trunk cabin from the cockpit was retained, as were the two round ports amidships on each side of the hull. Although unusual, this arrangement was perfectly workable and made *Alisande* unique.

Joel was on his own when it came time to draw the construction plan since there was no equivalent Hand drawing. Because Joel and his Brooklin Boat Yard crew were to build *Alisande*, his construction drawings are basic and lack the detail that Joel included in some of his later designs—especially ones for amateur builders that were to be sold through *WoodenBoat*. The Hand drawings didn't include anything regarding the cockpit and coaming or whether she steered by tiller or wheel. Joel called for a lovely, steam-bent oak coaming to surround the self-bailing footwell, and specified tiller steering.

I had the good fortune to be working for Joel the winter *Alisande* was built. Most of her spars including the bowsprit are my work, and I remember that after the woodwork on each spar was completed, Joel would measure for the circular metal bands to which the sheets and halyards would attach. These he'd draw out full size on whatever paper or cardboard was handy, and shoot them in to Hank Lawson who would heat, bend, weld, and grind steel flatbar to make each one. Near the end, when the spars were done and Hank had made all their metal fittings, the entire batch was sent

out for galvanizing. (Unfortunately, in retrospect, once Joel's shop drawings and sketches had served their purpose for this one boat, they were trashed.)

With her bronze-green hull, white waist and cabin sides, buff deck and housetops, and varnished spars, *Alisande* looked gorgeous on launching day. And when her engine proved balky, we raised sail and sailed her right off the launching cradle, around the harbor, and into the boatyard float where admirers awaited a closer look.

Kim used *Alisande* for a decade or so, then had the yard alter the trunk cabin and interior to a more conventional layout. Meanwhile, advised by Waldo Howland how fine a design this one was, Harry Bryan borrowed Joel's drawings and built a second boat, named *Patience*, in which he and his family cruised from their New Brunswick home through the Panama Canal and among the Pacific South Sea Islands and back again.

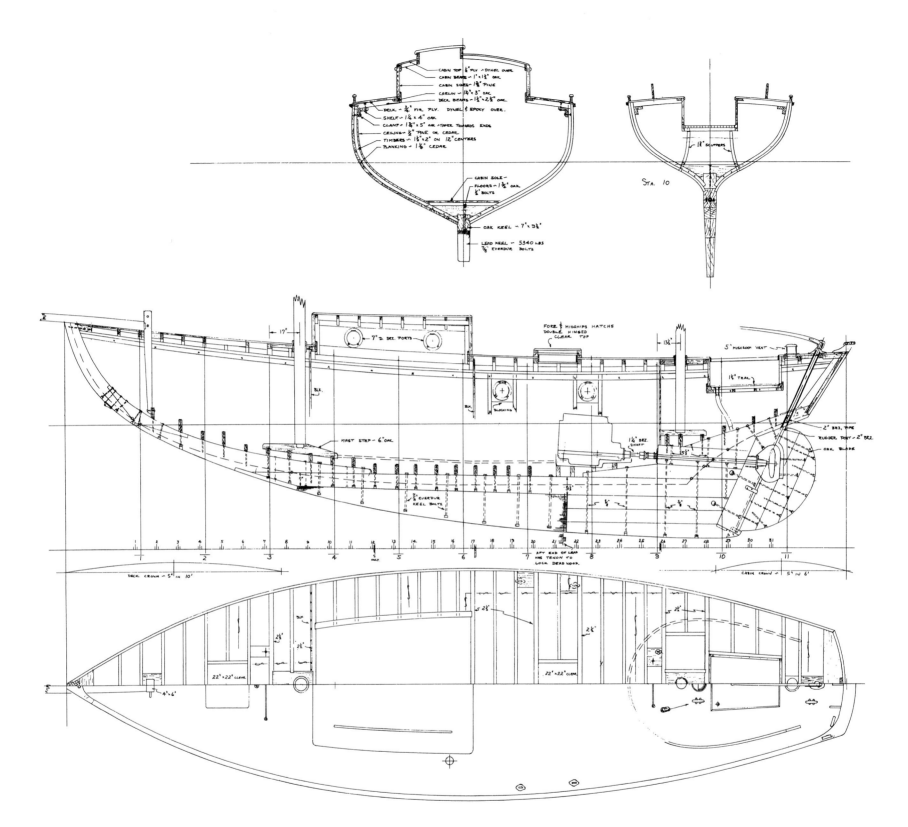

CONSTRUCTION PLAN

As a hands-on builder Joel realized the benefits of frames having a rectangular cross section—easier bending, less subsequent breakage, and more surface area for fastenings. Despite some yacht-building rules that called for square-sectioned frames, Joel's designs for plank-on-frame construction always specified frames that were wider than they were thick. *Alisande*'s, for example, are 2″ wide and 1¼″ thick.

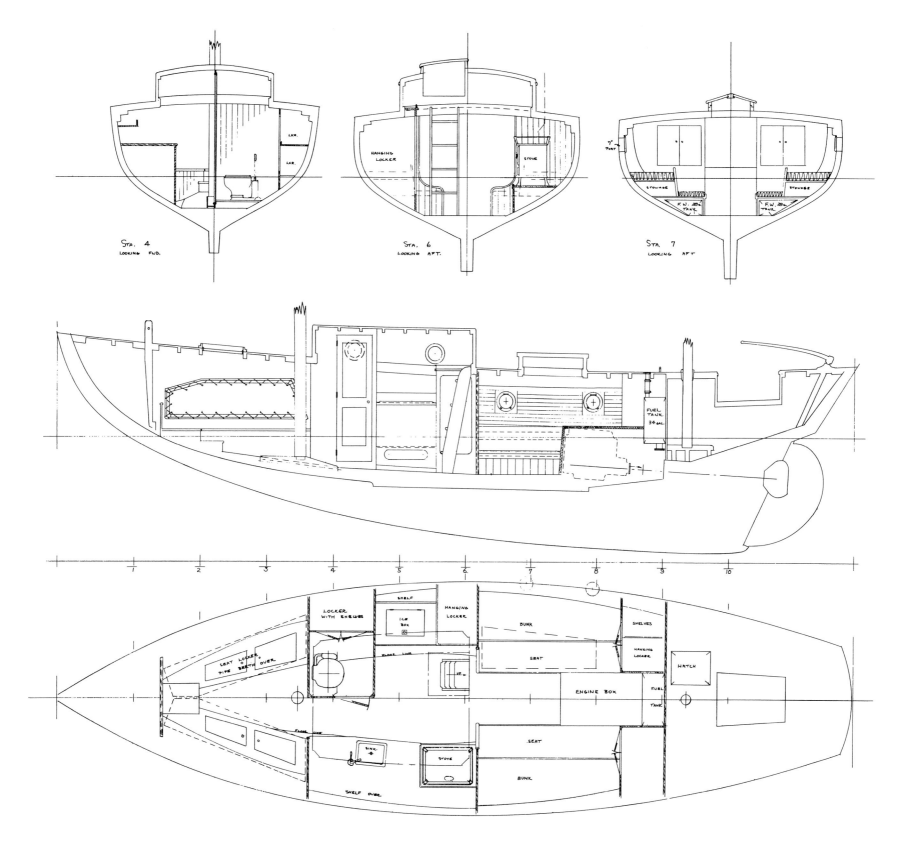

ARRANGEMENT PLAN

With the cabin entrance separated from the cockpit by a long bridge deck, *Alisande*'s original arrangement was unconventional. In drawing her plans Joel followed the same basic arrangement that designer William Hand had created many years before. It made for a distinctive profile and was in some ways quite practical, but in the end, owner Kim Faulkner abandoned this layout and had a longer trunk cabin designed and built, along with a conventional below-deck layout.

Bangor Packet

DESIGN NO. 14 (1981)

LOA	20'0"
LWL	18'4"
Beam	2'1"
Draft	4"
Weight	70 lbs.

Ted Leonard, a long-time friend of Joel's and client of Brooklin Boat Yard, sponsored this design. Ted resides in Bangor, a little over an hour's drive from Brooklin, but Brooklin is where he does his boating. His idea, which has proven itself over the past 20 years, was to keep his craft (aptly named the *Bangor Packet* by Joel), hauled out on a moored float in a shallow and little-used part of Center Harbor. From her float-mounted cradle, once her securing lines were cast off and her cockpit cover removed, Ted could simply shove her overboard and she'd be all ready for use. His idea in owning a boat like this was to gain some enjoyable exercise while losing a few pounds of weight. As of this writing, Ted still uses and treasures his *Bangor Packet*, painted with green topsides and a striking white bottom. Her sheerstrakes, guardrails, deck, coamings, and interior are varnished.

Joel loved designing this exercise boat, claiming it was easy because her hull was so long compared to her beam and freeboard. "What fun it was," he wrote "to draw lines for a boat of $\frac{1}{10}$ beam-to-length ratio—long, flowing waterlines and easy, *easy* buttocks." While creating it may have been simple for someone as talented as Joel, others might not have thought so. Judged against other exercise craft, I think she's better-looking because of her hollow bow and stern and her graceful sheer, accentuated as it is by the varnished sheerstrake. Having more freeboard forward than aft helps her looks as well.

The *Bangor Packet* is a fine compromise between a fixed-seat pulling boat and a shell that's for out-and-out competition. You sit *in* this boat rather than on it, keeping the center of gravity low and making the boat less tippy. Being closer to the water gives you a greater sensation of speed, and the extra beam, compared with the typical exercise boat (or wherry, as they are often called), not only increases stability but allows smaller outriggers to be used. The bare boat weighs but 55 pounds and the sliding seat, oars, and outriggers add another 15. For those needing a larger version of this same type, Joel designed what he termed the Gerry Wherry (Design No. 16) for two rowers. Both are of cold-molded construction and building them initiated the yard's involvement in hulls built by this method. Since then, cold-molded hulls have become a specialty of Steve White and the Brooklin Boat Yard crew.

This is a craft designed for salt water as well as fresh, and one that can stand a good deal of choppy water without scaring you to death or endangering you. In the unlikely event of a wave filling the cockpit, her watertight end compartments will keep her coaming well above water until she can be bailed out. (But if you recall the *Burt and I* recording from which Joel derived this boat's name, it's the *Bluebird II*, not the *Bangor Packet*, that fills with water after she's "smuck amidships" by the *Packet* in the fog.)

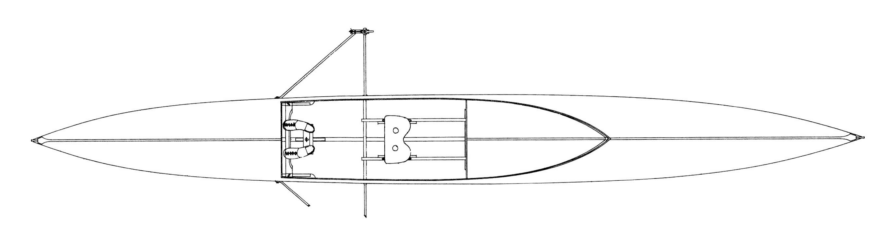

PROFILE & DECK PLAN

Good looks involve details as well as overall shape. Here Joel has accented the graceful sheerline with a simulated sheerstrake (a strip of varnished veneer glued to the cold-molded hull), and a half-round guardrail. He also shows both the forward and after stems projecting above the deck—always an attractive feature.

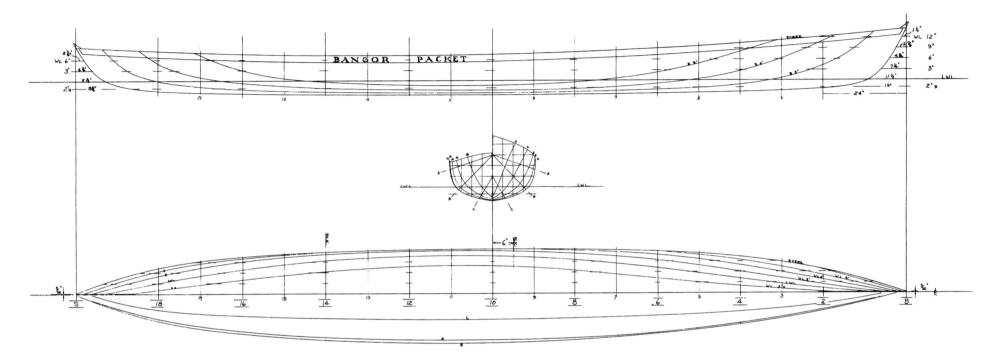

LINES PLAN

I've often thought what a great catamaran a pair of these striking hulls would make if joined together and fitted with a sailing rig. A small trimaran would be another possibility—one that used this hull fitted with a couple of similarly-shaped but smaller amas. Joel designed the longer Gerry Wherry (Design No. 16) for those wishing to row double.

Maine Idea

DESIGN NO. 15 (1981)

LOA	50'1"
LWL	46'0"
Beam	15'1"
Draft	5'3"
Displ.	50,000 lbs.
Power	375 hp Volvo diesel

At the time of her creation, the 50' *Maine Idea* was the largest craft Brooklin Boat Yard had ever built. And with the exception of the scallop dragger *Nicole* (Design No. 8), she represented the largest boat Joel had ever designed as well. I remember Joel fussing with several variations to get an acceptable profile—a difficult task in a power cruiser with a 'midship pilothouse and aft cabin. I don't believe he was completely happy with the result, even though the completed boat met his performance, arrangement, and structural goals. The clients seemed altogether pleased.

Maine Idea's planking is Douglas-fir, since Joel considered her too big a craft for soft cedar planking and at least one of Joel's boatbuilders had developed an allergy to mahogany. She's framed with native oak and her plywood decks are sheathed with Dynel laid in epoxy—the way of most of Joel's decks, and one that has proven virtually bulletproof over the years.

Mr. and Mrs. A.S. Martin, *Maine Idea*'s owners, kept the boat moored off their summer place near Blue Hill's harbor entrance, some 15 miles north of Brooklin, from late spring to early fall, then ran her south for the winter, always with a paid skipper onboard.

Maine Idea represents the kind of robust practicality that will always make her a wonderful coastal cruiser for whomever she belongs to.

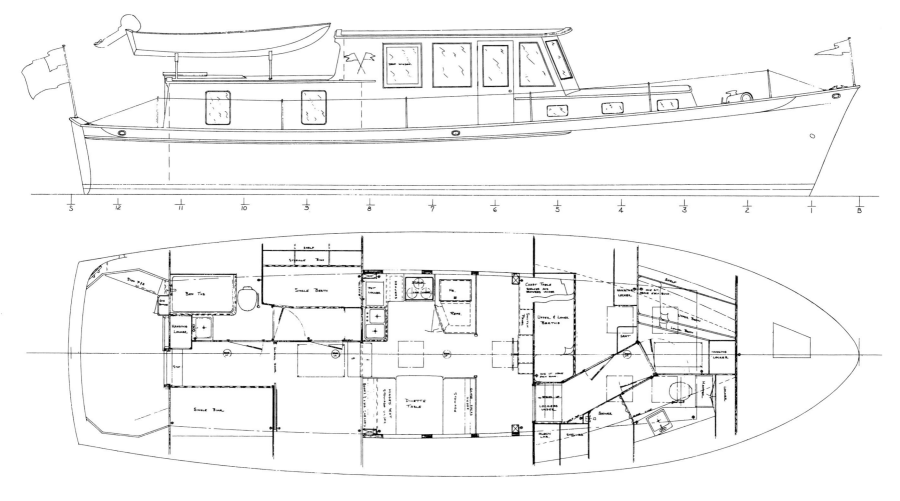

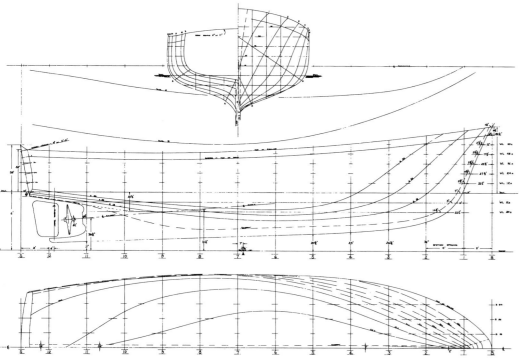

PROFILE & ARRANGEMENT PLAN

Joel called for three cabins on three levels to meet his clients' wishes for interior accommodations. Compromise occurs in every design, and in this one cockpit space gave way to cabin accommodations.

LINES PLAN

Maine Idea had harder bilges and a more flaring bow than Joel's previous powerboat designs. He also called for a stem that reversed in profile and became well rounded in plan view by the time it reached the sheerline.

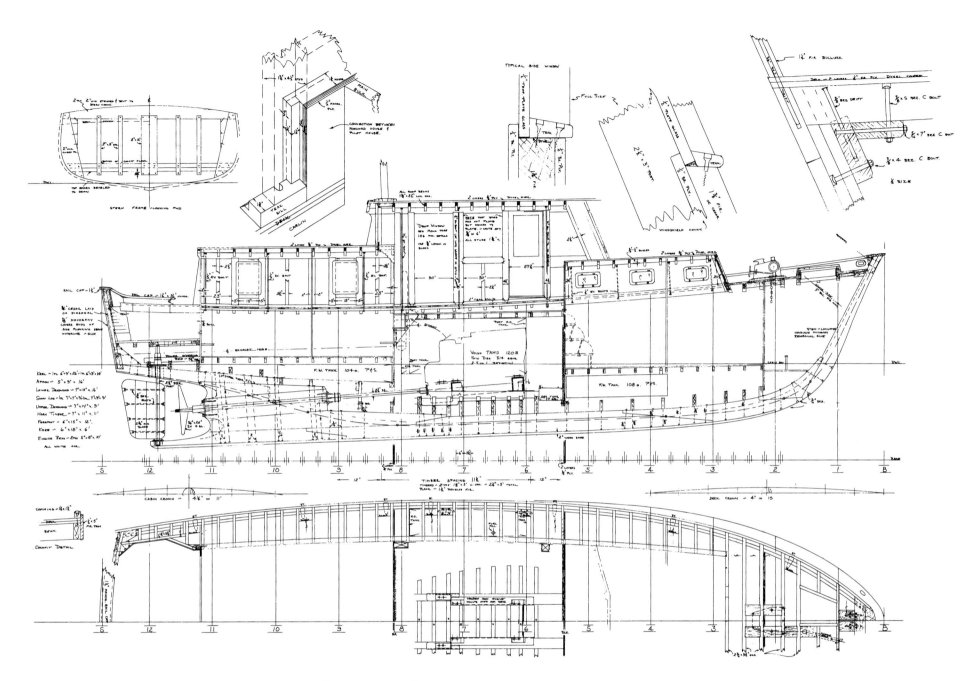

CONSTRUCTION PLAN

Maine Idea was not only larger than Joel's previous powerboats but more complex as well. As you can see, he developed a detailed construction plan that included specific details drawn to a larger scale.

Mimi Rose

DESIGN NO. 17 (1982)

LOA	*32'0"*
LWL	*28'8"*
Beam	*10'0"*
Draft	*5'0"*
Displ.	*17,000 lbs.*
Sail Area	*685 sq. ft.*

Joel shares the credit for this design with Bob Baker who had drawn the preliminary plans before he died. Bob's drawings established the boat's basic dimensions and its overall appearance. With Bob gone, owner Bill Page turned to Joel for the final drawings. As I recall, one of Joel's first moves was to dramatically cut back on the displacement from what Bob had shown on his lines plan. (Bob never had the time to do a weight study.) Thus Joel drew the boat's final lines, but retained the spirit of what Bob and Bill had had in mind. Based upon this hull shape, Joel worked out an arrangement to Bill's criteria, part of which was to provide berths for five—two of the five being Concordia fold-downs, include a cast-iron galley stove, and place the toilet out of sight (but not enclosed) forward of the main cabin bulkhead.

As with *Mimi Rose*'s design, the credit for her construction is also shared. Gordon Swift built the hull in his New Hampshire shop, and owner Bill Page finished it off, including the rig, at his home in Maine.

The result of this collaboration is one of the finest cruising boats I've ever seen. She's a boat you could go anywhere in, all the while sailing along at a good clip. Her cutter rig allows a variety of options for shortening sail in heavy winds. Below deck, thanks partly to the symmetry in Joel's arrangement, and partly to Bill's exceptional workmanship and detailing, you'll find a delightful cabin that you won't want to leave.

"Jaunty" comes to mind along with "salty" when you think about *Mimi Rose*. There's no boat quite like her, even though her dimensions are by no means unique. It's the confluence of elements like a springy sheer, raking mast, wineglass transom, cocked-up boom, and all those delightful Bill Page details that get to you. It's a credit to her designers and builders that *Mimi Rose* needs no shiny paint or varnish to make her a striking addition to any anchorage.

SAIL PLAN

Joel didn't have to be convinced to give *Mimi Rose*'s mast considerable rake as he was a proponent of this himself. He also believed in the high-cut headsails shown here.

LINES PLAN

Mimi Rose's heart-shaped transom not only looks good but provides a termination for the coamings. Notice the "sheer as built" notation in the upper right. It's one of the tweaks that Bill Page gives almost every design he builds from. "Just a whisker," he says, until it satisfies his eye.

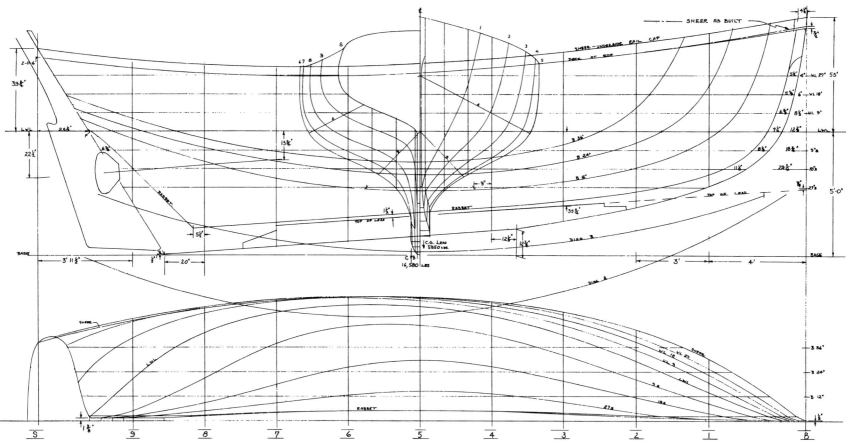

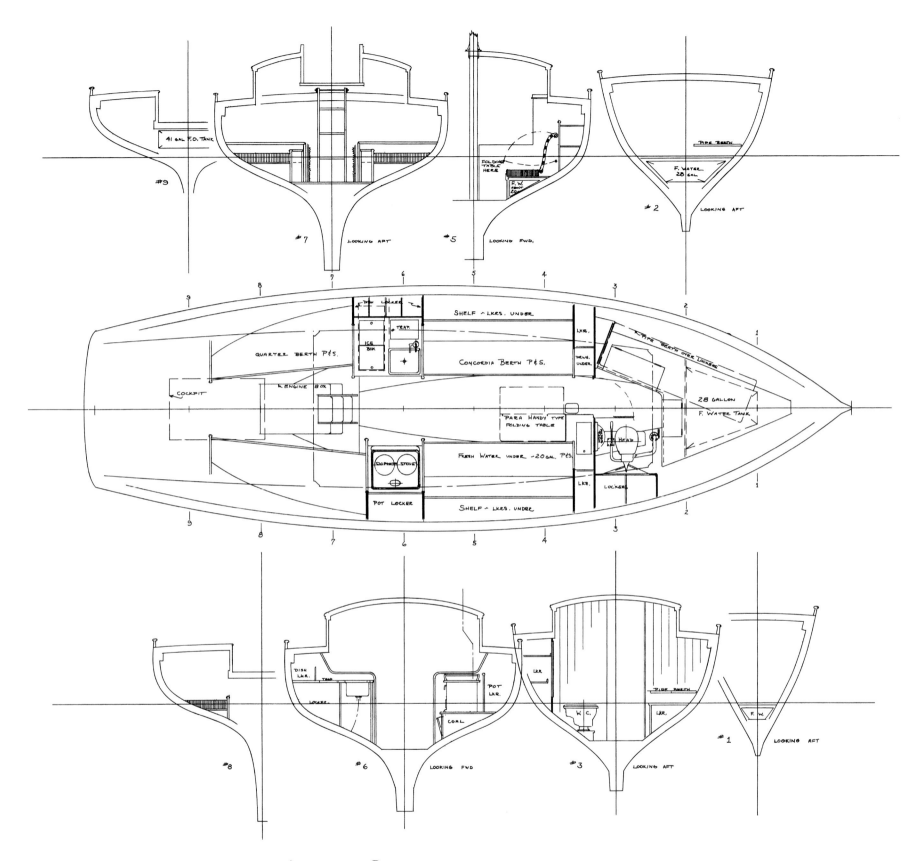

ARRANGEMENT PLAN

Concordia berths and a cast-iron woodstove surrounded by rubbed-effect varnish
help make this cabin inviting after a day's sail or during a foggy-day layover.

V-bottom Daysailer

DESIGN NO. 18 (1983)

LOA	20'0"
Beam	8'0"
Draft	1'0"
Displ.	1,780 lbs.
Sail Area	192 sq. ft.

When Joel drew this boat's plans, he was responding to a client who wanted an easy-to-build boat in which to teach sailing. The idea was for amateurs and beginners to help build as well as learn to sail in a decently-sized, jib-and-mainsail craft. Simplicity of design and construction was a major objective. Client Tod Cheney's goals changed, however, and he never went ahead with the building, although he still holds out hope for the future. Of the design, he wrote recently, "I can see how the little boat is a tribute to Joel's genius; how working from simple, almost mundane parameters he drew an elegant boat that, on paper at least, did everything asked of it." Joel prepared a full set of plans for this 20-footer whose chief eye-catching feature is its vertically planked, round stern. Less obvious are the structural items that Joel schemed up to make her strong and easy to build.

Joel designed the rudder blade to pivot so she can sail in only a foot of water. All you have to do is pull on its lanyard and belay it to the tiller-mounted cleat. This type of rudder goes hand-in-hand with the pivoted plywood centerboard, as both devices swing up of their own accord when the water gets shallow. Scooting along before the wind in, say, 18 inches of water, or sailing up on a beach for some shore-side exploring or picnicking are a snap in a boat like this.

Joel made the floorboards level and just big enough in area for sleeping so those who wish can go camp cruising. There's space for lots of camping gear under the foredeck, and I believe he intended the bulkhead to be watertight and thus free of bilge water that might accumulate from rain or salt spray. More dry storage can be found behind the aft bulkhead. With reasonably sealed bulkhead doors, the chambers beyond the two bulkheads will provide floatation in the unlikely event of a capsize.

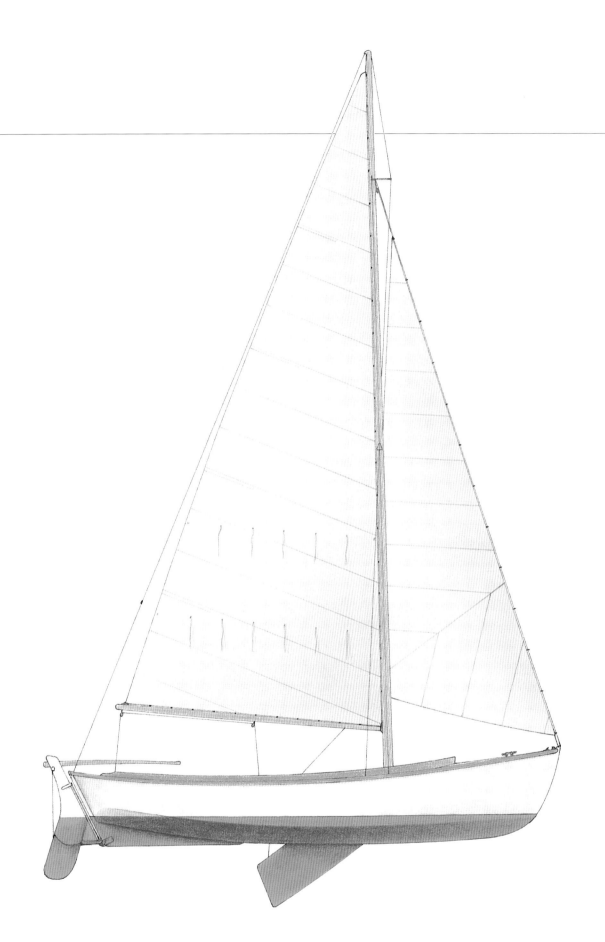

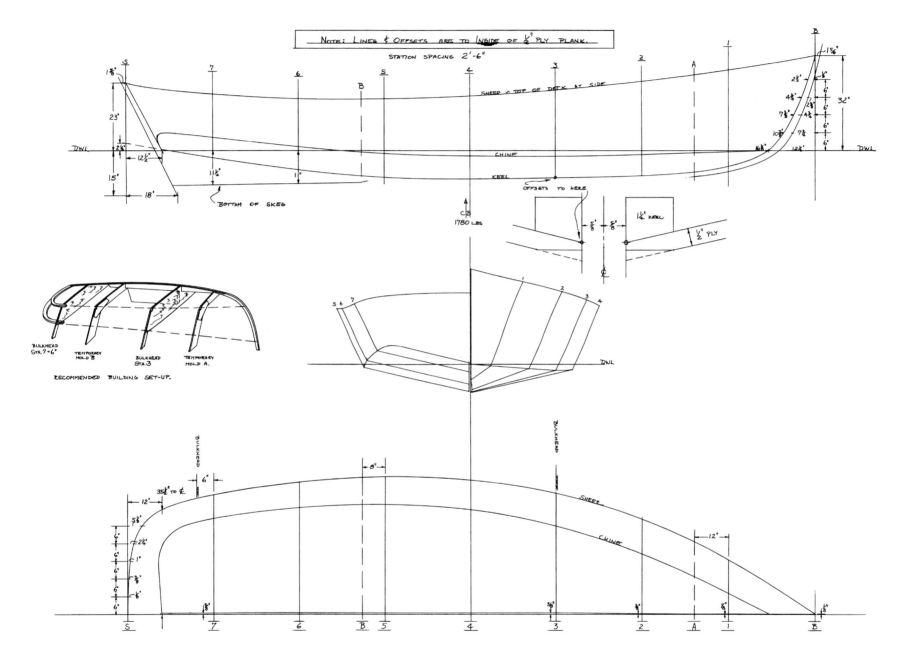

LINES PLAN

Joel gave this daysailer plenty of beam for stability, a high bow to keep at least some
of the spray from coming aboard, a chine that meets the stem at the waterline for a
clean-looking forebody, and of course, a graceful, springy sheer and that unusual round
stern. She's somewhat similar to the deadrise skiffs of Chesapeake Bay.

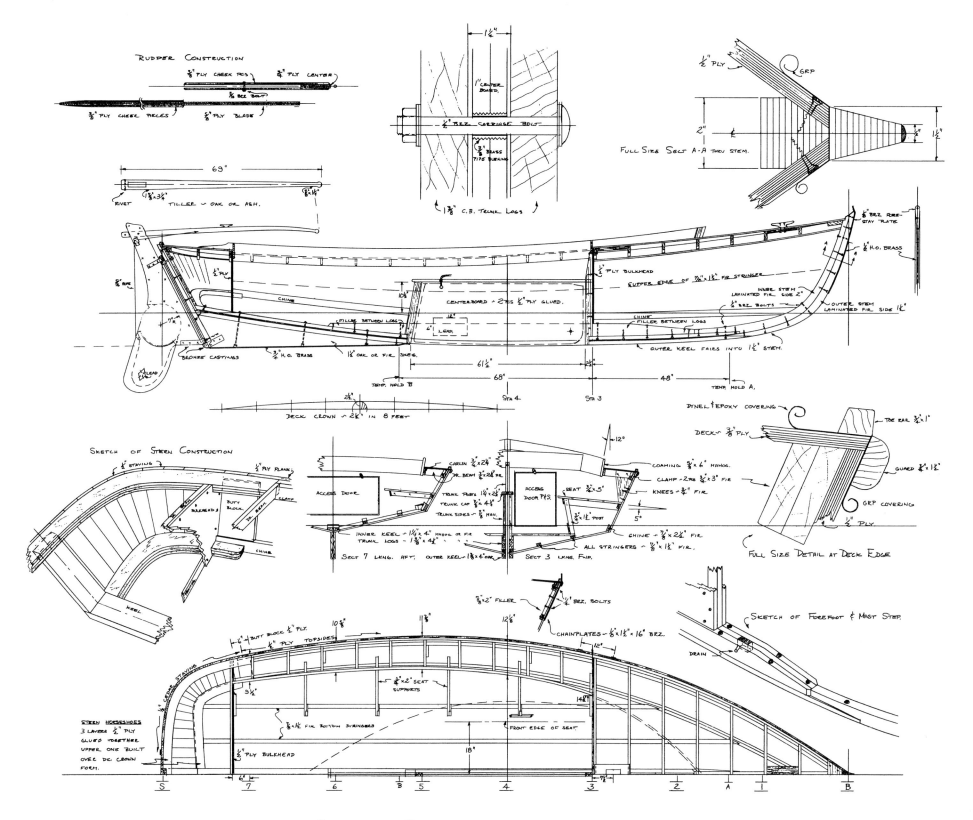

CONSTRUCTION PLAN

The hull is planked of ½" plywood and sheathed with fiberglass. Instead of the usual transverse, sawn frames common to most sheet plywood hulls, Joel calls for fore-and-aft stiffeners—these in addition to the two bulkheads that border the cockpit. Two stringers run along each bottom panel, and another sweeps along each side panel performing double duty as a seat riser.

Nutshell Prams

DESIGN NOS. 19 & 23 (1983 & 1984)

LOA	*7'7" & 9'6"*
Beam	*4'0" & 4'4"*
Weight	*90 lbs. & 100 lbs. (approx.)*
Sail Area	*37 sq. ft. & 55 sq. ft.*

I believe that Joel had this design pictured in his mind long before he decided to set it down on paper. One day he said simply that he had an idea for an improved pram that he'd like to try out. Soon afterwards he produced a drawing, then another, then one more—each one a refinement of the one before it. Somewhere along the line I thought to myself, "here is a Joel White boat I can afford," so I signed up for the first one, and was able to help tweak it with some features I thought would make it better. I suggested a marconi rig with a sprit-boom (bad idea, tried on the first boat and then abandoned), and also asked if Joel could make space for stowing the daggerboard, rudder, and tiller behind the after thwart (a good idea that was retained).

Lapstrake plywood construction offered lots of interesting possibilities, we all agreed, and that's no doubt what got Joel thinking about prams in the first place.

Joel built *Sarah's Swallow* for our daughter Sarah as a kind of prototype to see how his concept would work. Sarah, age 12, hung out at Brooklin Boat Yard awaiting any little jobs such as puttying that Joel could throw her way. After Joel had finished the building and the boat was at home, Sarah and I did the painting and Anne made the marconi sail. Bedecked with flags running up the mast and back down to the transom, Sarah cracked the traditional bottle and down the beach the boat went to float perfectly with her lower lap just kissing the water.

Trials indicated she was just a little tender, and that the tall rig wasn't working well in a boat having so much rocker in her bottom. (She pitched a lot, and alternately caused the tall sail to luff or stall out from overtrim.) The next boat Joel built for Jenny Mayher. Jenny named it *Nutshell*—a name so appropriate that it became the name of the design as well. Jenny's Nutshell Pram and those that followed carried a lug rig that improved performance under sail, had a wider bottom to increase stability, and had its mast stepped through a hole in the forward thwart so the rail-level mast partner, originally fitted to *Sarah's Swallow*, could be dispensed with. Joel also changed oarlocks so he could avoid making separate mounting blocks for them.

Nutshells are essentially frameless and depend upon their planking for most of their strength. Thus the interior is essentially clear of structure for easy cleaning and painting. They have but one 'midship frame which is laminated to the correct shape, making it amply strong and in no danger of splitting since the grain follows the frame's basic shape.

After designing, building, and testing the original 7′6″ Nutshell and making the refinements noted earlier, Joel went on to design a larger version to be built from 10′ long plywood instead of 8′. *WoodenBoat* sells the building plans for both versions which are also available in kit form. Hundreds of Nutshells have been built all over the world. In my opinion this is the best pram ever designed, and although it is one of Joel's smallest, it may be his most significant design because of all that have been built and the many, many people who have benefited from its exceptional beauty and utility.

LINES PLAN 7'7"

Joel increased the width of the bottom for more stability after the first Nutshell was built. The new outline is shown here as the dashed line in all three views and is labeled "bottom as built for WB." Without anyone aboard, Nutshells float with the lower lap just kissing the water; Joel's displacement curve indicates the deeper immersion with one person aboard bringing the total weight to 205 pounds.

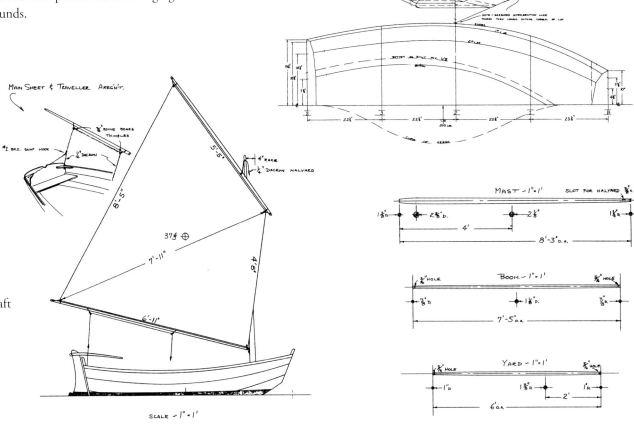

SAILING RIG DETAILS 7'7"

Extra pieces are needed to produce the sailing version. Joel designed the daggerboard, rudder, and tiller so that all three can be stowed out of the way aft of the stern seat. The mast, boom, and yard bundle into a neat package along with the sail.

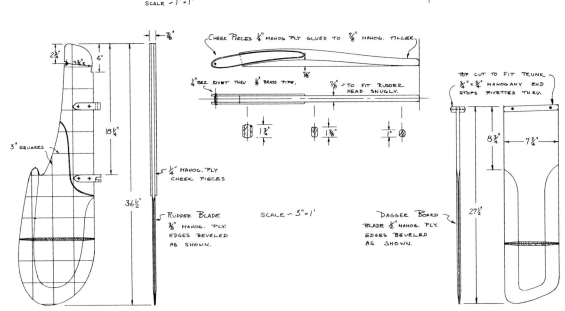

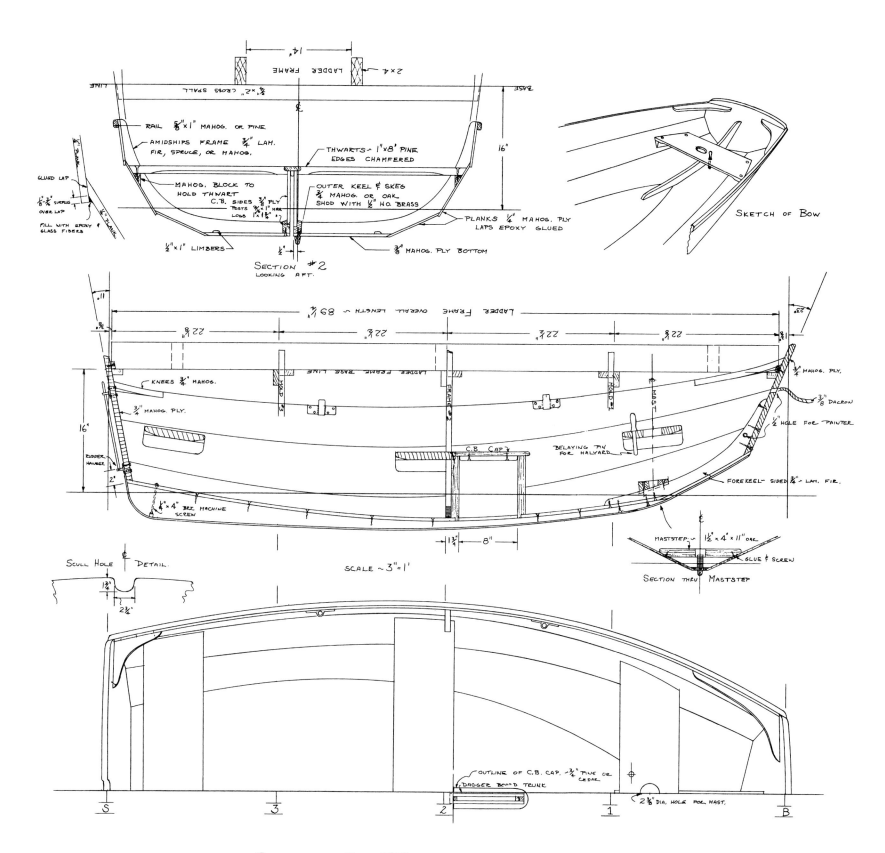

SKETCH OF BOW

SECTION #2
LOOKING AFT.

SCULL HOLE DETAIL.

SCALE ~ 3" = 1'

SECTION THRU MASTSTEP

CONSTRUCTION PLAN 7'7"

The construction drawing shows the Nutshell in its final form with its mast
stepped through the forward thwart as well as the use of standard oarlock sockets.
It also indicates the jig to be used in setting up the hull.

Planking Layout 7'7"

Ever mindful of the building process and always keeping simplicity as a priority, Joel drew this plan to show builders how to arrange the major pieces on two-and-a-half sheets of 4' x 8' plywood. He specified high grade, African mahogany plywood which, unlike Douglas-fir, will take paint or varnish extremely well.

Sail Plan 7'7"

Sarah's Swallow, the first Nutshell, carried a similar rig. It proved to be a bad choice for a boat that pitched as much as this one. Being lower, the final lugsail works just fine.

RUDDER   BLADE

⅜" (9MM) 4'x8' MAHOGANY PLYWOOD PANEL

BOTTOM

DAGGERBOARD TRUNK SIDES

¼" (6MM) 4'x8' MAHOGANY PLYWOOD PANEL

MIDDLE PLANK

BOW

REGISTRATION MARK — LINE UP WITH AFT EDGE MIDSHIP FRAME

SHEER PLANK

BOW

GARBOARD PLANK

BOW

STERN

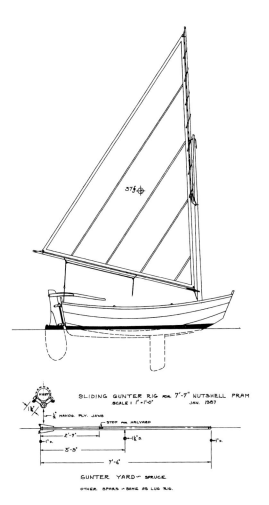

SLIDING GUNTER RIG FOR 7'-7" NUTSHELL PRAM
SCALE : 1"=1'-0"   JAN. 1987

GUNTER YARD - SPRUCE
OTHER SPARS - SAME AS LUG RIG.

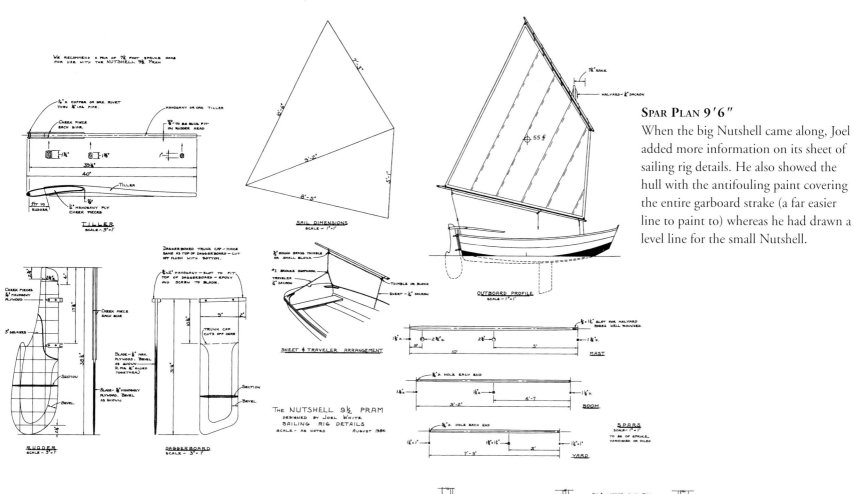

SPAR PLAN 9′6″

When the big Nutshell came along, Joel added more information on its sheet of sailing rig details. He also showed the hull with the antifouling paint covering the entire garboard strake (a far easier line to paint to) whereas he had drawn a level line for the small Nutshell.

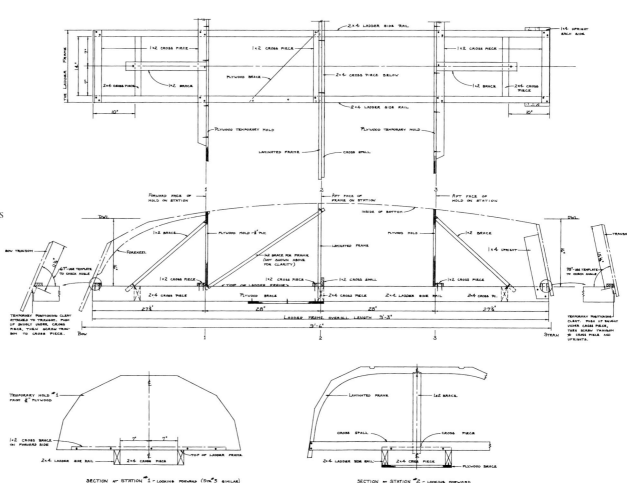

BUILDING JIG 9′6″

For the big Nutshell, Joel drew this plan for building the setup jig, responding to the feedback he had received from builders of the smaller boat. With a drawing like this, builders have more confidence and do a better job right from the start.

Forthright

DESIGN NO. 21 (1983)

LOA	35'0"
LWL	30'3"
Beam	11'0"
Draft	5'0"
Displ.	20,128 lbs.
Sail Area	748 sq. ft.

This cutter's design came about through her builder Gordon Swift. Swifty had a client who wanted him to build a cruising cutter of about 35 feet, but had no particular design in mind. Client John Carson had watched Bill Page's *Mimi Rose* take form in Swifty's shop and had come to admire her. So too had Swifty. With this in mind, they approached Joel for a larger version.

Forthright was the result, and as you can see, there's a lot of *Mimi Rose* in her as well as a lot of the late Sam Crocker, a designer whose work both Joel and Swifty respected. Joel gave *Forthright* a stem profile he favored—one that became straighter as it rose towards the deck. Even though *Forthright*'s stem had more overhang than a typical Crocker design or *Mimi Rose*, Joel made sure there was still a noticeable reverse in the waterlines as they approached the stem. He also gave this boat a radiused transom—a refinement he thought would look good. I think Jon Wilson's Concordia 33 *Free Spirit* may also have influenced Joel to some degree, as her mooring lay just outside his design office window. Both *Mimi Rose* and *Forthright* have the same 5' draft, but *Forthright* has less reverse in her sections. Joel didn't have to work as hard for full headroom in this larger boat: he didn't have to get the last inch from a lowered cabin sole because this hull was inherently more roomy. I'm guessing that the idea for the full-length, cast-iron ballast keel came indirectly from Swifty's mentor, Bud McIntosh, who strongly favored this as a means of damage control in case of an accidental grounding.

In *Forthright* Joel produced a basic yet handsome four-berth auxiliary cruiser with an enclosed toilet room, a bowsprit and boomkin, and with the cutter rig that was his favorite.

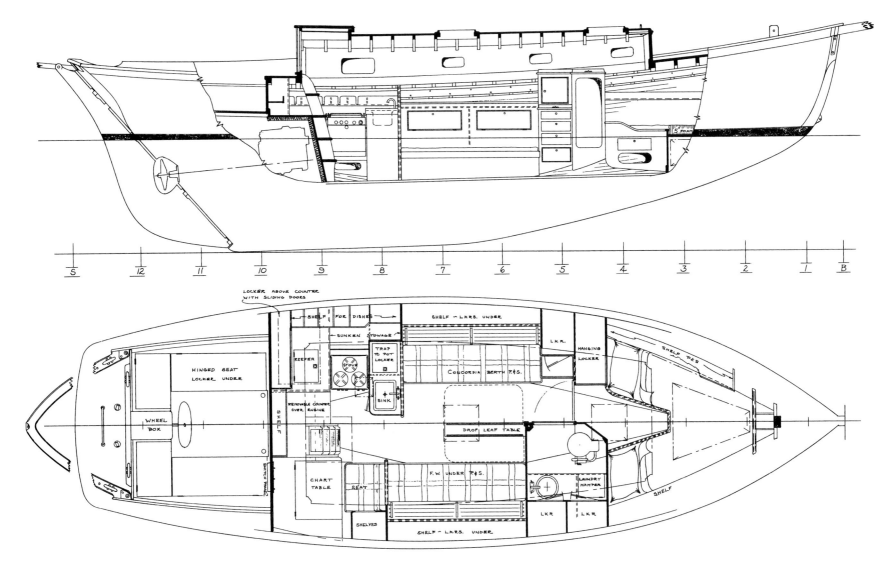

ARRANGEMENT PLAN

Forthright's size allowed a conventional interior that slept four persons, two in the main cabin on fold-down Concordia berths, and two in the forward V-berths. Joel also included an enclosed head and a navigation station.

FACING PAGE

LINES PLAN

Sailing performance became more of a priority for Joel around the time of *Forthright* and you can see his calculated values that predict speed under sail listed right on this drawing. From this time on such ratios as ballast-to-displacement, displacement-to-length, sail area-to-wetted surface, and sail area-to-displacement were given his careful consideration. With his MIT background, a new computer, and AeroHydro's software, Joel had an accurate and convenient means of determining a boat's stability as well.

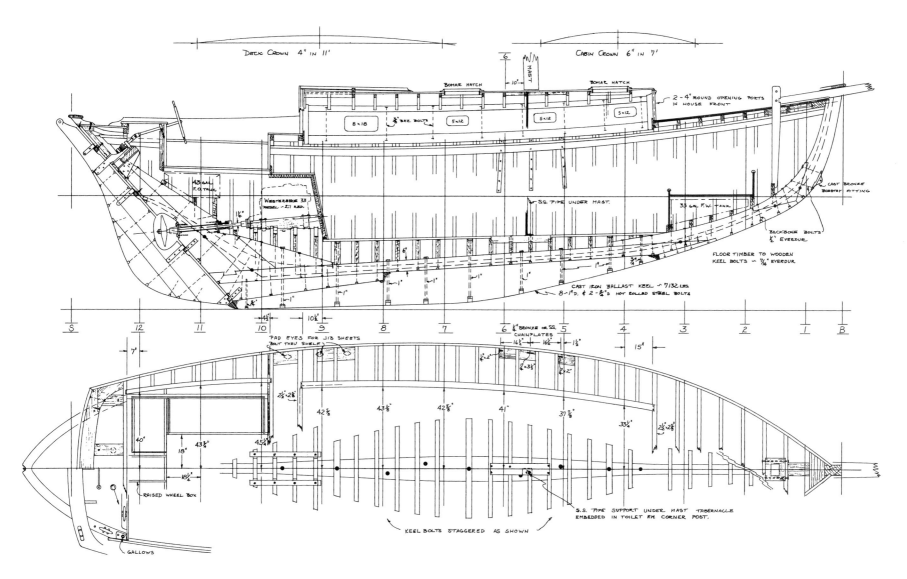

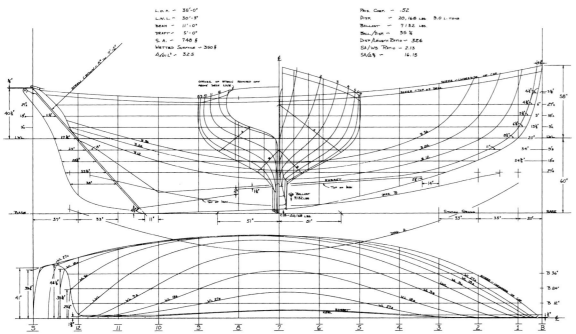

Construction Plan

A carefully-thought-out bolting layout as well as backbone members whose shapes are commonly available, are earmarks of a designer well versed in building. In this plan Joel has laid out the bolting so the backbone assembly can be built on its side where boring and fitting are easiest. After erecting the bolted-together backbone (the stem, stem knee, gripe, timber keel, sternpost, stern knee, and deadwood), the floor timbers and ballast keel get fitted and bolted into place.

Shearwater

DESIGN NO. 22 (1984)

LOA	16'0"
Beam	4'5"
Draft	7"
Weight	150 lbs.
Sail Area	69 sq. ft.

Realizing the potential of lapstrake plywood construction and fully aware that his recently designed Nutshell Pram—even enlarged to 9'6"—had limited potential for speed-under-oars, Joel drew this long double-ender. Her oarlocks are mounted on the rails and she has no sliding seat, ranking her below Joel's Bangor Packet design for speed, but she is a good deal faster than the Nutshell.

Shearwater started out as a pure rowboat. The sail was added subsequently, and with some reservation on Joel's part. She's slippery in either mode. Joel kept the hull narrow at the waterline, built her light as well as strong, and made her sufficiently long so that she'd move as fast as a good rower could row. In shaping Shearwater, Joel was inspired by the traditional rowing craft of Western Norway known as Oselvers. (Joel in fact first suggested "Joelselver" as this design's name, but predicting a Norwegian objection, ultimately decided on "Shearwater.") In use, she's tippy, surprisingly burdensome because of her flaring topsides, swift, and at times, because she is undecked, fairly wet. And for that same reason, you want to know what you're doing if you sail her when it's windy!

Shearwater would make a fine camp cruiser with or without the sailing rig. Floorboards brought to the level of the tops of the frames make an ideal platform for sleeping bags. The three thwarts simply lift out, and the boat is light enough to be lifted or dragged up on a beach above the high tide line. Although Joel kept the first Shearwater for a couple of years to evaluate its performance, his use never included cruising. As a tender, this boat's projecting stems are of continual concern unless fitted with some kind of soft fender.

At Joel's urging we sailed and rowed her a lot, and Anne and I have always regretted not seizing the opportunity when Joel decided to sell. Despite her limitations, she is so beautiful overall that we'd love having her in our small boat stable. I know we'd have used her often—mostly as a car-topper to be launched casually whenever we discovered interesting new waters.

LINES PLAN

The lines for a lapstrake boat are more useful if drawn to the inside of the planking so the builder can lay out and build the station molds directly from the table of offsets. That's what Joel has done here. And instead of using waterlines and buttock lines, his offsets are to the knuckles (identified as 1st lap, 2nd lap, and bottom of inner keel), to facilitate building.

CONSTRUCTION & ARRANGEMENT PLAN

To strengthen the ends of the hull Joel has called for "rangs" similar to those used in the Norwegian craft that inspired this design. From the same source he also adopted the removable seats with convex edges as well as the transverse floorboards.

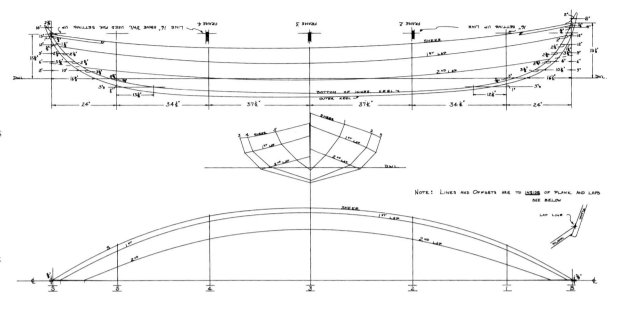

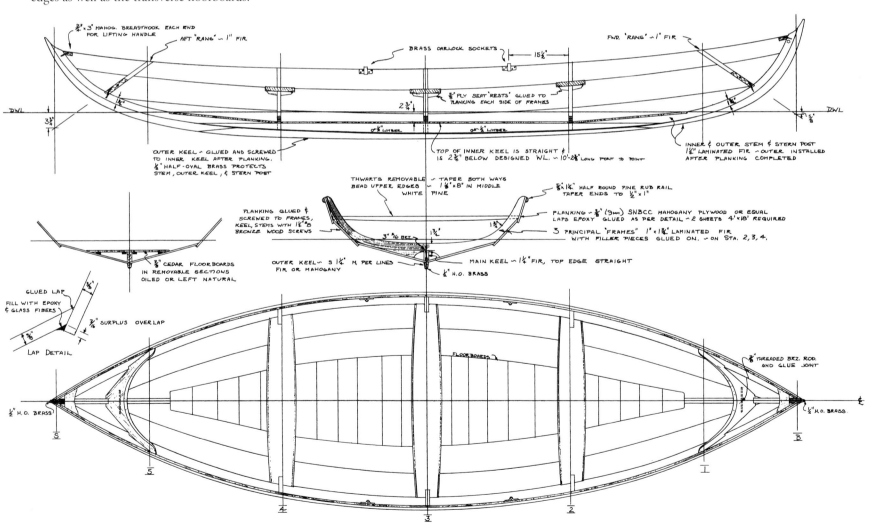

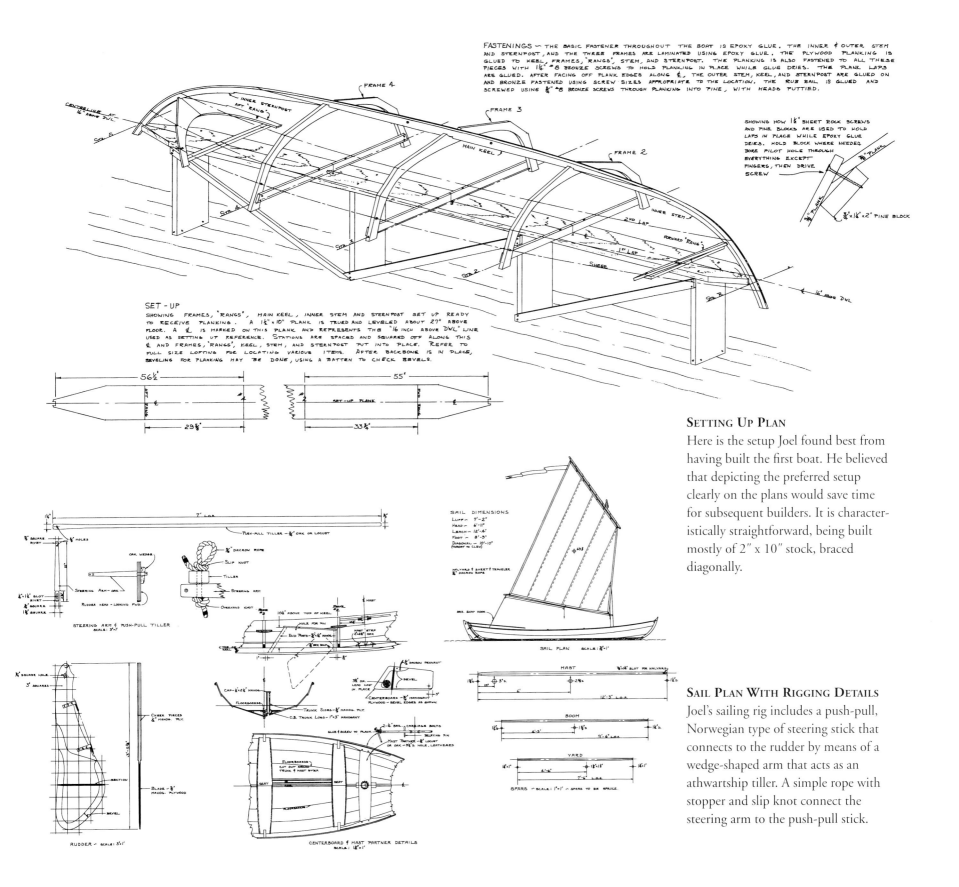

FASTENINGS — THE BASIC FASTENER THROUGHOUT THE BOAT IS EPOXY GLUE. THE INNER & OUTER STEM AND STERNPOST, AND THE THREE FRAMES ARE LAMINATED USING EPOXY GLUE. THE PLYWOOD PLANKING IS GLUED TO KEEL, FRAMES, "RANGS", STEM, AND STERNPOST. THE PLANKING IS ALSO FASTENED TO ALL THESE PIECES WITH 1¼" #8 BRONZE SCREWS TO HOLD PLANKING IN PLACE WHILE GLUE DRIES. THE PLANK LAPS ARE GLUED. AFTER FACING OFF PLANK EDGES ALONG ℄, THE OUTER STEM, KEEL, AND STERNPOST ARE GLUED ON AND BRONZE FASTENED USING SCREW SIZES APPROPRIATE TO THE LOCATION. THE RUB RAIL IS GLUED AND SCREWED USING ⅞" #8 BRONZE SCREWS THROUGH PLANKING INTO PINE, WITH HEADS PUTTIED.

SHOWING HOW 1⅛" SHEET ROCK SCREWS AND PINE BLOCKS ARE USED TO HOLD LAPS IN PLACE WHILE EPOXY GLUE DRIES. HOLD BLOCK WHERE NEEDED. BORE PILOT HOLE THROUGH EVERYTHING EXCEPT FINGERS, THEN DRIVE SCREW

¾" × 1⅛" × 2" PINE BLOCK

SET - UP
SHOWING FRAMES, "RANGS", MAIN KEEL, INNER STEM AND STERNPOST SET UP READY TO RECEIVE PLANKING. A 1½" × 10" PLANK IS TRUED AND LEVELED ABOUT 27" ABOVE FLOOR. A ℄ IS MARKED ON THIS PLANK AND REPRESENTS THE "16 INCH ABOVE DWL" LINE USED AS SETTING UP REFERENCE. STATIONS ARE SPACED AND SQUARED OFF ALONG THIS ℄ AND FRAMES, "RANGS", KEEL, STEM, AND STERNPOST PUT INTO PLACE. REFER TO FULL SIZE LOFTING FOR LOCATING VARIOUS ITEMS. AFTER BACKBONE IS IN PLACE, BEVELING FOR PLANKING MAY BE DONE, USING A BATTEN TO CHECK BEVELS.

SETTING UP PLAN
Here is the setup Joel found best from having built the first boat. He believed that depicting the preferred setup clearly on the plans would save time for subsequent builders. It is characteristically straightforward, being built mostly of 2″ x 10″ stock, braced diagonally.

SAIL PLAN WITH RIGGING DETAILS
Joel's sailing rig includes a push-pull, Norwegian type of steering stick that connects to the rudder by means of a wedge-shaped arm that acts as an athwartship tiller. A simple rope with stopper and slip knot connect the steering arm to the push-pull stick.

Bridges Point 24

DESIGN NO. 24 (1984)

LOA	*24'0"*
LWL	*18'8"*
Beam	*7'6"*
Draft	*3'5"*
Displ.	*3,944 lbs.*
Sail Area	*278 sq. ft.*

When a designer so favors one of his designs that he decides to have a boat built for himself, you know that the design must be an exceptionally good one. Such was the case with *Ellisha*, which Joel finished off and sailed often—right up through his final summer.

It all started when Brooklin native Wade Dow told Joel he wanted to try building fiberglass sailboats instead of the lobsterboats he'd previously specialized in. Joel thought this was a grand idea, mostly because of how he imagined it would benefit his friend Wade, but partly because of the opportunity it would give him to put down on paper some ideas that had been rattling around in his head for a boat of just this size and type.

Joel loved to tweak sheerlines, even though revising was not in his nature. I'm not sure how many sheerlines Joel fussed with for this design, but I do know that he favored strong sheers that swung upward noticeably as they approached the transom. That's the kind of sheer he gave the Bridges Point 24. The Herreshoff influence is strong in this boat and Joel made no secret of this source of inspiration. The forebody, 'midship section, and most of the underwater profile Joel developed from the Herreshoff 12½ footer. The short overhangs harked back to that design as well. But Joel preferred stems that grew straighter as they ran upwards, and for this boat, a generously wide and radiused transom with an inboard rudder. He gave this transom outline a little hollow along its lower edge as well.

Thus was born the Bridges Point 24. Over 50 have been built so far, almost all with the full cabin configuration. Joel gave *Ellisha* the alternate, smaller cabin—an extension of the coamings really—that forms a point at its forward end. This is another idea he borrowed from Herreshoff, one that makes for a more elegant appearance but with a sacrifice in interior space. In all Wade Dow's hulls is a perfectly-formed, molded-in cove line paralleling the sheer that can be either painted or gilded. (*Ellisha*'s is gilded.) This detail, along with a traditional teak toerail, gives the BP-24s a high-end, custom look. Some are fitted with little diesels placed under their self-bailing cockpits, and others have outboard motor wells. Joel's *Ellisha* used an outboard over the stern on an inconspicuous bracket.

If there's any breeze at all, the sails are all you need, as these are exceptionally fast boats that ghost along well in only a zephyr. The BP-24s also have comfortable cockpits with seats that are ergonomically contoured. Everything is within easy reach, even for single-handing. Thanks to the low cabin and high boom, the visibility is excellent. BPs are well balanced on any point of sail and in any wind. Of course, reefing (a simple matter with only a single line to pull) in strong winds is presumed here. Roller furling jibs are ordered by most owners, although Joel never favored such a feature (he considered them unreliable), preferring instead to hank on whichever of his three headsails seemed appropriate for the day's conditions.

About a dozen locally-owned BP-24s come back to the Dow shore for an annual race and get-together. Wade and his family put on a grand feed each year for the owners and crew who show up. It all has turned out the way Joel imagined it might.

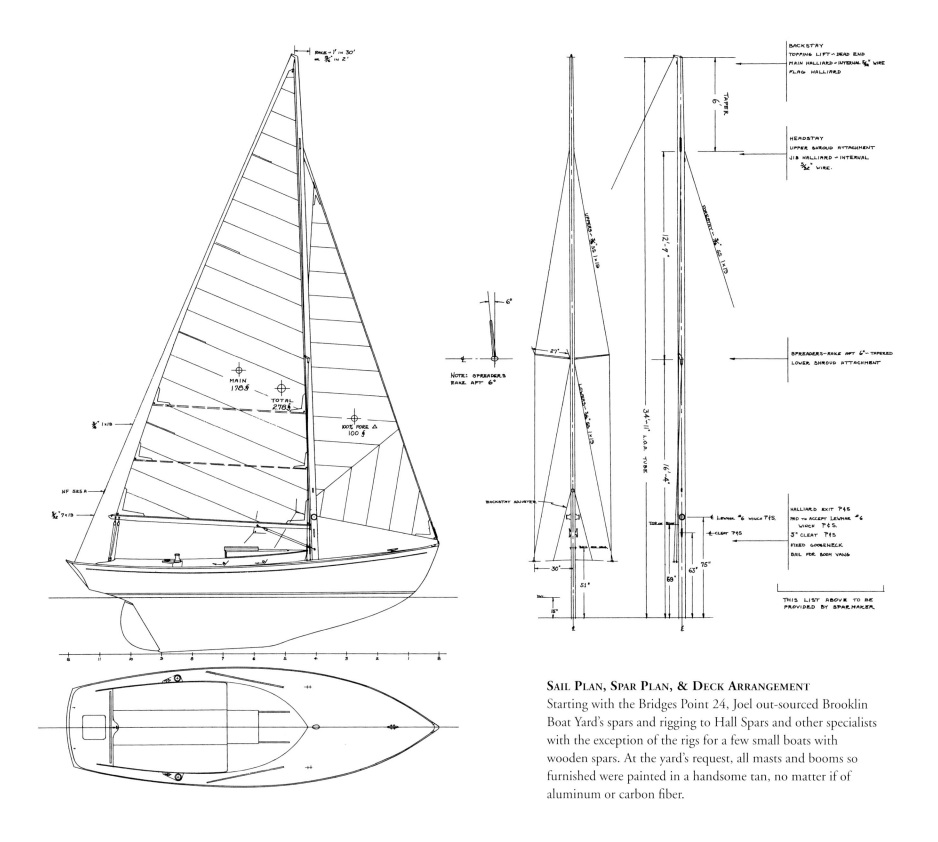

SAIL PLAN, SPAR PLAN, & DECK ARRANGEMENT

Starting with the Bridges Point 24, Joel out-sourced Brooklin Boat Yard's spars and rigging to Hall Spars and other specialists with the exception of the rigs for a few small boats with wooden spars. At the yard's request, all masts and booms so furnished were painted in a handsome tan, no matter if of aluminum or carbon fiber.

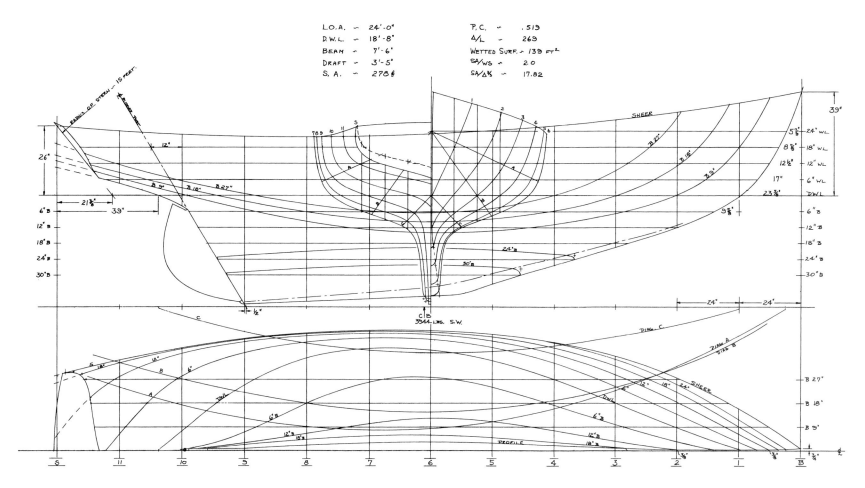

L.O.A.	~	24'-0"		P.C.	~	.519
D.W.L.	~	18'-8"		A/L	~	269
BEAM	~	7'-6"		WETTED SURF.	~	139 FT²
DRAFT	~	3'-5"		SA/WS	~	2.0
S.A.	~	278#		SA/Δ⅓	~	17.82

LINES PLAN

Beginning with *Forthright* Joel placed ever-increasing emphasis on stability, or sail-carrying power. His sail area-to-displacement ratios were important in this regard, and with help from a computer program he could determine, or at least closely estimate, how much sail could be effectively carried in a given wind.

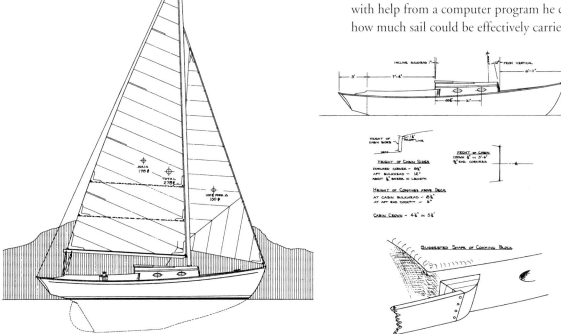

SAIL PLAN & DETAILS
FOR FIBERGLASS DECK & CABIN

As time went on, builder Wade Dow asked Joel to make this drawing for fiberglass deck/cabin assemblies. On it Joel specifies heights of cabin sides and coaming above the deck, rakes for the ends of the cabin, and the sheer along its top edge. He also shows window locations and cabintop crown. His rendered sail plan on this drawing is especially attractive.

Lark

DESIGN NO. 28 (1985)

LOA	*32'5"*
LWL	*29'7"*
Beam	*8'10"*
Draft	*2'11"*
Displ.	*9,887 lbs.*
Power	*103 hp Westerbeke diesel*

Selecting a builder before deciding on what is to be built is not a common occurrence, but that is what happened with *Lark*. After Tom Welsh decided that he wanted Gordon Swift to build him a small power cruiser, he approached Joel for a design. After a couple of proposals for larger boats that were beyond the budget, Tom and Joel settled on this 32-footer which Swifty went on to build.

Joel and Swifty had known each other for years, so when Swifty asked that Joel dispense with the time-consuming construction drawing, all parties including the owner were in agreement. Swifty had his own ways of doing things and years of experience. A construction drawing would only slow him down. Thus, for *Lark* Joel drew only the two sheets of plans shown here. I don't know how the offsets were handled, but I suspect that Joel picked them off his lines drawing, recorded them informally on a sheet of paper, which he then gave directly to Swifty.

Lark is laid out with basic accommodations for two persons. Besides the V-berths forward, there's an enclosed toilet room, a hanging locker, and a small galley. They share this space with the boxed-in engine. The cockpit is self-bailing, clear of obstructions, and partially sheltered by the open-backed pilothouse. In all, a simple craft that perfectly suited the Welches at the time.

Lark now hails from Brooklin, having been purchased by a summer resident who moors and stores her here.

PROFILE & ARRANGEMENT PLAN

Joel's profile drawings, of which *Lark's* is typical, show the client what his boat will look like when afloat and viewed from the side. Joel's profiles are not lavish, yet by careful use of line work—especially at the sheer—he succeeds in producing a rendering that a non-technical person can easily understand. Because powerboat profiles are a good deal longer than they are high, Joel and other designers often draw the interior arrangement on the same piece of paper as is done here.

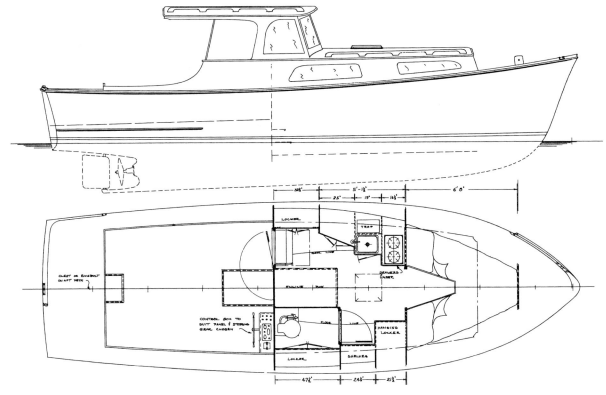

LINES PLAN

Lark's concave, rounded stem and flaring forward sections are reminiscent of *Maine Idea's*. Joel was a firm believer in the so-called, semi-built-down powerboat hull in which the rabbet line follows the keel for much of its length then sweeps upward across the deadwood and shaft log, and finally joins the horn timber above the propeller. In contrast to the "skeg-built" boats of the Jonesport, Maine, area these "semi's" provide a more suitable location for bilgewater (under the cockpit and not beneath the living space), yet they are easier to plank than a fully-built-down hull that carries its rabbet line straight aft to the sternpost.

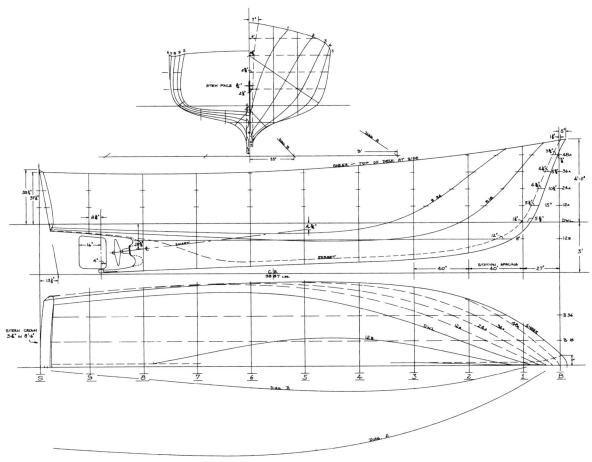

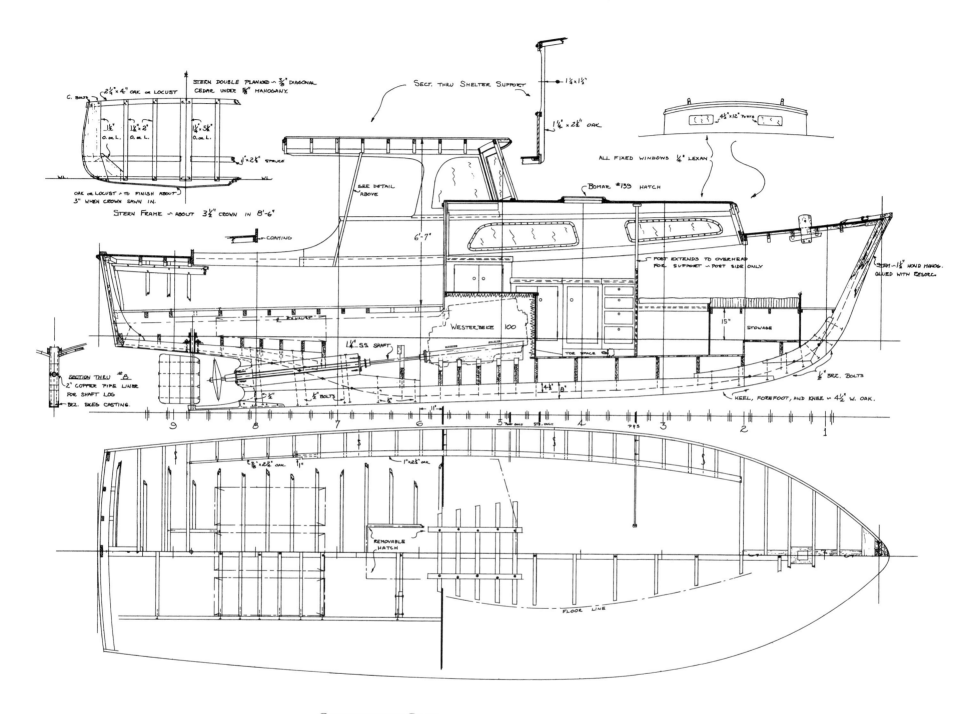

CONSTRUCTION PLAN

Because he knew who the builder would be, Joel drew only a basic construction plan that included the vital aspects of the interior arrangement shown in elevation. He and the client decided that the best compromise was to have the engine intrude into the living quarters—its presence minimized by enclosing it in a sound-dampened box. Joel also drew a stem with significant "swell" at the top as was first done on *Maine Idea*. This makes the hull easier to plank, and Joel loved the look.

Double-ended Cruising Sloop

DESIGN NO. 29 (1986)

LOA	29'4"
LWL	23'7"
Beam	9'2"
Draft	4'2"
Displ.	10,525 lbs.
Sail Area	430 sq. Ft.

Joel did most of his cruising in a boat of this same type named *Northern Crown*, an Aage Nielsen-designed cutter he owned for nearly 20 years. Over those years and his many miles of using *The Crown* (as she was often called), Joel came to respect the features of this striking 35-footer, so when Glenn Baldwin approached Joel with specific design criteria—one element of which was that the boat be double-ended—Joel quickly settled upon a kind of shrunk-down *Northern Crown*. He gave Baldwin's boat the same hollow waterlines as *The Crown* at both ends, but made the stern a little less dramatic so it would be easier to build.

Joel drew a fractional sloop rig, making it nice and tall for going to windward. Its proportions remind me of a Danish spidsgatter. You'll note that Joel has given her a full deckline, both forward and aft, which was one of *Northern Crown*'s prominent characteristics. But to make these curves eye-sweet from all vantage points he kicked up the sheerline at both ends of the boat as well. Without such compensating treatment, a boat's sheer can take on an unattractive reverse (called powderhorn) from certain perspectives.

It's difficult to achieve standing headroom in so small and shallow a boat without overdoing the freeboard and/or cabin height. But here Joel has struck a good compromise with those elements. He gained a few inches by eliminating the cabin roof beams and placing the cabin sole directly in contact with the boat's floor timbers. This means that the fuel and water tanks, instead of being under the cabin sole as they are in many boats, move to the bow and stern—the water tank in the forepeak and the fuel tank aft of the engine under the cockpit.

Designer and client, each of whom had definite ideas of what the intended boat should be, didn't see eye-to-eye on a number of features. He gave Glenn's boat (which Glenn built and named *Circle*) a masthead rig, along with an interior that included quarter berths and a nav. station. Glenn also opted for a bowsprit and a slightly lower trunk cabin—two features that went beyond the plans Joel had prepared for him. A couple of years later when he had the time, Joel drew the sail plan and the interior layout he thought the boat should have, and sent this version to *WoodenBoat* for a design review. It features a rather conventional arrangement for a two-person cruiser, with a third berth forward for the occasional guest.

LINES PLAN

Balanced ends and a generous displacement go hand-in-hand with seakindliness, and in this respect these lines are exemplary. They also show a nice distribution between what is under water and what is above.

CONSTRUCTION PLAN

Client Glenn Baldwin opted for glued strip construction for his boat—the first built to this design—and Joel retained it for the published version. Having seen the inevitable checks that develop over time in deadwood made of oak, Joel also opted for glued-together planks of mahogany for this boat's backbone.

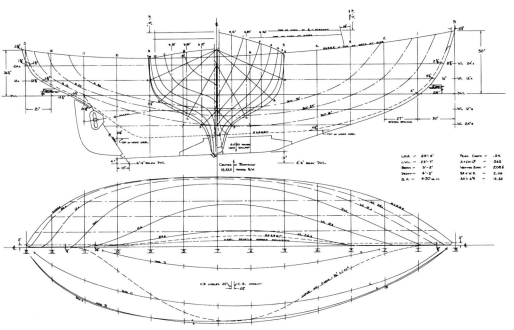

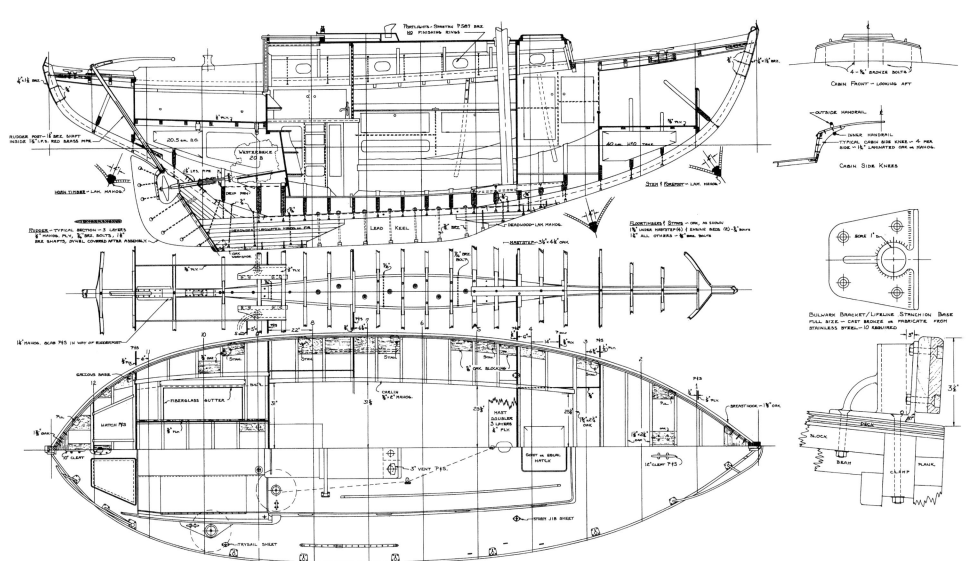

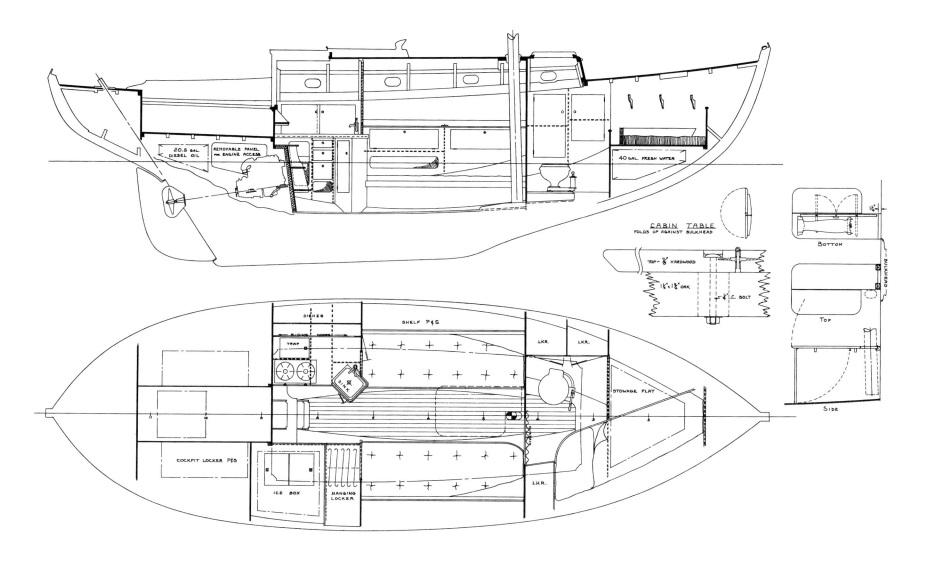

CABIN TABLE
FOLDS UP AGAINST BULKHEAD

ARRANGEMENT PLAN

Symmetrical interiors are more restful than helter-skelter ones, and having the settee/berths directly opposite each other predicts a welcoming cabin that stimulates thoughtful conversation. To maximize the living space, Joel has tucked the little diesel as far aft as it will go, yet has managed to make it accessible.

Fox Island Class Sloop

DESIGN NO. 30 (1986)

LOA	22'0"
LWL	19'6"
Beam	6'1"
Draft	3'3"
Displ.	1,955 lbs.
Sail Area	160 sq. ft.

Joel's aim here was to avail himself of lapstrake plywood construction, and to come up with a design that would lend itself to semi mass production at a price that was affordable. The original client/builder turned out only a single boat before moving on to other pursuits. Building Fox Islanders was then taken on by Skiff Craft of Plain City, Ohio, which completed two boats and hoped to build more. Promoting sailboats within their existing powerboat market proved difficult, but Skiff Craft retained the plank patterns and will make them available for anyone wishing to build to this design.

The Fox Islander is a speedy daysailer that is so fine-lined that she needs a fixed lead keel to keep her on her feet. A fin keel along with a spade rudder make for a maneuverable craft that will spin in its own length and give you an exciting sail and beat most boats of her size. The downside is that she's not easily placed on a trailer. Likewise, she needs over 3' of water depth to go sailing, which is considerably more than a centerboarder such as Joel's Design No. 47 (*Lala*) would require.

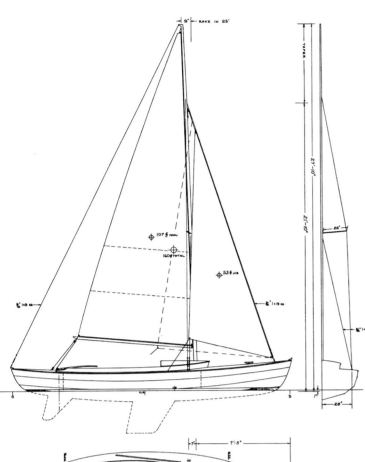

Sail & Deck Plan

In his later designs such as this one Joel placed the shroud chainplates inboard of the rail. This improved the headsail sheeting and made the passage from cockpit to foredeck easier. A person could now pass outside the shrouds instead of having to duck under them.

Offsets to Inside of Plank—inches • denotes heights below DWL.

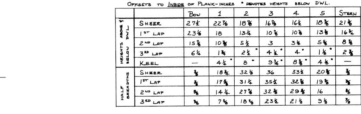

		Bow	1	2	3	4	5	Stern
Heights above & below DWL	Sheer	27 1/2	22 7/8	18 7/8	16 7/8	16 1/2	18 3/8	21 3/8
	1st Lap	23 1/8	18	13 1/4	10 7/8	10 3/8	13 1/8	16 3/4
	2nd Lap	15 7/8	10 5/8	5 1/2	3	3 1/8	5 5/8	8 7/8
	3rd Lap	6 1/4	1 3/4	2 1/2 •	4 1/2 •	4 •	1 1/8 •	2 3/8
	Keel	—	4 1/4 •	8 •	9 3/4 •	8 3/8 •	4 1/8 •	—
Half Breadths	Sheer	3/8	18 3/4	32 1/8	36	33 1/2	20 5/8	3/8
	1st Lap	3/8	17 5/8	31 1/4	35 1/2	32 7/8	19 5/8	3/8
	2nd Lap	3/8	14 1/4	27 7/8	32 3/8	29 5/8	16	3/8
	3rd Lap	3/8	7 5/8	18 3/8	23 1/2	21 1/8	9 1/8	3/8

Lines Plan

Five station molds, their shapes taken directly from the Table of Offsets, and the bow and stern stems—all well-braced in their respective locations—make up the structure around which this hull is planked. Any minor fairing this setup requires can be easily done by shaving or shimming the molds before the planks are hung. These station molds, in fact, stay with the completed hull as frames 1, 2, 5, 7 & 8.

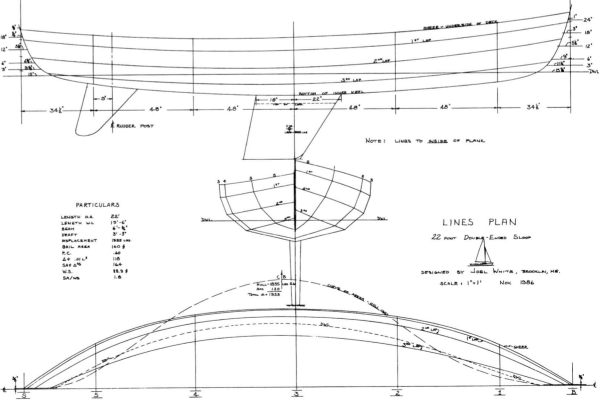

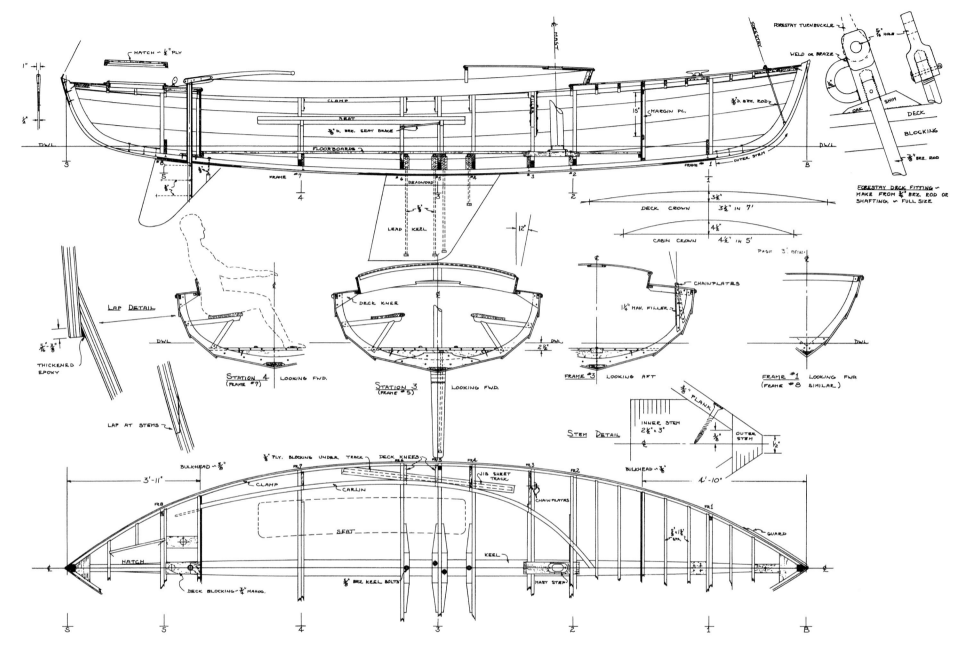

CONSTRUCTION PLAN

Joel has supplemented the evenly-spaced, "station mold" frames with additional frames at the mast and over the ballast keel—the primary areas of stress under sail. The two bulkheads form bow and stern flotation chambers to keep the boat afloat if she takes a knockdown. Joel's "dotman" at station 4 demonstrates the comfort of the sloped seats and outward-raking coamings.

Marsh Cat

DESIGN NO. 31 (1987)

LOA	15'0"
LWL	14'0"
Beam	6'11"
Draft	9"
Displ.	1,309 lbs.
Sail Area	152 sq. ft.

Both Joel and client Sam Holdsworth knew about Beetle Cats when they established the parameters for the Marsh Cat. A Beetle wouldn't quite make the grade for the use Sam had in mind. He wanted more space in the cockpit so there'd be room for his whole family. This meant a bigger boat with a proportionally larger cockpit.

Joel had his own ideas as to sheerline and bow profile and incorporated them into the Marsh Cat. He liked noticeably more freeboard at the bow than at the stern and a slightly overhanging stem whose curve straightened as it rose from the waterline. The short, curved bowsprit adds a distinctive look and also gets the forestay clear of the bow chocks as well as forming a mooring cleat (known around here as a "Jonesport cleat") at its aft end.

You sit right on the floorboards of a Marsh Cat; the freeboard is too low and the clearance under the boom too scant for cockpit seats. Sprawling on cushions and leaning back against the coaming isn't all that bad, and Joel has kept the floorboards level and sufficiently high to keep any bilge water down in the boat's belly where it belongs instead of sloshing around and wetting the occupants.

I can't say why Joel opted for a rope traveler. Perhaps, because it blocks off the aft end of the cockpit, it's to keep people from sitting too far aft and upsetting the boat's trim. There's no afterdeck which leaves the transom fully exposed to facilitate mounting an outboard motor.

Sam Holdsworth sails among the shallow marshes north of Cape Ann, Massachusetts—places near Ipswich and Essex—where there are acres and acres of thin water waiting to be explored. With her pivoted centerboard and kick-up rudder, the Marsh Cat automatically adapts to shallow water. Sam keeps his Marsh Cat out of the water when she's not in use, sometimes for weeks on end. That's why Joel called for a cold-molded hull instead of a conventionally planked one that might dry out, open its seams, and leak when launched.

Thinking that the boat that worked for Sam Holdsworth might find use in similar environments, Joel developed detailed drawings (there's a total of six sheets) and arranged to have them sold through *WoodenBoat*.

SAIL PLAN

Shallow draft and an expansive, level platform make the Marsh Cat an ideal camp-cruiser. I can see her drawn up on a gently-sloping beach, a tent rigged over the furled sail, coffee brewing on a single-burner camp stove, her crew enjoying the early morning view over the stern as they sit cushioned on their folded sleeping bags. A snug and pleasant place to be, even in bad weather.

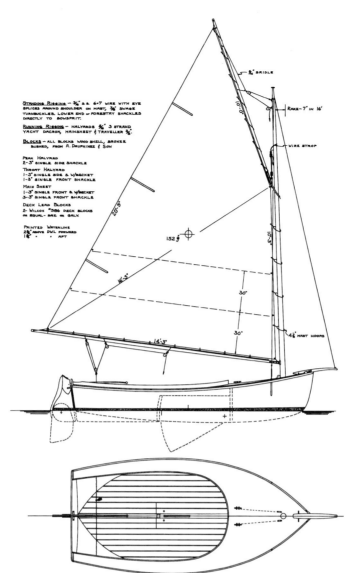

LINES PLAN

Concerned that some builders might miss the important point, Joel underlined his notation that these lines were drawn to the inside of the planking—except for the profile, which is to the outside. His "DIAG. B" may look odd applied to the forebody (on the right-hand side of the body plan), but he placed it there to ensure fairness at the turn of the bilge near the transom where boats occasionally go wrong and end up with a lean and hungry look a few feet from the stern.

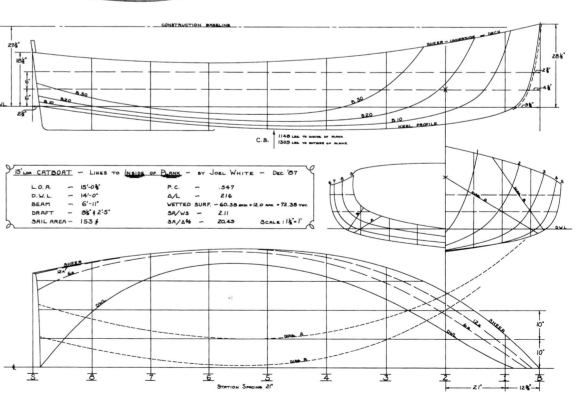

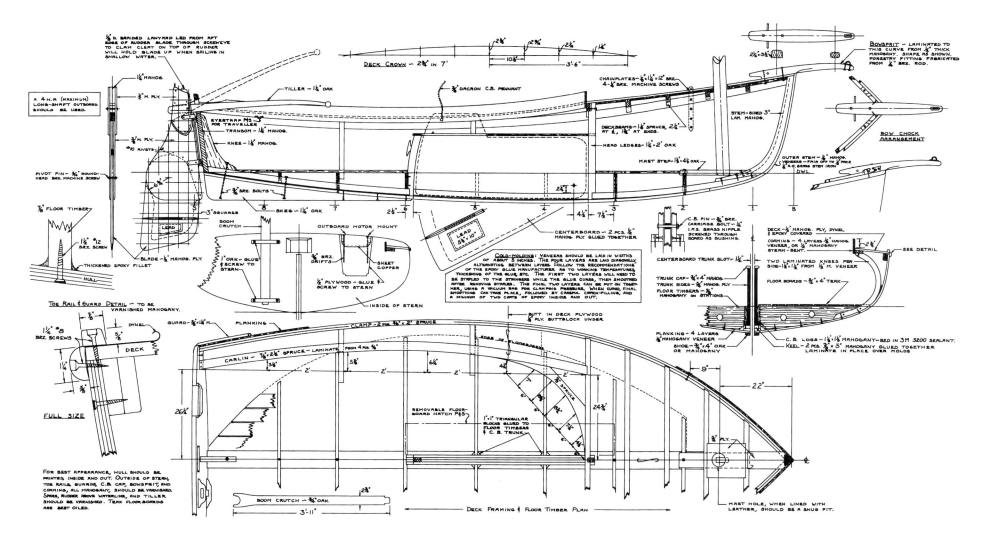

CONSTRUCTION PLAN

Although this cold-molded hull is virtually frameless, Joel reinforced it with floor timbers and a couple of sizeable laminated knees adjacent to the cockpit. Joel inked the Marsh Cat drawings so they'd make better prints, but in subsequent designs returned to his beloved #3 pencil with which he could more rapidly express on paper what was in his mind's eye. He felt the inking made only an incremental improvement in printing quality, and the inking process failed to sufficiently engage his creative juices.

Mosquito Boats

DESIGN NOS. 32 & 33 (1988)

MARIKA

LOA	20'0"
Beam	4'10"
Draft	7½"
Displ.	1,200 lbs.

VENITA

LOA	30'11"
Beam	7'7"
Draft	1'6"
Displ.	4,338 lbs.

Their names might be the same, but these cross-planked open boats are about as far from the Mosquito Boats of World War II as it's possible to get. Joel produced these designs as alternatives to the time-honored dugouts of the La Mosquita Indians of Central America. The big trees from which dugouts are hewn were becoming scarce.

"Trimaran" Jim Brown brought this situation to *WoodenBoat*'s attention in the fall of 1987. The following autumn upon the close of the regular WoodenBoat School, 15 Mosquito Indians, funded by a grant from USAID, spent six weeks building these two boats, taught by Brown and instructors Greg Rössel, Paul Balbin, and Mike Bonfigli. The plank-on-frame process represented a new skill that had to be learned, and suitable designs had to be worked up. That was where Joel came in. Hearing the predicament and the topography described, Joel suggested two boats, a large one to be powered by a small inboard diesel and a small one propelled either by paddles or an outboard motor.

Both boats were launched shortly before the Indians departed and both appeared to perform as hoped. By then the Indians had mastered the plank-on-frame building process so that, with necessary materials, more boats like them could be fashioned back in home territory. Both prototypes were shipped home for inspiration as well as everyday use.

The Pipante, as the 20'*Marika*'s type is known, was to represent a plank-on-frame version of the dugout, while *Venita* (the type called a Tuk-Tuk) was more of a cargo-carrying sea boat shaped much like a dory. For the often-encountered shallow water, Joel gave *Venita* a tunnel stern, and ran the skeg (or outer keel) all the way aft to protect the propeller.

As was often his custom when it came to humanitarian endeavors, Joel donated all his time for developing these designs and for the consulting that accompanied the construction.

Lines Plan (*Marika*)
Joel believed strongly that flat-bottomed boats should have lots of rocker, or curvature in underwater profile. *Marika* is so shaped and moves easily through the water, turns quickly, and can be nosed well up onto a beach for loading or unloading. Intended either for outboard or paddle power, she's a substitute for the Indians' traditional dugouts.

Construction Plan (*Marika*)
Joel called for skiff construction in which the bottom planks run athwartships. Rather than using chine stringers, he specified that the lower strake of side planking be extra thick so the bottom planks could be fastened directly to it. Because this "chine plank" diminishes to nothingness at the curved-up bow, a pair of interior "bow chines" take over and give the forward bottom plank fastenings the necessary substance to drive into.

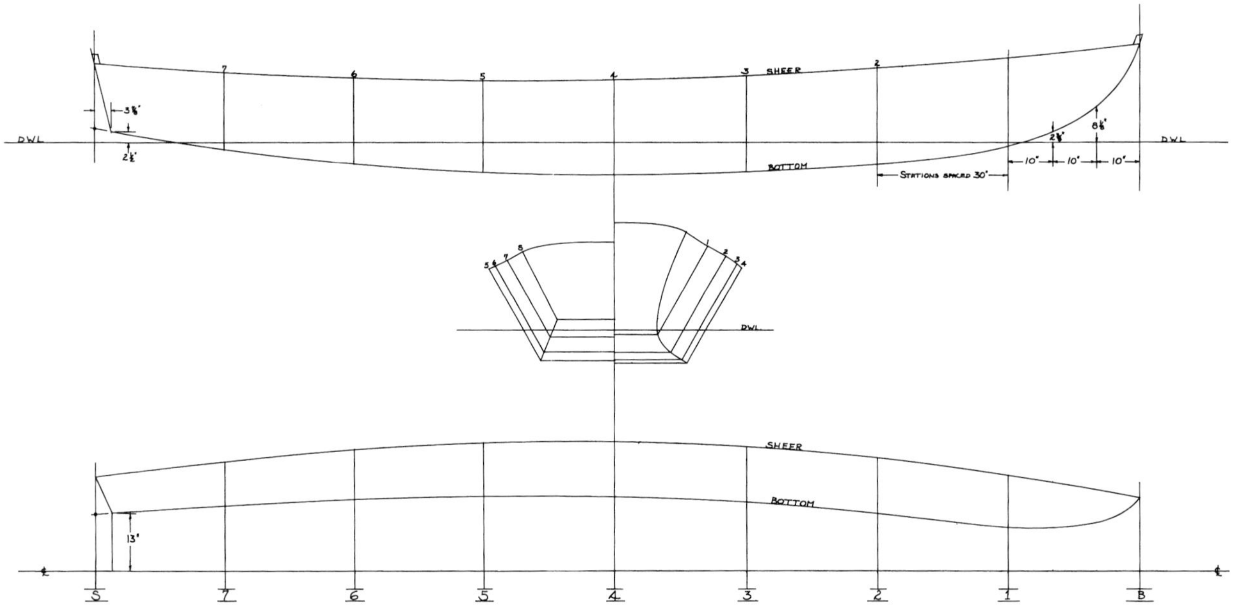

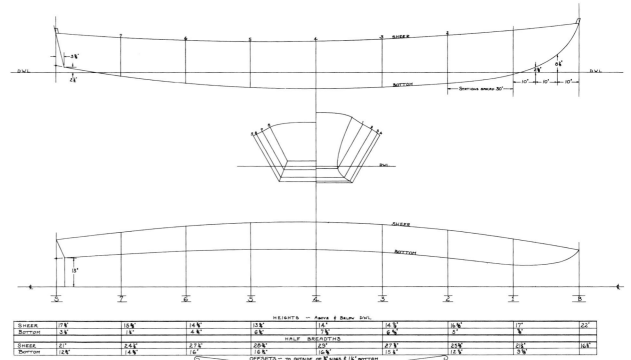

	S	7	6	5	4	3	2	1	B
HEIGHTS ~ ABOVE & BELOW DWL									
SHEER	17 5/8"	15 5/8"	14 3/8"	13 3/4"	14"	14 7/8"	16 5/8"	17"	22"
BOTTOM	3 1/8"	1 1/2"	4 3/4"	6 3/4"	7 3/8"	6 5/8"	5"	7/8"	
HALF BREADTHS									
SHEER	21"	24 1/2"	27 1/4"	28 3/4"	29"	27 7/8"	25 3/8"	21 1/2"	16 1/2"
BOTTOM	12 3/4"	14 5/8"	16"	16 3/4"	16 5/8"	15 1/2"	12 7/8"	9 7/8"	

OFFSETS ~ TO OUTSIDE OF 7/8" SIDES & 1 1/8" BOTTOM

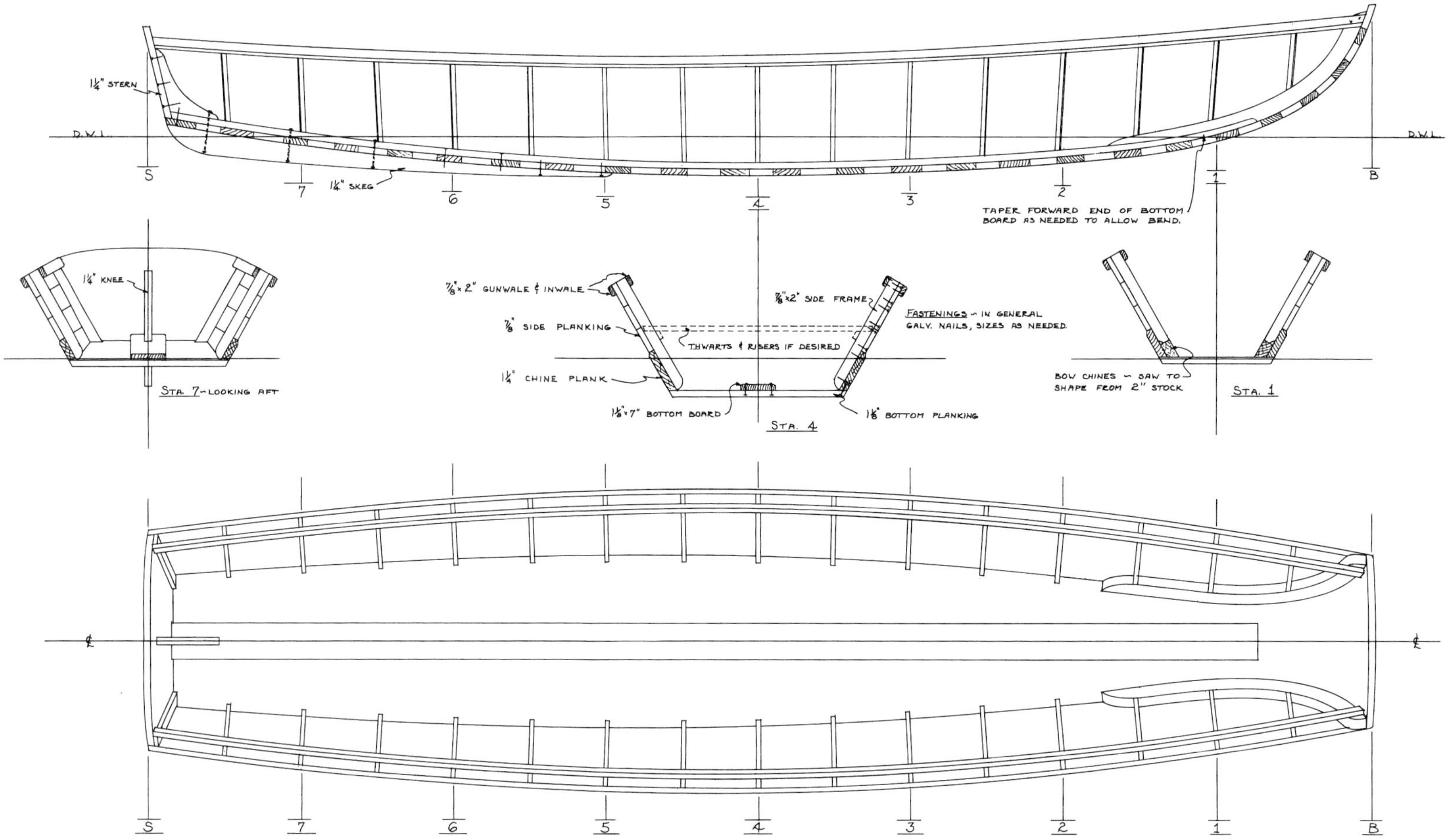

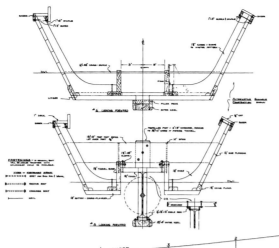

CONSTRUCTION SECTIONS AFT (*VENITA*)

This shows how the propeller tunnel is constructed and how the engine is to be supported. Anticipating rough usage, Joel made this boat exceptionally rugged. She'll take the ground often, so has an outer keel (2½ x 8″) that runs all the way aft to protect the propeller and rudder.

LINES PLAN (*VENITA*)

This 30-footer draws a scant 18″ of water and her propeller is protected by a stout outer keel. Her sides flare a constant 63 degrees from stern to stem so that a master pattern could be used in building the frames. The stem rake is the natural result of the flaring sides coming together at the centerline.

CONSTRUCTION PLAN (*VENITA*)

Although *Venita*'s bottom is crossplanked, her hull is set up like a dory on its "grown crook" frames around which the side planking bends and fastens. Joel used the same type of "chine plank" in this design as in *Marika*, but further strengthened the bottom with a pair of longitudinal bottom boards inside and an outer keel outside.

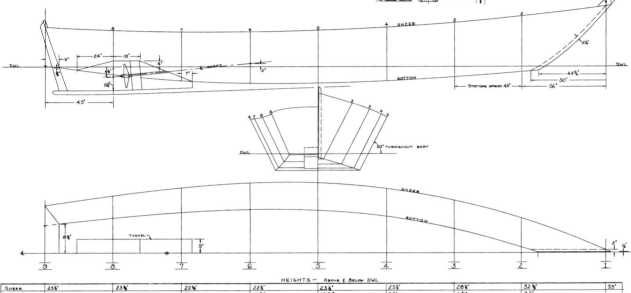

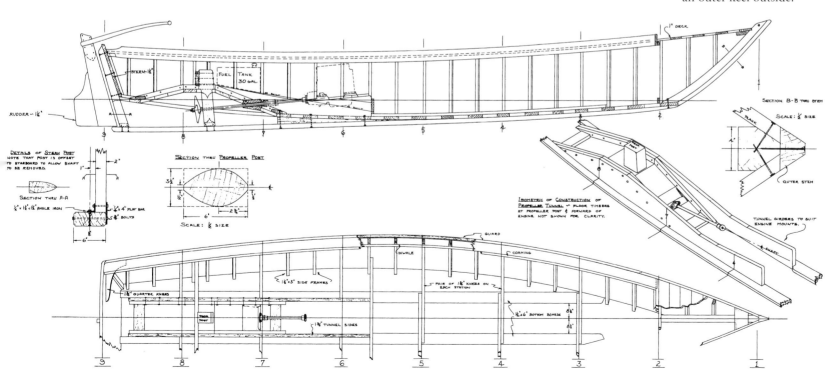

Pauline (Conversion)

DESIGN NO. 34 (1988)

LOA	*83'0"*
Beam	*18'0"*
Draft	*7' approx.*

Pauline took shape at the Thomaston, Maine, yard of Newbert & Wallace when I was an eighth-grader from nearby Rockland. I watched her being built and have followed her career ever since. North Lubec Canning Co. was the first and longest owner. *Pauline* carried that Rockland-based sardine plant's fish for four decades and was kept in tiptop shape, well painted and spotlessly clean. Of the six carriers of this model from this builder, *Pauline* was always my favorite. When she was offered for sale I took the time to measure her above the waterline as she lay out of service for the first time in her career. Since Roy Wallace shaped her directly from a half model there were never drawings, so I set about committing what I could of her to paper.

After a few months Ken and Ellen Barnes made an offer and bought the boat, intending to convert her for carrying passengers along mid-coast Maine. They already owned the cruise schooner *Stephen Taber*, so looked upon *Pauline* as a means of branching out into a power-driven coastal cruiser for twelve. But she needed reconfiguring first and I suggested they meet with Joel White.

Joel had long admired *Pauline* and her five sisters and welcomed the opportunity to draw her conversion plans, using hull shape measurements that had recently been taken of the underbody by Woodin and Marean for Coast Guard certification, and my previously-mentioned above-water plan. It was obvious from the start that she'd need a good-sized deckhouse; the existing sardine carrier configuration, much as we liked it, would have to go. Various options were considered but the concept that seemed to fit best was to make her look like a passenger steamer of pre-World War I vintage. This resulted in a pleasing profile, a generous deckhouse, a raised pilot-house, a stack, and a couple of masts. By the time Joel started drawing, he had before him many illustrations (mostly old photographs) of what these old-time steamers looked like.

He worked quickly and within a few days completed what he'd been asked to do: draw an outboard profile and make some arrangement studies in both plan and sectional views. The owners themselves and their conversion team leader, Tom Bournival, would handle the construction and arrangement details as they went along. Joel had set the stage, and others

with complementary talents finished the conversion over the course of a single winter.

Maintained in Bristol fashion, dressed out with flags, and with her diesel engine exhausting up through the hollow mizzen mast, leaving the deck in near silence, *Pauline* gets a warm welcome wherever she goes.

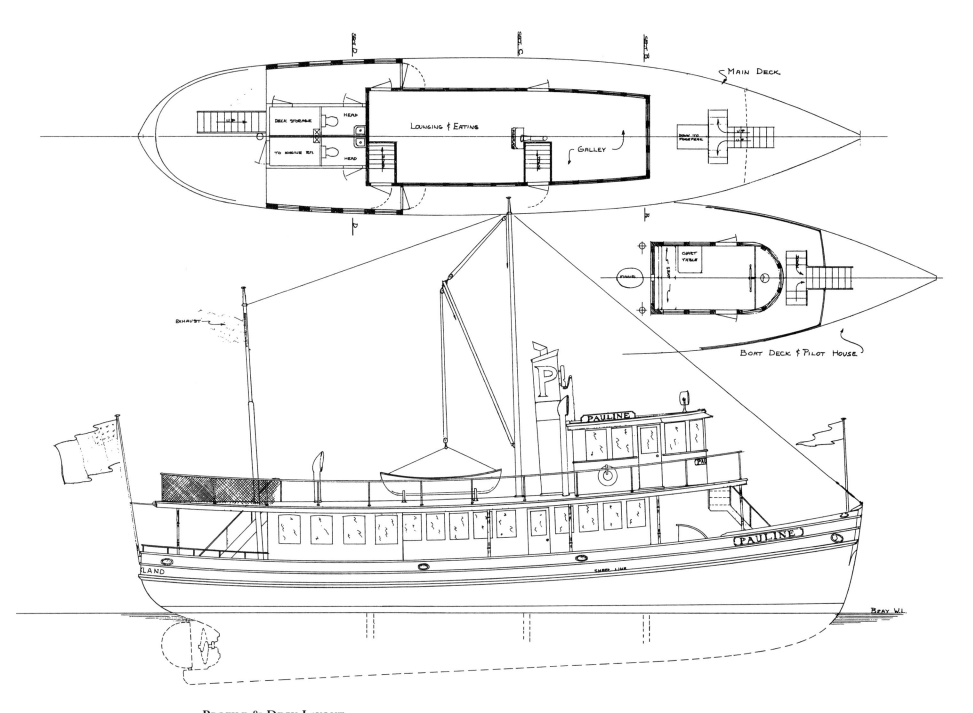

PROFILE & DECK LAYOUT

Although *Pauline*'s sardine carrier wheelhouse had to be eliminated in order to
make sufficient cabin space above the main deck, Joel was able to develop a layout
that would accommodate the existing engine and bulkhead locations. The engine
noise is minimized by having the engine exhaust run up the hollow mizzenmast.

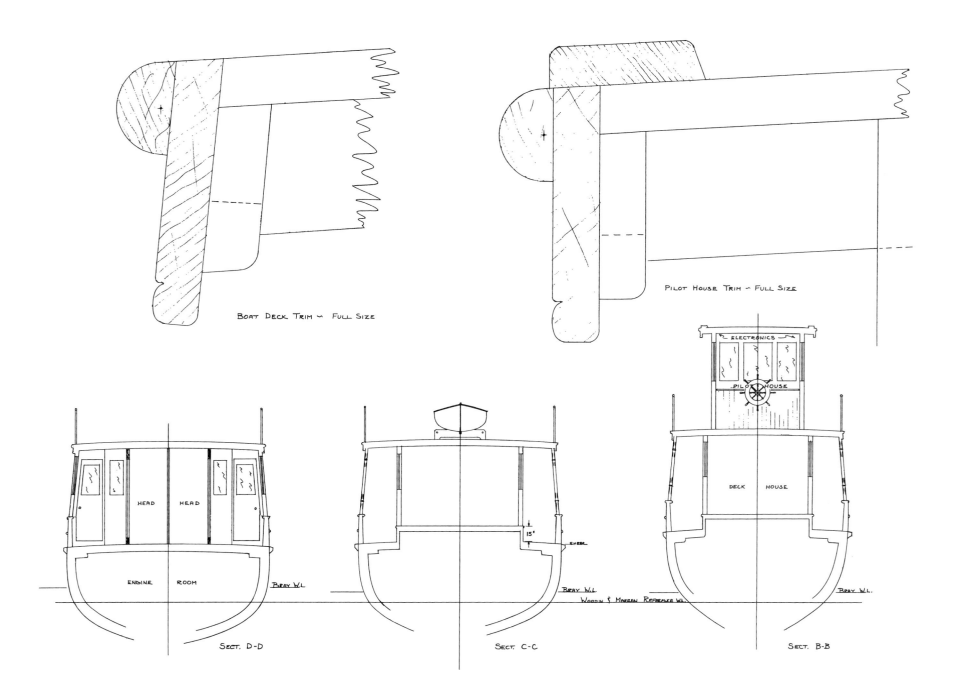

BOAT DECK TRIM ~ FULL SIZE

PILOT HOUSE TRIM ~ FULL SIZE

ELECTRONICS

PILOT HOUSE

HEAD HEAD

ENGINE ROOM

BRAY W.L.

SECT. D-D

15"

SHEER

BRAY W.L.

WOODIN & MARRAN REFERENCE W.L.

SECT. C-C

DECK HOUSE

BRAY W.L.

SECT. B-B

TYPICAL SECTIONS

A boxy appearance is prevented by giving plenty of tumblehome to the cabin sides that extend to the rails. Generous overhangs, suitably finished with beaded skirtboards and a half-round molding are traditional steamer details and avoid a "baldheaded" look.

Haven 12½ and Flatfish

DESIGN NOS. 35 & 52 (1989 & 1995)

HAVEN		*FLATFISH*	
LOA	*16'0"*	*LOA*	*20'3"*
LWL	*12'6"*	*LWL*	*16'1"*
Beam	*6'1"*	*Beam*	*7'6"*
Draft	*1'6"*	*Draft*	*2'2"*
Displ.	*1,400 lbs.*	*Displ.*	*3,094 lbs.*
Sail Area	*133 sq. ft.*	*Sail Area*	*268 sq. ft.*

Joel designed the Haven as a centerboard version of the famous Herreshoff 12½ footers, one of which he'd owned for nearly half a century. Because he so respected the original design, having sailed his *Shadow* in all conditions for many years, he set out to make the Haven perform exactly like the Herreshoff. With a little more beam and slightly filled-out bilges, Joel's numbers indicated identical stability. Wetted surface remained about the same and the sail plan identical, so it came as no surprise that Joel achieved what he set out to do. The local yacht club intermingles Havens and Herreshoffs on the racecourse without handicap, just as the club allows the gaff and marconi versions to compete together.

The chief advantage of the Haven over the Herreshoff is, of course, the shallow draft and with it the long, straight keel. She'll float in only a foot and a half of water, whereas it takes two and a half feet for the Herreshoff. This opens more acreage for thin-water sailing, and allows for easy trailering, a requirement of Sam Neel who ordered the first Haven. You can take her from one body of water to another distant one behind the family car. Or you can "dry sail" her by taking her home and sticking her in the garage during idle times. Some Havens are now being built with cold-molded hulls to better resist the drying out and leaking that sometimes accompanies long-term storage ashore.

The deeper keel and wineglass-shaped sections of the Herreshoff may make her look more elegant than the Haven when you see them together out of the water, but this is of small concern once they're overboard and their underbodies are hidden from view. Then the two are indistinguishable unless you seek out the telltale centerboard trunk. They have the same wonderfully roomy cockpit and comfortable seating, and the same safe feeling when the wind breezes up. Most are plank-on-frame boats where the structural elements such as the frames are clearly visible. You get as much of a visual treat when you're in the boat as you do when watching one sail past.

Although Havens employ lots of individual pieces of wood in their construction, and building one represents a challenge to the inexperienced builder, Joel's drawings include all the necessary detail including full-size patterns for the 22 timber molds and dimensions for the custom cast-bronze hardware. Lofting is optional and skipping this step saves a good deal of

time and allows the builder to start right in shaping wood. Despite the Haven's complexity, hundreds have been built, many of them by Brooklin-based builder Eric Dow. Eric's shop is pictured on the following pages.

As for Haven's larger sister, the Flatfish, Joel gave her exactly the same treatment using the Herreshoff Fish Class sloops as a starting point. Not having a Fish boat handy for measuring or for examining the details, Joel used information I picked off one of the original and unaltered boats, *Merry Hell*,

which is in Mystic Seaport's watercraft collection. As with the Haven, Joel's drawings include the details necessary to produce a proper boat for builders unfamiliar with the Herreshoff ambiance. Because the Haven and Flatfish are so similar, the Haven 12½ instruction book serves for the latter's construction.

While Joel never claimed complete credit for designing these two boats (he always attributed the majority to N.G. Herreshoff), he made it possible for more boats of these wonderful designs to be created, albeit with slight modifications. Making them centerboarders only increases their adaptability. Joel has added value to Herreshoff's original—a perfect move for today's peripatetic boat owners.

One can build a Flatfish in about the same number of hours as a Haven—there are only a few additional pieces—and the materials required are not much different in size or shape. You can adapt a Flatfish for coastal cruising using a boom tent or by extending the cabintop as Herreshoff did in the Fish's later years, naming the resulting creation a Marlin. Compared to the smaller Haven, the Flatfish is a faster craft as well, which is an important consideration for those faced with a tide-induced current.

SAIL PLAN (FLATFISH)

Although the Flatfish is the Haven's big sister, there are some differences besides size. The Flatfish's stem is straighter and overhangs more; the forward portion of the coaming is decked over to form a useful although tiny cabin, and running backstays have been added. (Joel's backstay push-pole detail also echoes Herreshoff's.)

LINES PLAN (FLATFISH)

These lines are drawn only for the even-numbered frames, and would result in half the number of "timber molds" used by the Herreshoffs for their multiple hulls. (HMCo's general practice was to have a separate mold to bend each pair of frames around.) Builders can go either way (the alternate is fewer molds, with ribbands added, over which to bend the alternate frames), but will have to end up with the specified 24 pairs of frames.

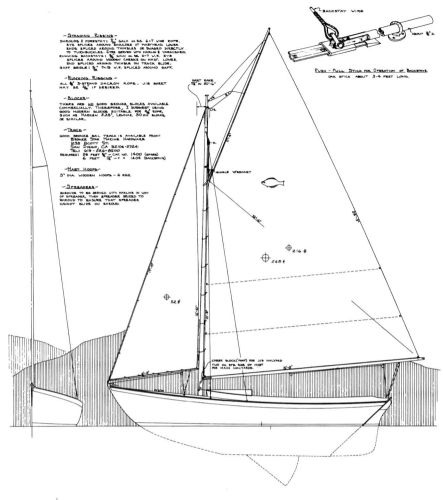

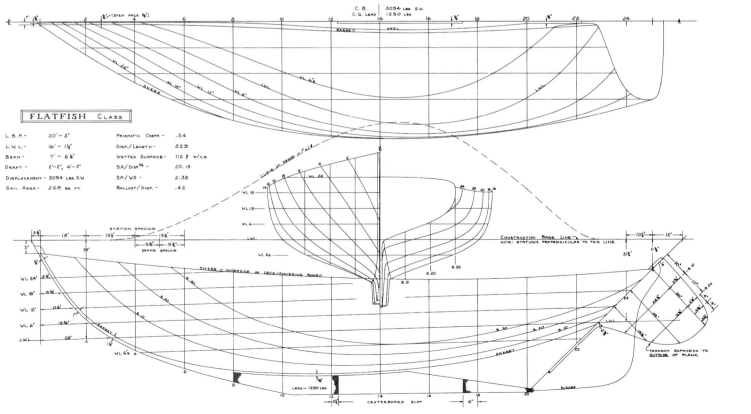

FLATFISH Class

L.B.P. -	20' - 3"	Prismatic Coeff. -	.54
L.W.L. -	16' - 1½"	Disp./Length -	329
Beam -	7' - 6⅝"	Wetted Surface -	112 ⌀ w/c.b.
Draft -	2'-2", 4'-3"	SA/Disp.^⅔ -	20.13
Displacement -	3094 lbs. S.W.	SA/WS -	2.33
Sail Area -	268 sq. ft.	Ballast/Disp. -	.42

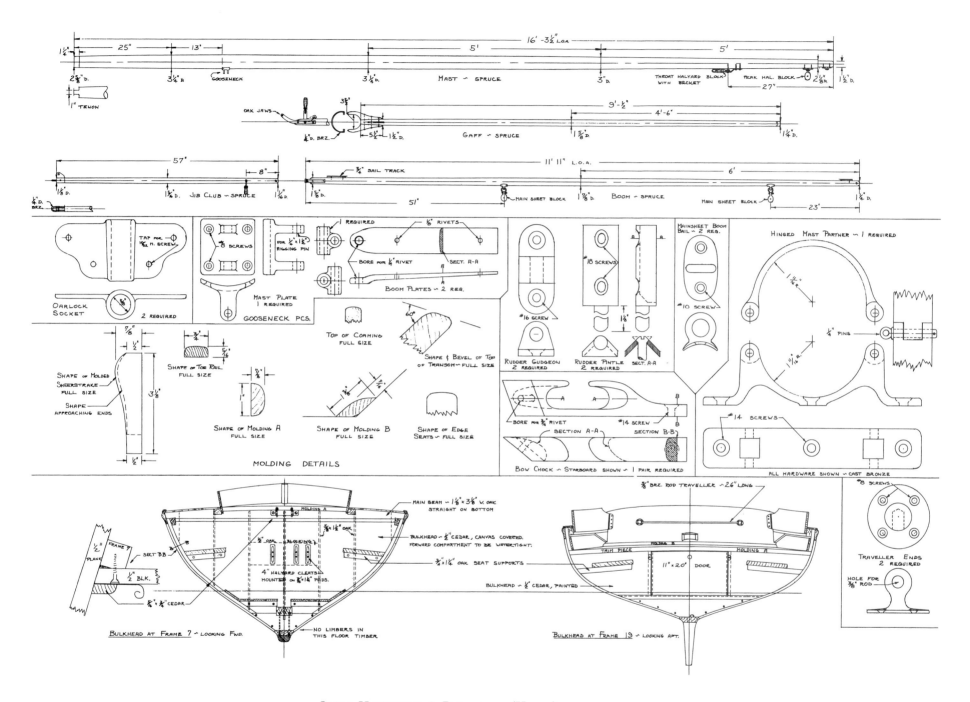

SPARS, HARDWARE, & BULKHEADS (HAVEN)

No matter how elegant its hull shape, a new boat will be a disappointment if its details aren't correctly executed. Joel knew this and was also aware that this particular design was especially detail sensitive. For this reason he carefully depicted the Haven's details including all the hardware.

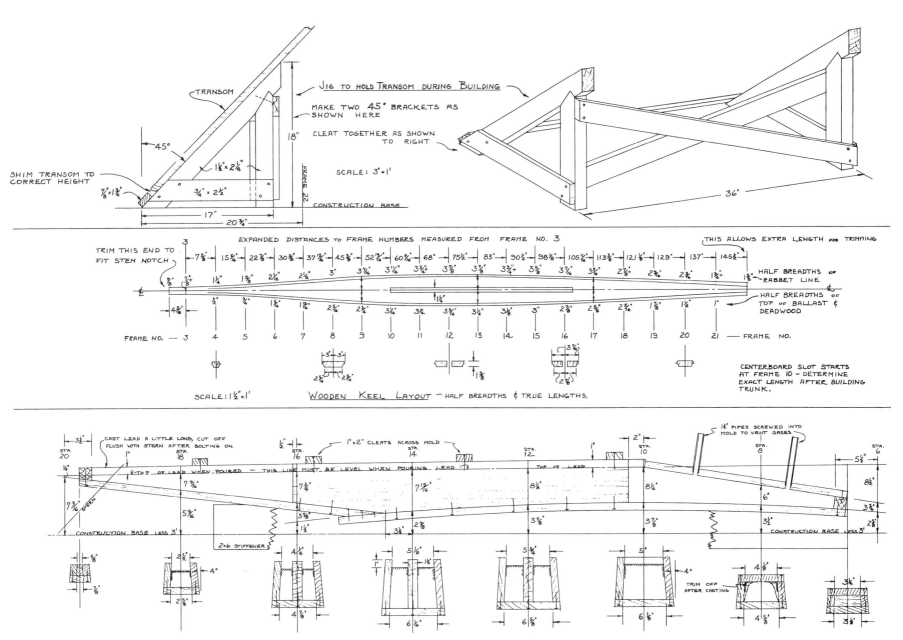

Transom Jig & Keel Details (Haven)

Joel drew up this supporting jig to hold the transom at its 45 degree angle and to help in other aspects to position it correctly. Likewise he depicted the wooden mold for pouring the lead ballast keel—after it had been proven successful for the first Haven. To save builders from lofting the wooden keel timber, its cross-sectional dimensions at each station are included here as well as its true (expanded) length between stations.

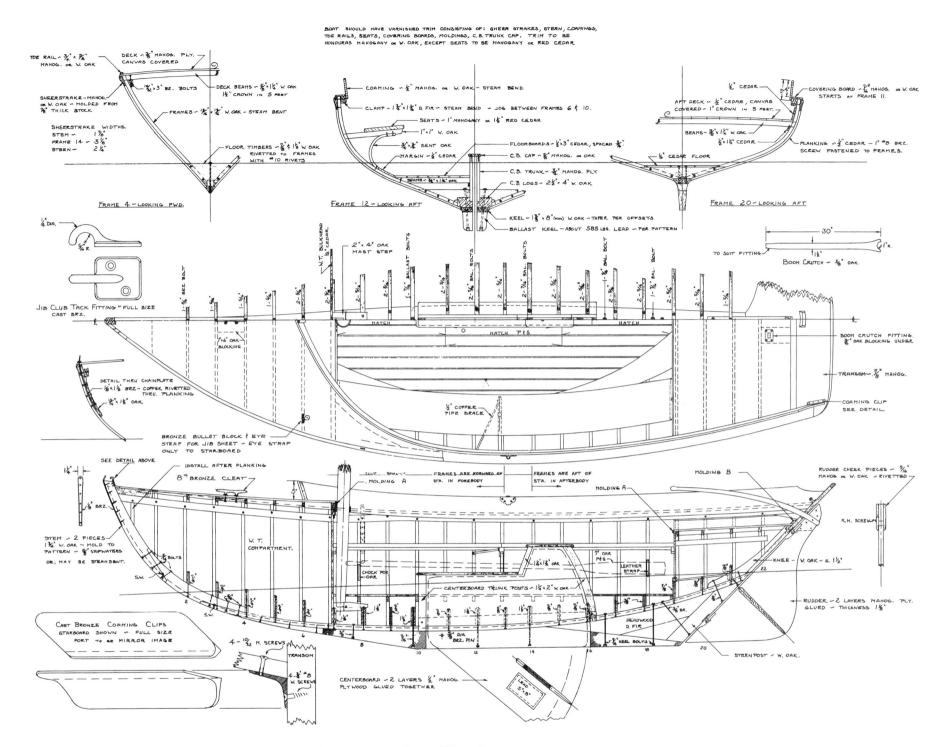

CONSTRUCTION PLAN (HAVEN)

Despite the Haven's complexity, many drawings have been sold through *WoodenBoat* and many boats have been built. Because the level of detail is so extensive, builders unfamiliar with Herreshoff standard practices can turn out these little jewels and have them look just as if they came out of that famed Bristol, Rhode Island, shop.

Sweet Olive

DESIGN NO. 37 (1989)

LOA	43'0"
LWL	32'0"
Beam	12'0"
Draft	6'3"
Displ.	26,300 lbs.
Sail Area	957 sq. ft.

When Kim Faulkner decided to do some offshore cruising he not only needed a bigger crew, he also needed a bigger boat. His gaff ketch *Alisande* (Joel's Design No. 11) was simply too small. Joel proposed a 43' ketch for which he drew preliminary plans, but in the end he and Kim decided on a cutter. This rig would provide nearly as many options for shortening sail as a ketch, and be a good bit faster under sail. *Sweet Olive* was the result and I am not alone in considering this one of Joel's best designs.

As with most new construction projects at Brooklin Boat Yard, this handsome cutter was turned out over the course of a single winter. Her hull was traditionally built with steam-bent oak frames, an oak backbone, and double planking of Douglas-fir over cedar, laid fore and aft. All fastenings were bronze and her ballast keel was of cast lead. There was no skimping on materials—*Sweet Olive* had the very best.

Sweet Olive is exceedingly handsome, with a slight hollow in her hull near the waterline as it approaches the stem, an elegant underbody with easy bilges and reversing sections down low near the keel. Joel gave her transom just enough reverse along its lower edge to be interesting. She has a time-honored, keel-mounted rudder whose heel has been slightly raised so as to help it stay operable in the event of an accidental grounding.

Joel called for a few bronze fabrications such as the maststep and the 'midship floors to make space for the water tank. In his subsequent designs with fin keel appendages, Joel's bronze fabrications would evolve into far more complex assemblies than those shown here.

Sweet Olive's hull is penetrated each side by a pair of round portholes—a distinctive, yet controversial detail that not all admirers approve of. They are a carryover from *Alisande* that Kim found highly desirable. They allowed one to see outside without going on deck, and brought in fresh air and light. A feature that meets with pretty much universal acclaim is the deck-level, bronze-sheathed guardrail that protects the hull when coming alongside a pile-faced wharf. It compliments the boat's sheer and adds some visual interest as well.

Although *Sweet Olive* was designed and built solely for cruising and has done little if any racing, Joel's sail area vs. displacement calculations indicate that she'd be a match for any boat her size and general shape.

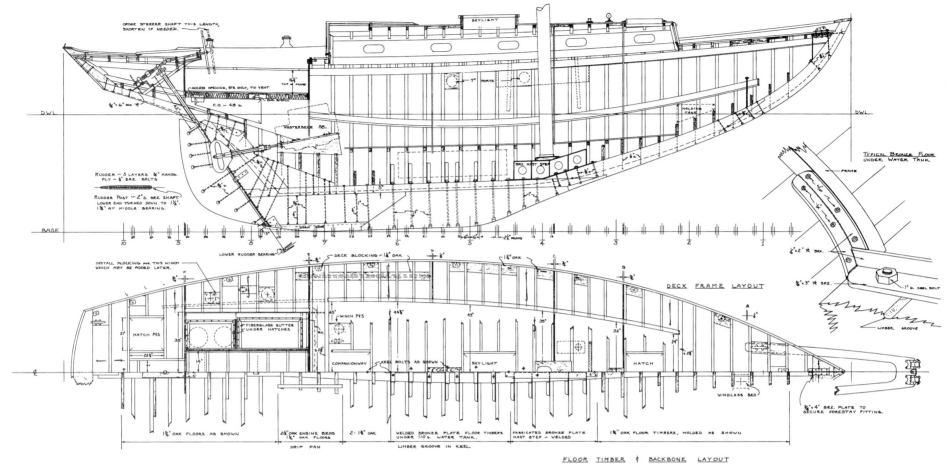

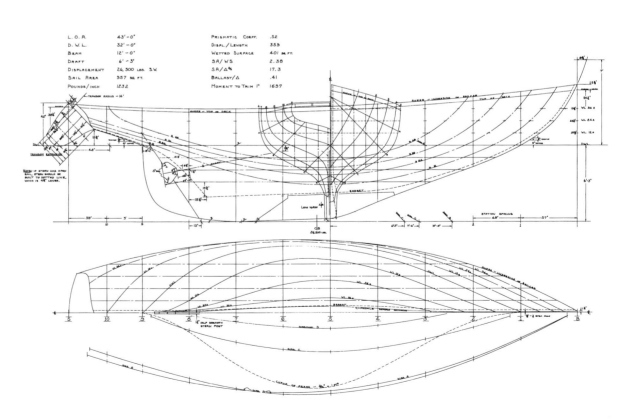

CONSTRUCTION PLAN

At this point in his career Joel drew a detailed construction plan for each new design. Besides his careful positioning of the backbone bolts and stopwaters, Joel has also shown a bilge stringer. The ceiling (interior planking) is interrupted by structural bulkheads, contributing no longitudinal strength, so the bilge stringers are meant to compensate.

LINES PLAN

Sweet Olive is a supremely lovely shape, and one not far from *Cirrus*—the Brooklin-based Fishers Island 31 that Joel admired from boyhood. He was well into computer-generated performance numbers by 1989 and the results tabulated here predict *Sweet Olive* will sail smartly, even though she was conceived as a pure cruiser.

L.O.A.	43'-0"	Prismatic Coeff.	.52
D.W.L.	32'-0"	Displ./Length	353
Beam	12'-0"	Wetted Surface	401 sq. ft.
Draft	6'-3"	SA/WS	2.38
Displacement	26,300 lbs. SW	SA/Δ⅔	17.3
Sail Area	957 sq. ft.	Ballast/Δ	.41
Pounds/Inch	1232	Moment to Trim 1"	1657

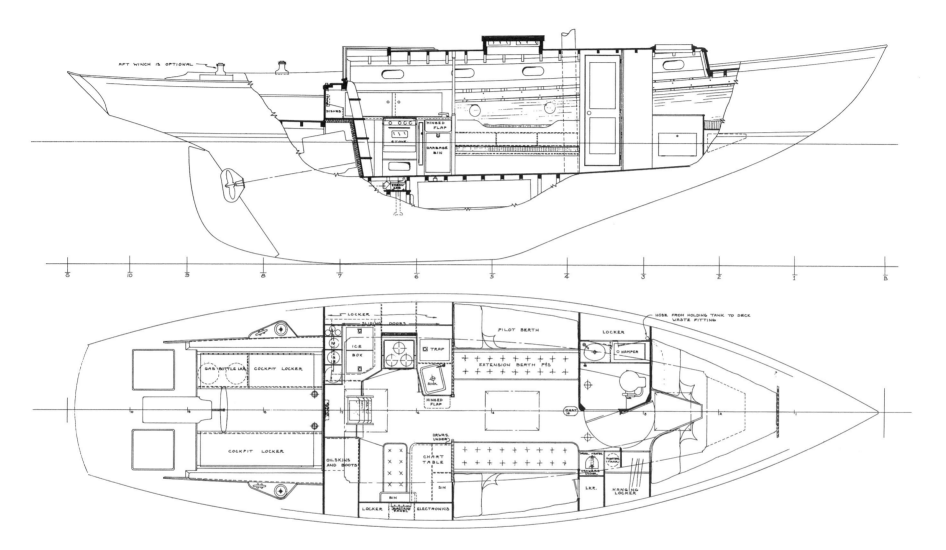

ACCOMMODATION PLAN

There's no cabin arrangement that fits a mid-sized sailing yacht's cross-sectional shape better than pilot berths fronted by settees, and Joel has adopted this layout in *Sweet Olive*'s main cabin. The galley and navigation station lie just aft, and an enclosed head and hanging lockers are ahead of the main cabin space. The V-berths way forward complete the boat's interior.

Shellback and Pooduck Skiff

DESIGN NOS. 38 & 40 (1989 & 1990)

SHELLBACK

LOA	*11'2"*
Beam	*4'5"*
Draft	*about 6"*
Weight	*100 lbs.*
Sail Area	*56 sq. ft.*

POODUCK

LOA	*12'10"*
Beam	*4'6"*
Draft	*about 6"*
Weight	*130 lbs.*
Sail Area	*65 or 79 sq. ft.*

Here are two rowing and sailing boats built of lapstrake plywood in the same manner as Joel's Nutshell Pram—the theme from which the Shellback takes its name. (The Pooduck's name comes from a beach in Brooklin.) Of these two, Joel developed the Shellback first, soon after the Nutshell. He was after a faster boat under sail and one that was more spacious and would row more easily. This meant abandoning the pram shape and employing a pointed bow as well as sharpening the stern at the waterline. As in the Nutshells, both these boats have but a single, laminated 'midship frame which is inconspicuously located under the middle thwart. The Shellback weighs the same as the big Nutshell and carries the same sail area, but is faster in most conditions. Both have daggerboards.

Soon after Joel built the first Shellback, his boatyard crew started turning out more for themselves using the same building jig. These 6 or 8 boats became a local fleet for after-work weekly races which Joel usually won. The Pooduck Skiff was a *WoodenBoat*-inspired evolution of the Shellback, built 30% heavier (thicker planks), 20" longer, and with around 20% more sail area. Joel gave her a lead-weighted, pivoting centerboard and the option of increasing the mast rake and setting a small jib. In the Pooduck Skiff, he went for more stability, roominess, and overall ruggedness, while only slightly sacrificing performance. Because of the Shellback's promotion—there's a how-to-build manual as well as a kit—it is by far the more popular of the two designs.

Joel's drawings for both the Shellback and the Pooduck are exceptionally detailed so either boat makes a wonderful wintertime project for builders who are short on experience. Once completed you'll have a boat that rows, tows, sculls, and sails extremely well. Joel never liked outboards, and deliberately designed his small boats so they'd do poorly with motors clamped to their sterns.

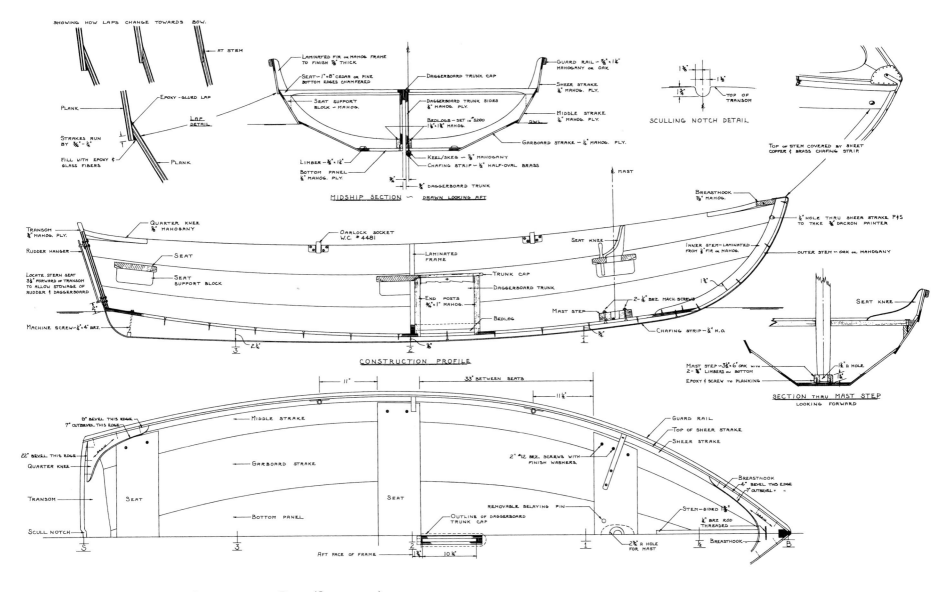

CONSTRUCTION PLAN (SHELLBACK)

The daggerboard trunk is slightly off-center so the board, when lowered, clears the keel. The forward thwart serves as the mast partner, so to strengthen it Joel added a pair of knees—oriented square with the sheerstrake for easier fitting. All three thwarts harmonize with the run of the plank laps rather than being parallel with the waterline.

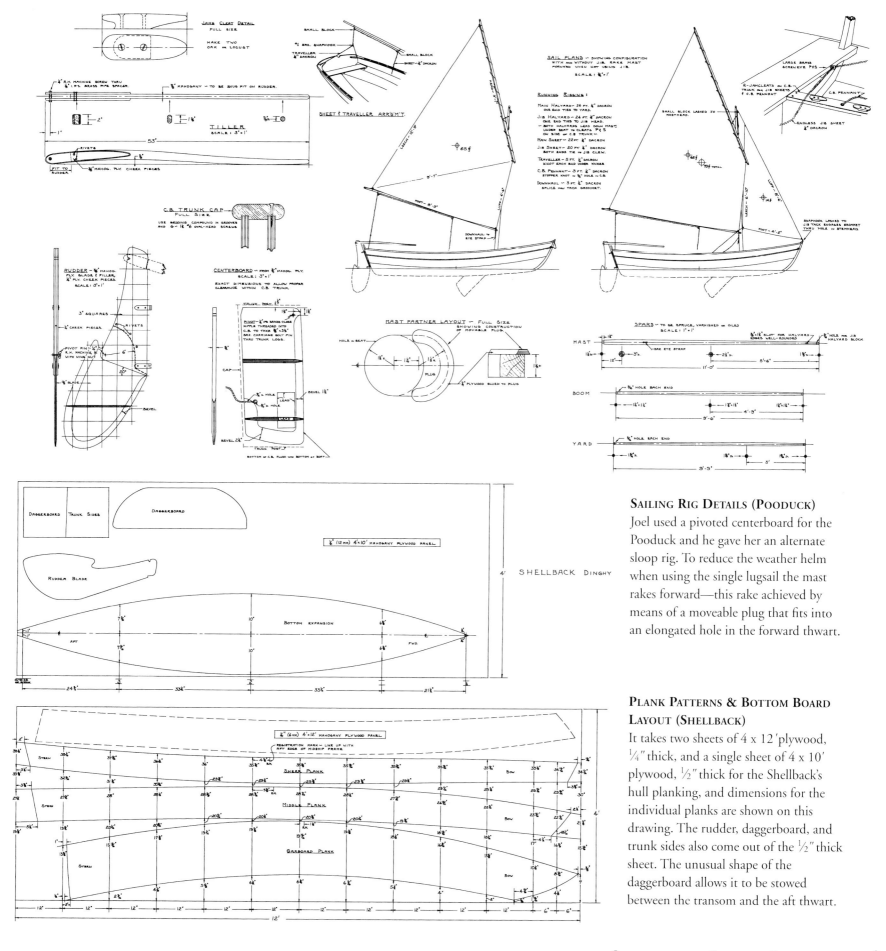

SAILING RIG DETAILS (POODUCK)

Joel used a pivoted centerboard for the Pooduck and he gave her an alternate sloop rig. To reduce the weather helm when using the single lugsail the mast rakes forward—this rake achieved by means of a moveable plug that fits into an elongated hole in the forward thwart.

PLANK PATTERNS & BOTTOM BOARD LAYOUT (SHELLBACK)

It takes two sheets of 4 x 12′ plywood, ¼″ thick, and a single sheet of 4 x 10′ plywood, ½″ thick for the Shellback's hull planking, and dimensions for the individual planks are shown on this drawing. The rudder, daggerboard, and trunk sides also come out of the ½″ thick sheet. The unusual shape of the daggerboard allows it to be stowed between the transom and the aft thwart.

Lala

DESIGN NO. 47 (1992)

LOA	23'0"
LWL	18'8"
Beam	6'1"
Draft	1'10"
Displ.	2,000 lbs.
Sail Area	193 sq. ft.

A designer should count himself lucky when his daydreams can be shared with others and boats like *Lala* are the result." This is how Joel ended his write-up on designing this speedy double-ended daysailer in *WoodenBoat*.

Being light and narrow, *Lala* and her sisters depend on the combination of a ballasted centerboard and crew weight on the windward rail to keep her on her feet when it breezes up. She carries a tall rig of generous area and can really move when the wind blows. Shallow and with a straight keel she is easy to trailer, a characteristic Joel purposely built into this design.

Author Tom McGuane ordered the first boat built by Joe Norton and named her *Lala*. *WoodenBoat* began selling other sets of drawings and the design was off and running. Hamilton Boatworks of Concord, New Hampshire, offers complete cold-molded boats finely finished off in wood that they call the "White 23." Edy and Duff of Mattapoisett, Massachusetts, (builders of the Stone Horse Jrs.) began producing these boats in fiberglass soon after *Lala*'s debut. Their version, the "Sakonnet 23," has proven popular, and as of this writing more than 40 boats have been turned out. All so far are double-enders, but after Joe Norton mentioned what a bear *Lala*'s stern was to plank in wood, Joel responded with a transom-sterned option.

As was Joel's custom with these later designs, the plans show lots of detail. He puts it this way: "Experience has taught me that more detail leads to fewer telephone calls from distressed builders." Joe Norton claims they were the most detailed drawings he had ever received.

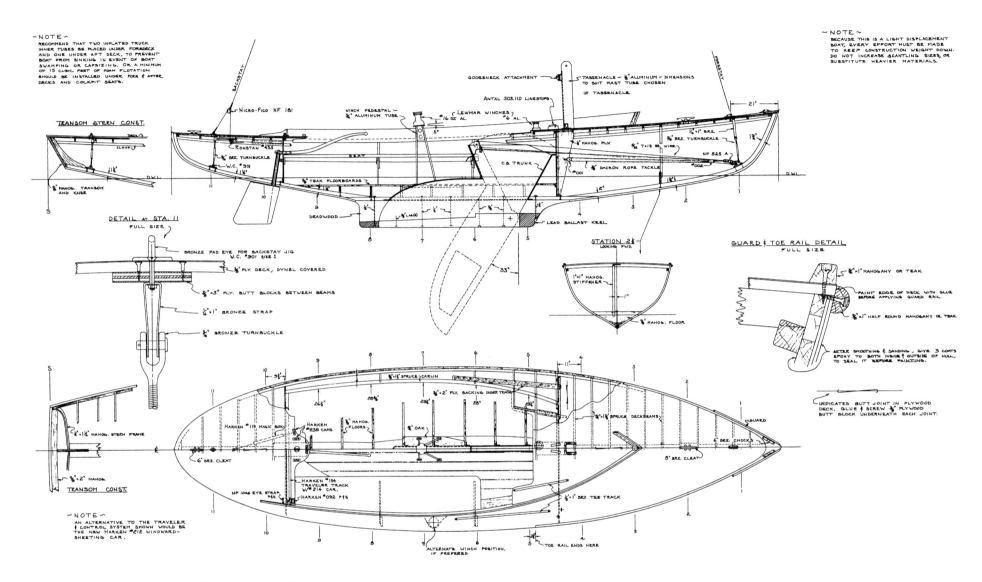

CONSTRUCTION PLAN

To ease the task of hoisting the heavy, ballasted centerboard, there's a 6-to-1 mechanical advantage by means of a wire-to-rope tackle, most of which hides under the foredeck. So as not to interfere with this, the mast is deck stepped (and pivoted on a tabernacle) and supported by a pair of knees, leaving the space between them clear for the centerboard hoisting tackle.

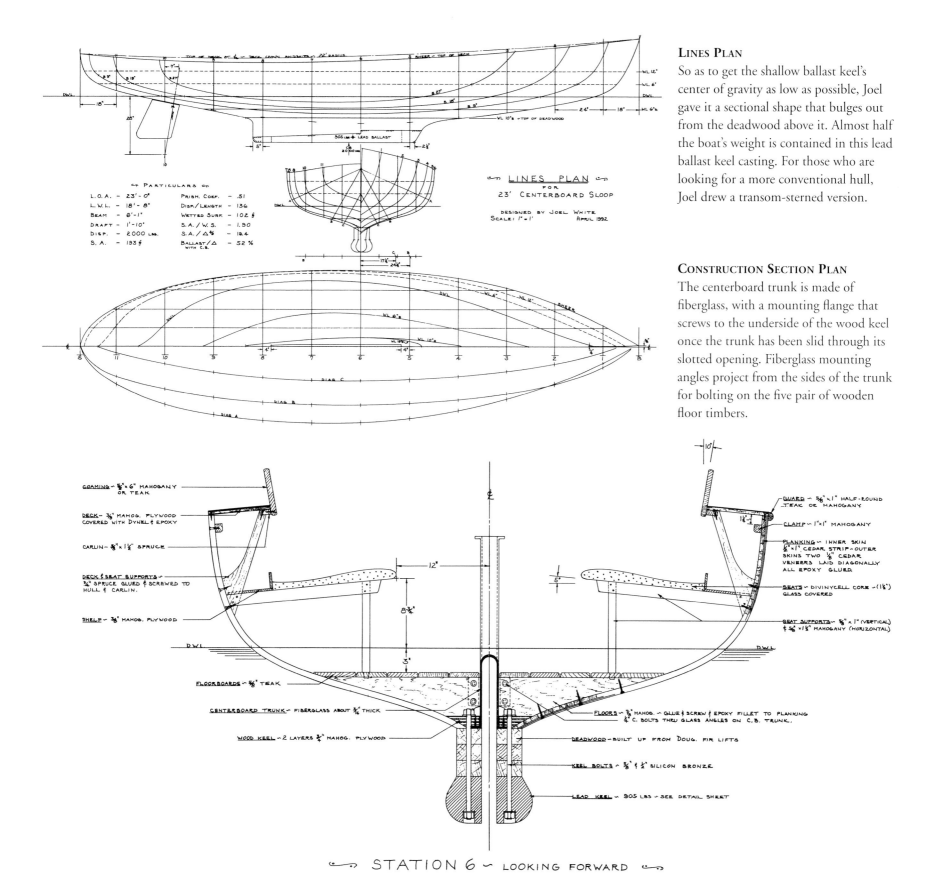

LINES PLAN

So as to get the shallow ballast keel's center of gravity as low as possible, Joel gave it a sectional shape that bulges out from the deadwood above it. Almost half the boat's weight is contained in this lead ballast keel casting. For those who are looking for a more conventional hull, Joel drew a transom-sterned version.

CONSTRUCTION SECTION PLAN

The centerboard trunk is made of fiberglass, with a mounting flange that screws to the underside of the wood keel once the trunk has been slid through its slotted opening. Fiberglass mounting angles project from the sides of the trunk for bolting on the five pair of wooden floor timbers.

LINES PLAN
FOR
23' CENTERBOARD SLOOP

DESIGNED BY JOEL WHITE
SCALE: 1"=1'   APRIL 1992

Particulars

L.O.A. — 23'-0"	PRISM. COEF. — .51
L.W.L. — 18'-8"	DISP./LENGTH — 136
BEAM — 6'-1"	WETTED SURF. — 102 ∮
DRAFT — 1'-10"	S.A./W.S. — 1.90
DISP. — 2000 LBS.	S.A./△⅔ — 18.4
S.A. — 193 ∮	BALLAST/△ WITH C.B. — 52 %

COAMING — ⅝"× 6" MAHOGANY OR TEAK

DECK — ⅜" MAHOG. PLYWOOD COVERED WITH DYNEL & EPOXY

CARLIN — ⅞"× 1½" SPRUCE

DECK & SEAT SUPPORTS — ¾" SPRUCE GLUED & SCREWED TO HULL & CARLIN.

SHELF — ⅜" MAHOG. PLYWOOD

FLOORBOARDS — ⅝" TEAK

CENTERBOARD TRUNK — FIBERGLASS ABOUT ⅜" THICK

WOOD KEEL — 2 LAYERS ¾" MAHOG. PLYWOOD

GUARD — ⅝"× 1" HALF-ROUND TEAK OR MAHOGANY

CLAMP — 1"× 1" MAHOGANY

PLANKING — INNER SKIN ¼"× 1" CEDAR STRIP—OUTER SKINS TWO ⅛" CEDAR VENEERS LAID DIAGONALLY ALL EPOXY GLUED

SEATS — DIVINYCELL CORE —(1⅛") GLASS COVERED

SEAT SUPPORTS — ⅝"× 1" (VERTICAL) & ⅝"× 1⅛" MAHOGANY (HORIZONTAL)

FLOORS — ⅞" MAHOG. — GLUE & SCREW & EPOXY FILLET TO PLANKING ¼" C. BOLTS THRU GLASS ANGLES ON C.B. TRUNK.

DEADWOOD — BUILT UP FROM DOUG. FIR LIFTS

KEEL BOLTS — ⅝" & ½" SILICON BRONZE

LEAD KEEL — 905 LBS — SEE DETAIL SHEET

STATION 6 — LOOKING FORWARD

Dragonera

DESIGN NO. 49 (1993)

LOA	74'0"
LWL	59'0"
Beam	15'0"
Draft	7'6"
Displ.	62,000 lbs.
Sail Area	1,800 sq. ft.

Dragonera was Joel's largest design when he began working on her drawings in spring of 1992. Client Bruce Stevens said he wanted a fast and easily-handled boat of about this size, and essentially left the other decisions to Joel. *Dragonera* benefited from Joel's recent trials and tribulations of having to prepare shop drawings for a couple of big sailing yachts the yard had built to plans of other designers—designers who hadn't done much thinking about streamlining the building process. Joel always brought a builder's perspective to whatever he drew, but he was especially determined to make *Dragonera*'s construction as trouble-free and efficient as possible. The drawings for the bulkheads, for example, specified where the plywood was to be scarfed, and occasional perspective sketches helped the workers better understand complex assemblies. Joel depicted items that needed special attention on sheet after sheet of detailed drawings.

Joel, his son Steve, and the boatyard crew built *Dragonera* in only about a year in spite of her size. With only the barest of sea trials, *Dragonera* set out for Bermuda where she encountered a fierce Gulf Stream gale that required heaving to under staysail and reefed mizzen for some twenty-one hours. That she came through undamaged except for a bent stern pulpit speaks volumes about her sound design and construction.

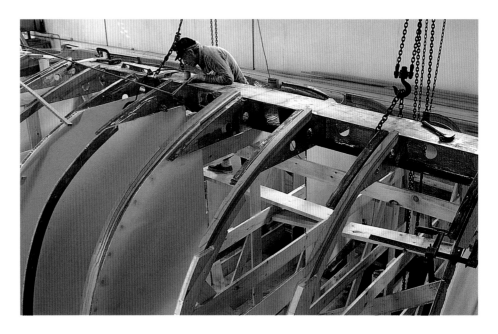

SAIL PLAN

An advantage of the ketch rig is that the sails are fairly even in area and shortening sail in a blow becomes simply a case of dropping and furling one or more of them. (Getting rid of the roller-furling jib is even easier.) A ketch's chief disadvantage—its mainsail backwinding the mizzen—is mitigated in *Dragonera* because there's good separation between these two sails, and the mizzen is relatively small, making her more like a yawl than a ketch. After a few years of use the staysail club was replaced with a self-tacking jib— a feature used in Design No. 53S.

LINES PLAN

Dragonera's hull slips easily through the water because her underbody is so lean and so relatively light in weight. This means that in spite of her length her sail area remains small and easily handled by only a few people. As with all his designs for cold-molded construction no matter what their size, Joel utilized a fin-type of keel and a spade-type rudder.

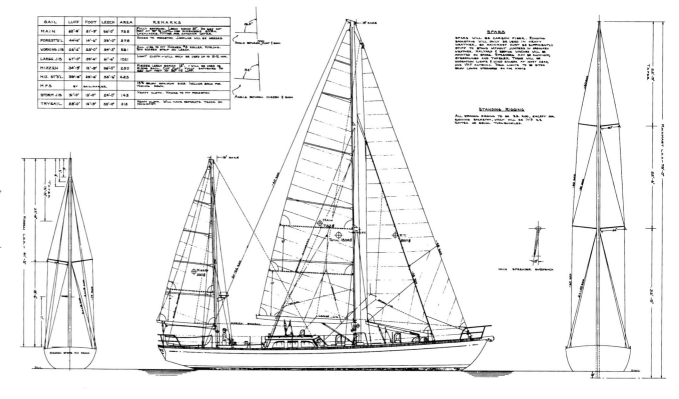

PARTICULARS

L. O. A.	74'-0"	PRISMATIC COEFF.	.55 (HULL ONLY)
L. W. L.	59'-0"	DISP./ LENGTH	134
BEAM	15'-0".	WETTED SURFACE	769 SQ. FT.
DRAFT	7'-6"	S. A. / W. S.	2.36
DISPLACEMENT	61,483 LBS. S.W.	S. A. / DISP. ⅔	18.7
SAIL AREA	1822 SQ. FT.	BALLAST / DISP.	36%
POUNDS/INCH	2850 LBS.	MOMENT TO TRIM 1"	8375 FT. LBS.

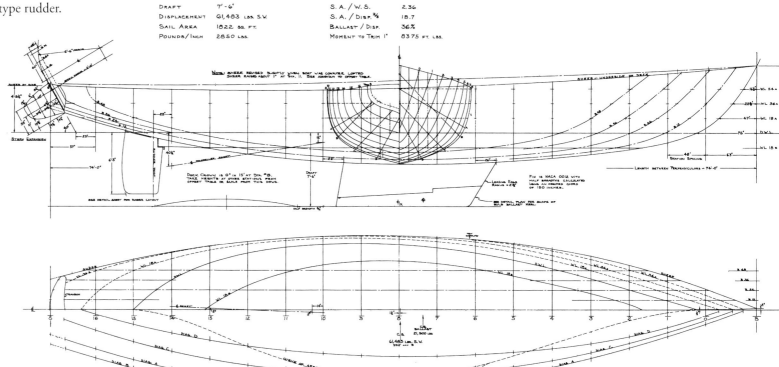

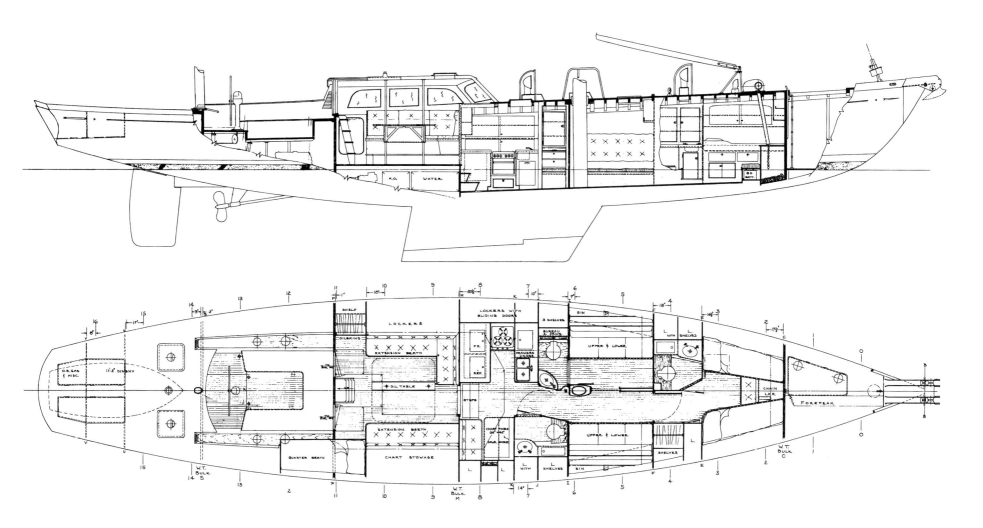

ARRANGEMENT PLAN

In a yacht the size of *Dragonera* there's sufficient headroom under the deck without having a trunk cabin. Her deckhouse allows for a raised platform under which the water and fuel tanks can be placed. A V-drive makes it possible for the engine to be aft of the living space and under the cockpit sole. Joel kept the mizzen small and its mast aft of the cockpit where it's out of the way.

Fast Cruising Sloop

DESIGN NO. 50 (1994)

LOA	62'2"
LWL	45'11"
Beam	11'8"
Draft	8'0"
Displ.	26,400 lbs.
Sail Area	1,200 sq. ft.

Joel worked up this design for Kim and Sue Bottles who very much loved what had been created but never went ahead with construction. Designed near the end of Joel's career, by which time he and Brooklin Boat Yard had gained a lot of experience in building beautiful cold-molded hulls and in turning out high grade yachts of this size, this is one of my favorites—a boat I'd really like to own.

Simplicity, aesthetics, and performance were design criteria that held lots of appeal for Joel, so he and the clients fussed over this design until it represented what they all believed in. Light air or windy conditions, no matter which, this boat would be up to it and lick about any boat of her size hands down. And in spite of her size, she'd be an easy boat to sail. Joel piled on plenty of area in her working sails, so that big, light-weather kites could be dispensed with. Her normal working jib and a poleless, single-luff spinnaker would do just fine. Furling the 700 sq. ft. mainsail would be the biggest job onboard since the plans already call for a roller furling headsail.

The idea for Design No. 50 stemmed from an article in *WoodenBoat* about Steve and Laurie White's Swede 55 *Vortex*, a long and skinny design of Knud Reimers' that Steve and his Brooklin Boat Yard crew built in 1990. Sue and Kim Bottles already owned a 30-square-meter sloop of about the same proportions, so were pretty well sold on the advantages of narrow, easily-driven hulls with relatively small sail areas. For them the *Vortex* story really hit home, and in fact was the basis for Joel's first Design No. 50 proposal. At first he tried to hold to about the same 52' overall length and general proportions, with added cruising accommodations, but couldn't come up with enough interior space for their needs.

The final design was based more on Joel's *Dragonera* shrunk down from a 59' waterline length to one of about 46'. To meet the clients' wish for a long-ended profile, Joel pulled out the bow and stern overhangs and even worked in a bit of reverse in the forward waterline. He also refined the shape of the ballast keel to give it more lift when going to windward. All parties agreed that this was more like it. Not only did this boat retain the desired racy look, but featured what I think is an exceptionally nice layout—one that includes two double berths. It's an ideal boat for two couples to cruise aboard, and by utilizing the main cabin there are berths for three more persons.

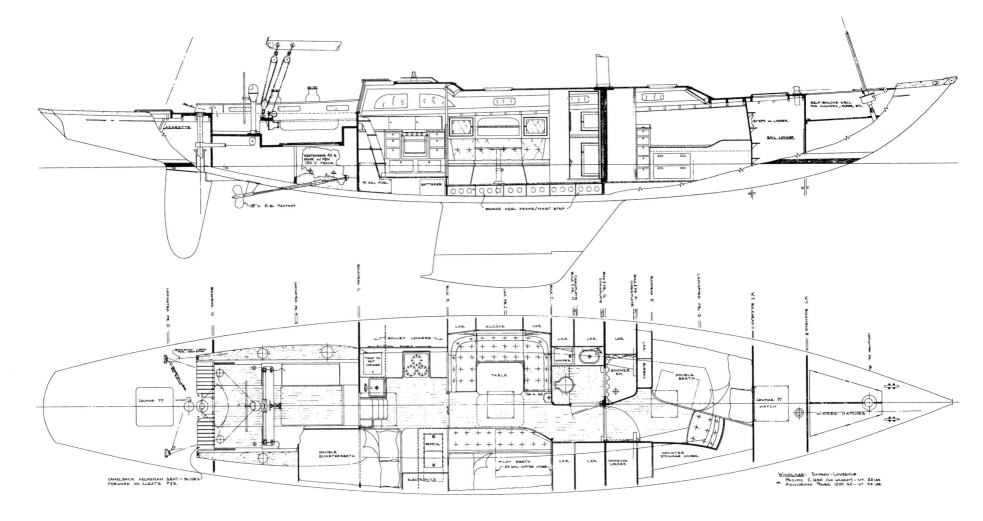

ARRANGEMENT PLAN

A V-drive works well here because it places the engine under the cockpit instead of taking up valuable living space. There is precious little bilge in modern, fin-keeled hulls, so to provide space for the batteries and fuel tank—both of which are best placed low—Joel incorporated a doghouse which permitted him to raise the cabin sole and take advantage of the space under it.

LINES PLAN

Beginning with this design Joel kept all his calculations and notes in a bound booklet instead of on separate pieces of paper. This produced a chronology and kept related material organized and always at hand. His notebook and designer/client correspondence file, which I borrowed for a short time, were tremendously helpful in writing a design review for *WoodenBoat* #131.

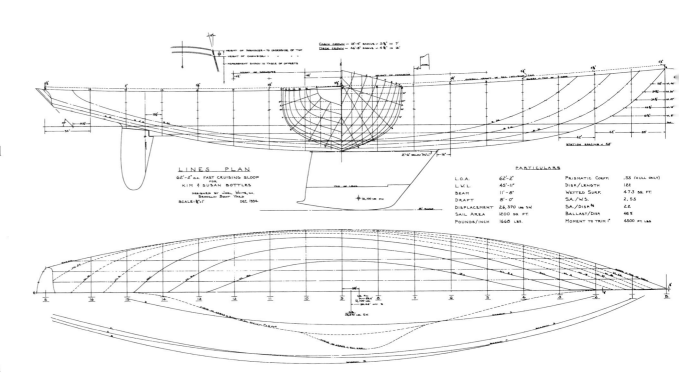

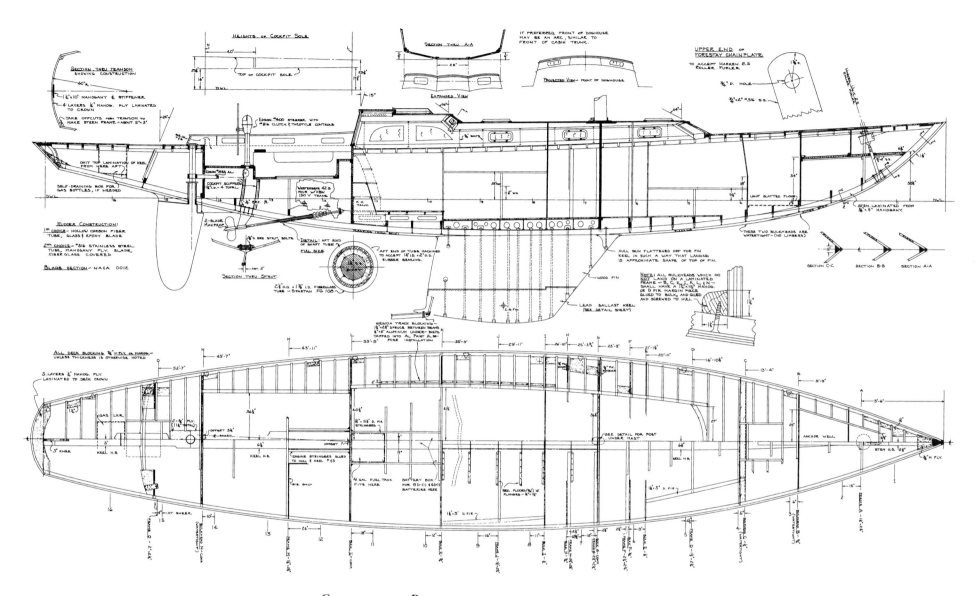

CONSTRUCTION PLAN

Fully appreciating the need for a secure attachment of the fin keel to the cigar-shaped hull, Joel called for a massive bronze weldment within the lower hull that also helps support the mast. This assembly distributes the load from the fin-and-ballast appendage over a good portion of the boat's bottom so the two don't separate in the case of an accidental grounding or during extreme sailing conditions.

Everglades

DESIGN NO. 51 (1994)

LOA	42'1"
LWL	36'10"
Beam	10'0"
Draft	3'0"
Displ.	15,610 lbs.
Power	Two 38.5 hp Yanmar diesels

Designing for elegance rather than speed, Joel gave this unusual craft a hull shaped almost like a sailboat. I especially like her transom with its rake and radius. The bow is more like traditional displacement power launches with its nearly plumb stem, narrow deck line (when viewed from above), and a hollow near the waterline. Although the general trend in yacht design is for more balanced ends (overhangs that are more-or-less equal bow and stern), a good designer can depart, just as Joel has done here, and produce a handsome and novel result.

This is a boat for sheltered waters; one that's never intended to smash into a big head sea. When used as a lake or river cruiser those big windows aren't a cause for concern and provide the boat's interior with lots of light when closed, and plenty of fresh air when open. These windows are of the drop sash type that lower into pockets within the cabin sides for opening. When underway you can choose between the two cockpits, one forward and another aft. If you prefer to sit inside there's good seating at the dinette and limited seating within the pilothouse.

Two small diesels, one under each of the berths, propel this boat through V-drives. The propellers and linked-together rudders are tucked up against the hull where they get protection from the centerline skeg should there be an accidental grounding. The rudders benefit from the wash of the propellers to enhance the boat's steering.

Despite her elegance, this is a tough little boat. Besides the usual center-line backbone, two fore and aft girders beneath the cabin sole begin near the forward end of the pilothouse and run nearly all the way to the stern. They're cleverly arranged to help support the engine as well as stiffen the hull. Adding strength to the hull at the sheer are full-length clamp and shelf assemblies.

To look good, the rakes of the cabin structure and windows have to be considered, and Joel's treatment in this regard looks just right. He drew the uprights of the cabin and pilothouse square with the boat's sheer—meaning that as the sheer changes so does the angle of the uprights. He noted right on the drawing that the window openings are supposed to be wider at the bottom than at the top but that the posts or uprights between them are of constant cross section. There'll be curved glass in the pilothouse windows as well. It's this attention to detail that makes or breaks a design.

Everglades will make a wonderful boat to explore the waterway that runs along our Eastern Seaboard, and that's exactly what Mike and Ann Matheson had in mind when they asked Joel to design her. She'll be a comfortable liveaboard even for extended periods, drawing many admirers. Even *Everglades'* two roof-mounted tenders will be special: *Palmetto* is a 12' lapstrake dinghy, and *Bug* is a Wee Lassie double-paddle canoe that will nest inside of *Palmetto*.

LINES PLAN

I never asked Joel why he drew this boat facing left instead of right, right-facing being the accepted convention. Perhaps he thought he could better evaluate her shape and appearance, or maybe he simply wanted some variety. Heading in either direction, *Everglades* has a lovely hull as these lines clearly show.

CONSTRUCTION PLAN

To achieve the desired rake, Joel specified each of the varying angles for all six posts on this drawing, and noted that the windows are wider at the bottom than at the top. Because this is a cold-molded hull, Joel could abandon the usual structure of a plank-on-frame yacht and strengthen the bottom with a pair of longitudinal stringers whose aft portions perform double duty as engine beds.

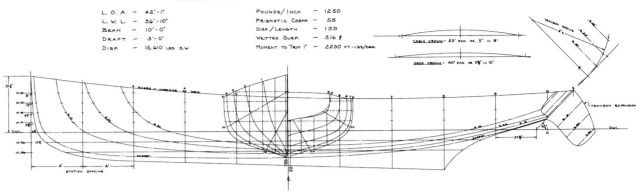

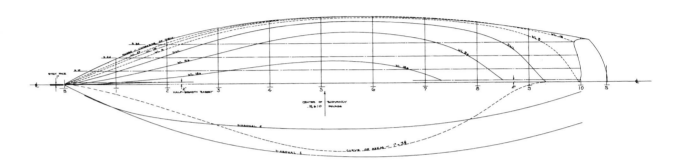

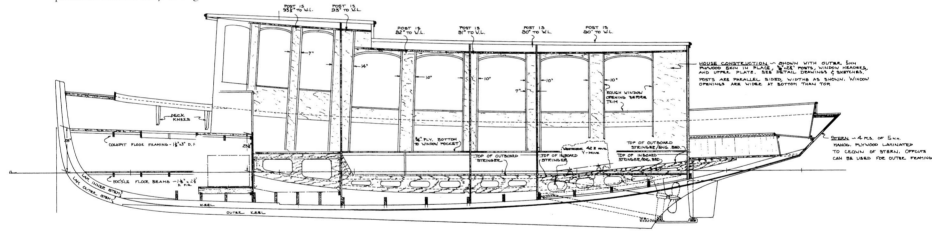

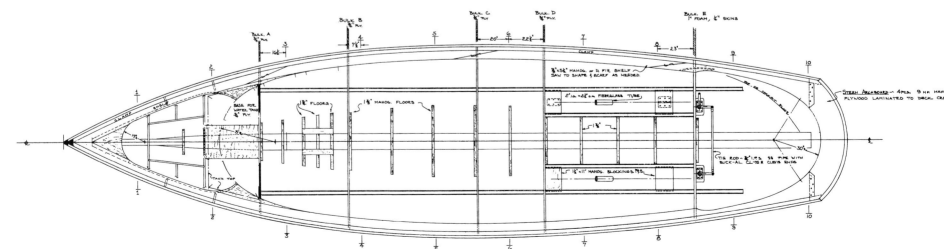

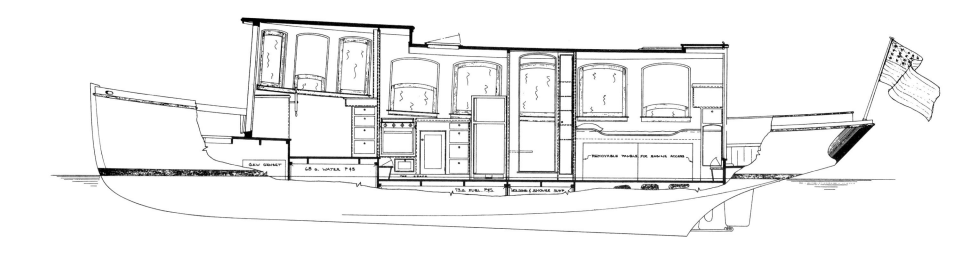

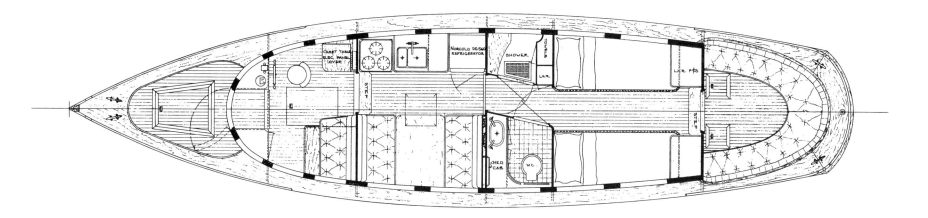

ARRANGEMENT PLAN

The noise underway will be largely confined to the unoccupied sleeping cabin where the engines are located—boxed in under the berths. The aft part of the boat will be quiet and habitable while shut down and anchored, especially the cushioned cockpit which is in the lee of the cabin and can be shaded by an awning.

Grace and the Center Harbor 31s

DESIGN NO. 53 (1995)
GRACE (KETCH NO. 53H)

LOA	31'1"
LWL	25'2"
Beam	8'5"
Draft	4'11"
Sail Area	441 sq. ft.
Displ.	7,916 lbs.

LINDA (SLOOP NO. 53S)

LOA	32'3"
LWL	25'2"
Beam	8'5"
Draft	6'0"
Sail Area	473 sq. ft.
Displ.	7,916 lbs.

THE MANTLEPIECE (SLOOP NO. 53G)

LOA	32'0"
LWL	25'2"
Beam	8'5"
Draft	6'0" (6'8" with new keel)
Sail Area	473 sq. ft.
Displ.	7,916 lbs.

PUDDING (SLOOP NO. 53D)

LOA	31'2"
LWL	25'2"
Beam	8'5"
Draft	6'0"
Sail Area	498 sq. ft.
Displ.	7,916 lbs.

The idea behind *Grace*, the first boat of Joel's and Bob Stephens' "Center Harbor" series, was to update L. Francis Herreshoff's *Quiet Tune* to improve her performance and make use of Brooklin Boat Yard's skill at cold-molded construction. She'd have the same short-ended hull with low free-board and low trunk cabin, but her underbody would be very different. The ballast keel and rudder would be appendages—separate pieces from the hull itself. This configuration moves through the water with less resistance than the full keel/attached rudder underbody of *Quiet Tune*, and because the hollows are minimized, the shape better lends itself to cold-molding. It's the way most sailboats are designed these days, no matter what the hull material.

Owner Frank Henry requested a ketch rig similar to *Quiet Tune*, but after Joel made some stability studies he concluded that his new design could handle a good deal more sail area. Even *Quiet Tune* could have carried more sail, Joel figured, and inquiries about that boat's light weather performance bore this out. As it turned out, *Grace* was a little larger all around, being about two feet longer overall and a little wider as well. Her cockpit is deep (non-self-baling) with comfortable seating and Joel added some basic cruising accommodations. He also fitted a small diesel between the seats at the forward end of the cockpit.

Before *Grace* came to fruition a second boat of the same type had been ordered. She was to be a sloop instead of a ketch, and given all the sail area she could handle. A deeper keel helped make this possible as did slightly greater bow and stern overhangs. She became *Linda* and was launched in company with *Grace* the very same June day. A number of onlookers agreed that this pair were the loveliest boats yet turned out by Brooklin Boat Yard.

More boats using the same concept followed, each slightly different, and all of them sloop-rigged. So far the favored color scheme has been green bottom and boottop, off-white topsides with a gilded covestripe, varnished toerails and cabin sides, and tan decks and spars. The 35' sloop *Kells* is similar in concept, but is considered an entirely new design of Bob Stephens.

For the summer of 2000 *Grace* was fitted with a new, free-standing, carbon fiber-reinforced-wood mizzenmast to clear the cockpit of the original mast's standing rigging.

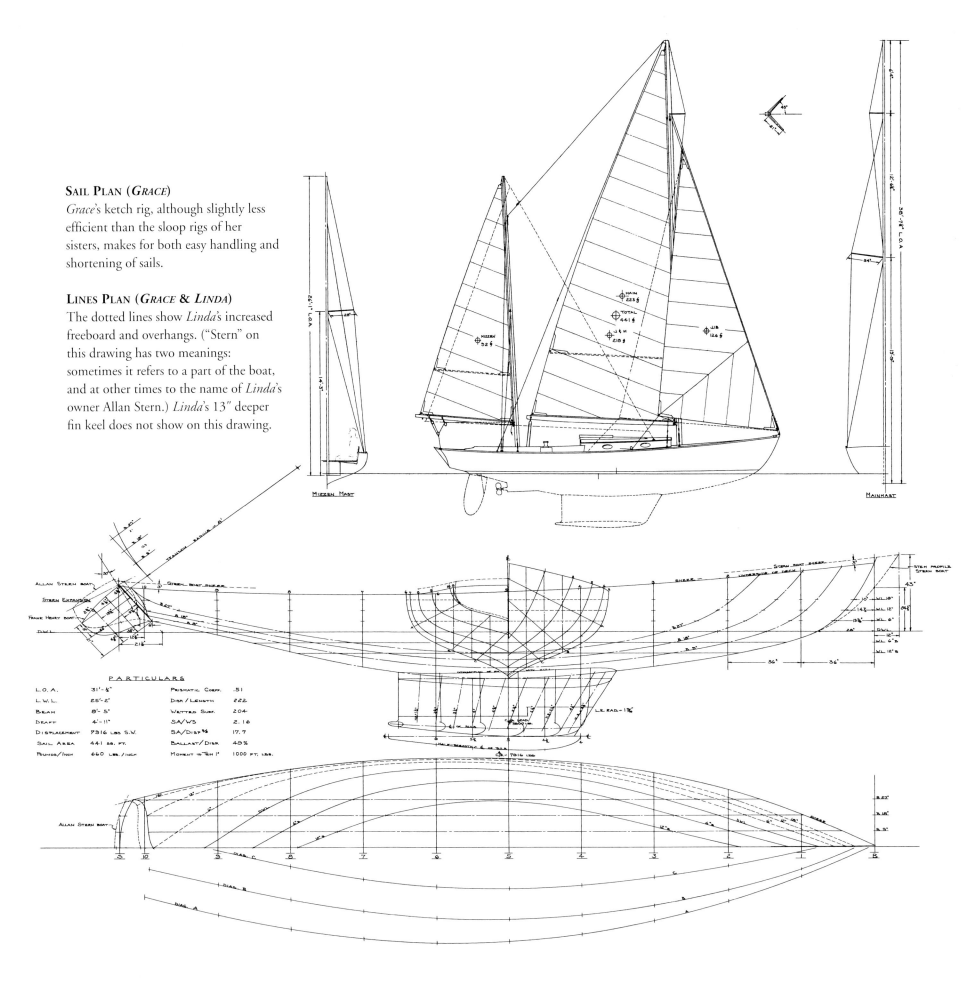

Sail Plan (*Grace*)

Grace's ketch rig, although slightly less efficient than the sloop rigs of her sisters, makes for both easy handling and shortening of sails.

Lines Plan (*Grace* & *Linda*)

The dotted lines show *Linda*'s increased freeboard and overhangs. ("Stern" on this drawing has two meanings: sometimes it refers to a part of the boat, and at other times to the name of *Linda*'s owner Allan Stern.) *Linda*'s 13″ deeper fin keel does not show on this drawing.

PARTICULARS

L.O.A.	31'-½"	Prismatic Coeff.	.51
L.W.L.	25'-2"	Disp/Length	222
Beam	8'-5"	Wetted Surf.	204
Draft	4'-11"	SA/WS	2.16
Displacement	7316 lbs S.W.	SA/Disp ⅓	17.7
Sail Area	441 sq. ft.	Ballast/Disp	49%
Pounds/Inch	660 lbs./inch	Moment to Trim 1"	1000 ft. lbs.

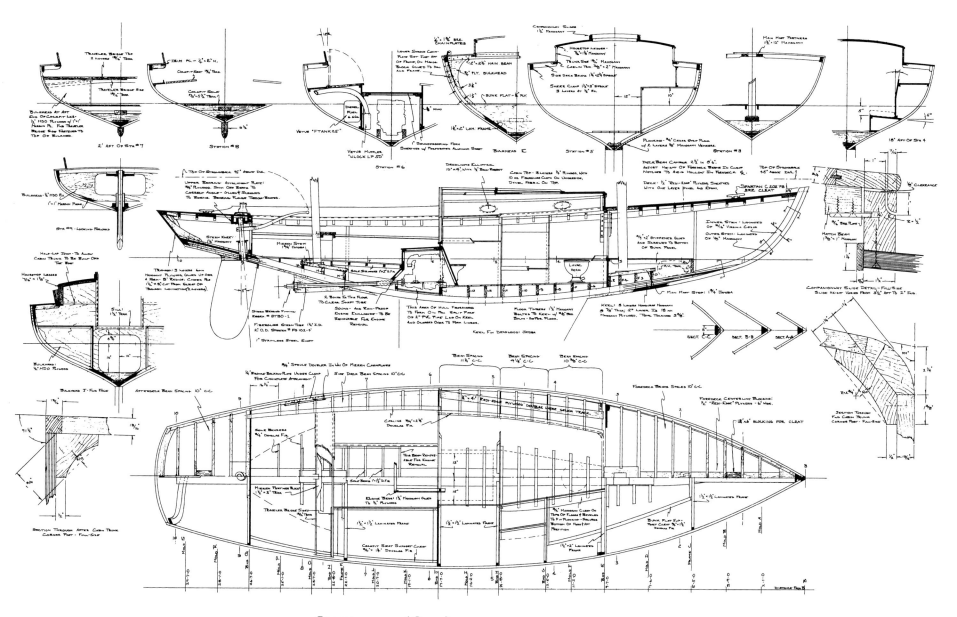

CONSTRUCTION (GRACE)

The Center Harbor 31s are small enough for floor timbers of wood instead of bronze to carry and distribute the fin keel's stresses. Conventional floor timbers also support the masts, and the type of elaborate bronze weldment Joel used for *Dragonera* and the Bottles' sloop has been eliminated here. To speed construction, the Center Harbor 31 trunk cabins are built separately over a jig and installed after the deck is completed.

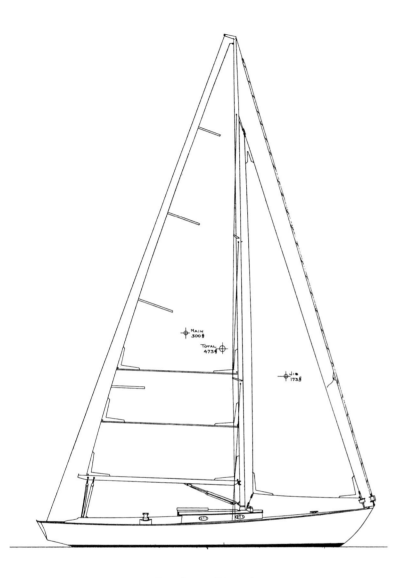

SAIL PLAN (*LINDA*)

Linda's tall rig makes her a potentially
fast boat. Her blade jib is self-tending,
made so by a radiused sheet track and a
jibsheet hauling part that is led up the
mast to a turning block. A roller furler
also helps dealing with the jib efficiently.

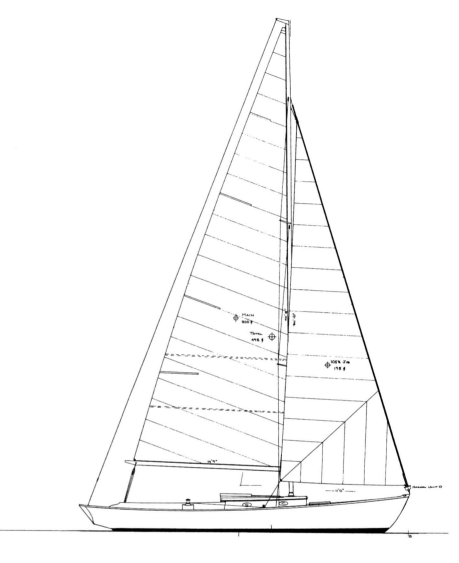

SAIL PLAN (*PUDDING*)

Pudding's tall rig is essentially the same
as *Linda*'s, but without the self-tending
jib. This gives her an incrementally larger
sail area. Minimalist cruising for two is
possible in this design, but the intended
use is primarily day sailing.

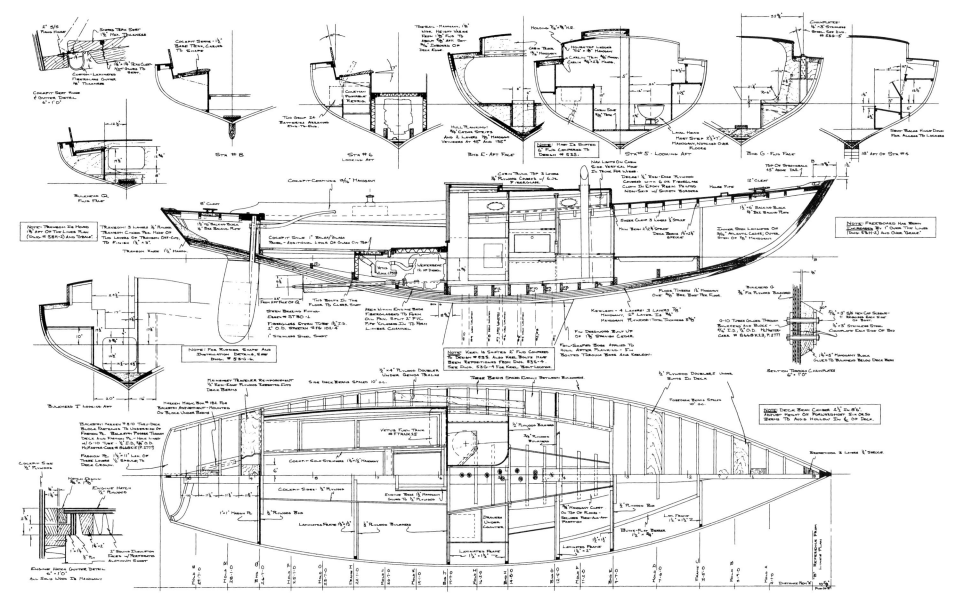

CONSTRUCTION PLAN (THE MANTLEPIECE)

In comparing this drawing with that of *Grace*, you'll find that an enclosed head has been added and the cockpit has been made roomier by eliminating the mizzenmast. This plan, as well as the corresponding plan for *Grace* and the sail plan for *Pudding*— all shown on previous pages—was drawn by Bob Stephens.

Wild Horses and *White Wings*

DESIGN NO. 55 (1995)

LOA	76'8"
LWL	53'11"
Beam	16'1"
Draft	11'0"
Displ.	52,000 lbs.
Sail Area	2,239 sq. ft.

Joel didn't have much faith in this project in the beginning, but he was intrigued with the type of boat that client Donald Tofias had in mind. The W-Class story begins in 1995 after Tofias bought the venerable double-ended, Burgess-designed cutter *Christmas*, renamed her *Arawak*, and asked Joel to make her faster by designing a new lead ballast keel to replace her original iron one, and a taller, more modern rig to go with it. In the process, Donald got to know Joel and Steve White, as well as Taylor Allen whose Rockport, Maine, yard would be executing Joel's redesign.

Tofias, having observed through Elizabeth Meyer and her J-boats how much fun really big boats can be, came up with the idea of reintroducing big class, one-design racing to the current and potential yacht racing fraternity. He logically based his thinking on New York 50 class sloops, a fleet of nine identical 72′ long gaff-rigged lovelies designed and built by Herreshoff in 1913. The 50s were one of the last big class one-designs—a type of yacht that died out after the First World War.

By 1913 Herreshoff had adopted an abrupt aft overhang that held little appeal for Joel and Donald. Both agreed that they'd prefer longer, more graceful sterns, and Joel mentioned as well that he didn't just want to tweak another Herreshoff design (as he had already done with the Haven and Flatfish), but preferred to create an entirely new boat, maybe based on certain Herreshoff elements, but not on a single Herreshoff design.

Joel had drawn some proposals and there'd been a few meetings between Donald, Joel, Steve, and Taylor with the idea that once they had a suitable design there'd be two identical boats built: one by Brooklin Boat Yard and the other by Rockport Marine. Joel and Donald also agreed that all rights to the final design would be owned by Donald's company Padanaram Yacht Co., LLC (subsequently renamed W-Class Yacht Co., LLC) instead of the designer, which is the usual custom. Joel could proceed with the design work without risk of the project being abandoned somewhere along the way. He'd be compensated whether or not the boats were ever built.

Joel soon homed in on a shape he and the others really liked. He'd become fond of Herreshoff's Buzzards Bay 25s which Steve's crew had recently turned out with cold-molded hulls. To assist in their construction, Joel had drawn their lines from the original Herreshoff offsets. For the

W-Class sloops he figured that if he adopted the general shape of the BB25 midsection and forebody then gave the rest of the boat his own treatment, he'd end up with a pretty good-looking design. What this meant was a long, raking, and fairly straight stem profile; considerable hollow to the bow, especially at the waterline; a steep and straight deadrise, a long and graceful aft overhang, low freeboard, and a subtle sheer that was noticeably higher at the bow than at the stern. He paid particular attention to shaping the ends of the boat, making the stem face increase in width as it rose from waterline to deckline, and giving the transom a reverse curve (a wineglass shape) near its low point and a touch of tumblehome at its upper corners as they approached the taffrail. Since the hull was to be cold-molded, Joel had to minimize severe concavity and shape the underbody to handle the fin keel and the spade rudder.

Even in this 76-footer, headroom is scant partly because of the low free-board and partly because of the shape of this boat's underbody. (With reversing sections, hollow garboards, a wineglass midbody, or however else

you choose to describe "old-fashioned" hull shapes, the cabin sole can be a good deal lower than in a canoe-bodied fin-keeler.) For headroom, Joel gave the W's a trunk cabin whereas Herreshoff's yachts of this size would have entirely flush decks, pierced only by skylights, hatches, and companionways. Other limiting size constraints were the length of Brooklin Boat Yard's shop and the width between its granite Travelift support piers.

Joel achieved a spectacularly beautiful result in what turned out to be his last design. With the hull shape, sail plan, and interior arrangement pinned down, Joel forged ahead with the remaining plans, assisted significantly by Bob Stephens, the upcoming and talented designer/builder who'd begun to take over designing and drafting as Joel's health gradually deteriorated.

To everyone's amazement, Donald Tofias announced in June of 1997 at the first Mystic Seaport-based WoodenBoat Show that he was ordering two W-76 sloops and that the first would be ready by spring of the following year. Exactly a year later, on June 23rd, 1998, *Wild Horses* took to the water ready to sail. Joel didn't live to see this, although he did witness the early stages of the first hull which was planked and ready to turn rightside up when he died in December.

White Wings followed at the end of that same summer, by which time *Wild Horses* had proven that this design sailed as fast as it was beautiful to look at. Taylor Allen and I helped Donald Tofias steer *Wild Horses* to a resounding victory in the Eggemoggin Reach Regatta, one of that boat's first big races. Since then, the W's have scored many wins and have demonstrated that despite low freeboard and large sail area, they are well-mannered at sea as well as swift around the race course.

As I sit in Antigua writing this early in 2001, both W's are here and have just crossed the starting line of the second day's 'Round the Island Race. There's a snapping good breeze, the crews know what they're doing, and we're waiting to watch them cross the finish line in Falmouth Harbor.

I expect they'll cross the line first. I believe they might also do well on corrected time in spite of their high rating. As it turned out, both W's broke the elapsed-time record for this race, *Wild Horses* by 40 minutes with *White Wings* close on her heels.

Next day the W's headed off for another race, this one in Grenada. The next will be St. Martin, then it's back to Antigua for the Classic Yacht Regatta at the end of April. Tofias then plans to ship them to the Mediterranean for their second summer of intense racing and promotion. How wonderful that so worthy a design, Joel White's finest, gets this kind of exposure.

Sail Plan

A carbon fiber mast and rod standing rigging constitute the part of the specifications that Joel included on this drawing. Although the contract for fabricating the entire rig would be farmed out—to Hall Spars in this case—Joel provided the key design parameters. The spar color isn't pinned down here, but the mast and boom were ordered in a lovely medium tan which does much to enhance the W's overall beauty. Likewise with the traditionally-cut sails all of which, including the spinnaker, were white. The two headsails are Joel's idea based on ease of handling and appearance, but in practice, the single genoa has prevailed.

Lines Plan

Specifying the exact shape of the stem face and transom becomes necessary if the finished yacht is to be faithful to her designer's intentions. In this drawing, Joel calls for a stem face that flares to 2½" at the deck, and a transom and aft overhang with reversing curves that have been precisely dimensioned. Although such design effort has little effect on performance since the upper stem and transom are both clear of the water, this kind of bow and stern depiction greatly influences a boat's beauty.

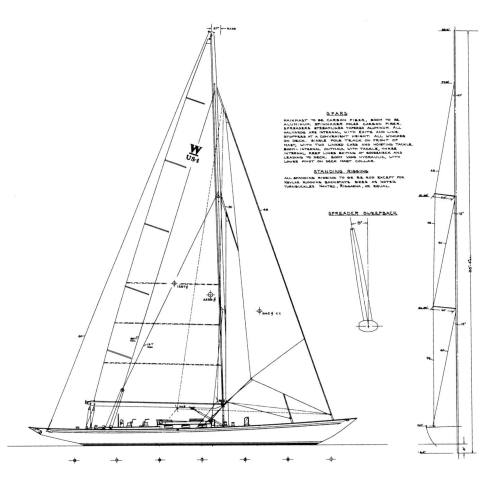

~ PARTICULARS ~

L. O. A.	~76'- 4"	PRISMATIC COEFF.	~.56	
L. W. L.	~53'- 11"	DISP./LENGTH	~149	
BEAM	~16'- 1"	WETTED SURF.	~778 SQ. FT.	
DRAFT	~11'- 0"	SA./W.S.	~2.87	
DISPLACEMENT	~52,800 LBS. S.W.	S.A./DISP ⅔	~25.6	
SAIL AREA	~2239 SQ. FT.	BALLAST/DISP.	~50%	
POUNDS/INCH	~2584 LBS.	MOMENT TO TRIM 1"	~9000 FT. LBS	

LINES to OUTSIDE of PLANK

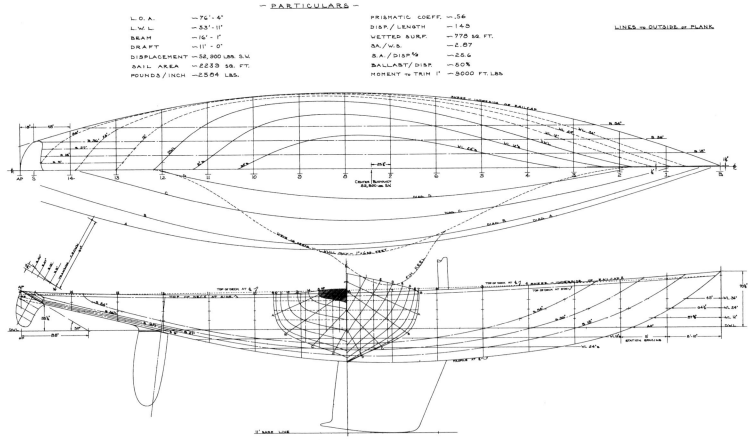

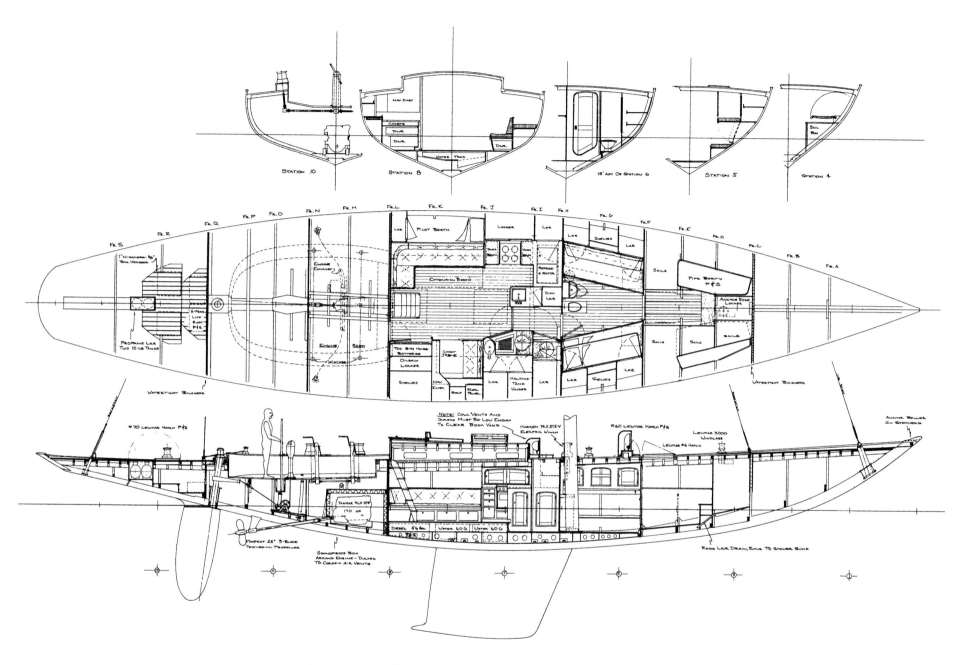

ARRANGEMENT PLAN

As is clear from this drawing, the living spaces are concentrated in the middle part of the hull directly over the fin keel where the motion at sea is the least. This keeps the weight out of the bow and stern which in turn reduces wave-induced pitching. The cockpit is huge with seating atop the coamings and a pair of two-speed, coffee-grinder winch pedestals on centerline ahead of the steering wheel. Linked together and clutched to one of the four single, coaming-mounted winch drums there'd be plenty of sheet-tending power and plenty of exercise for the crew.

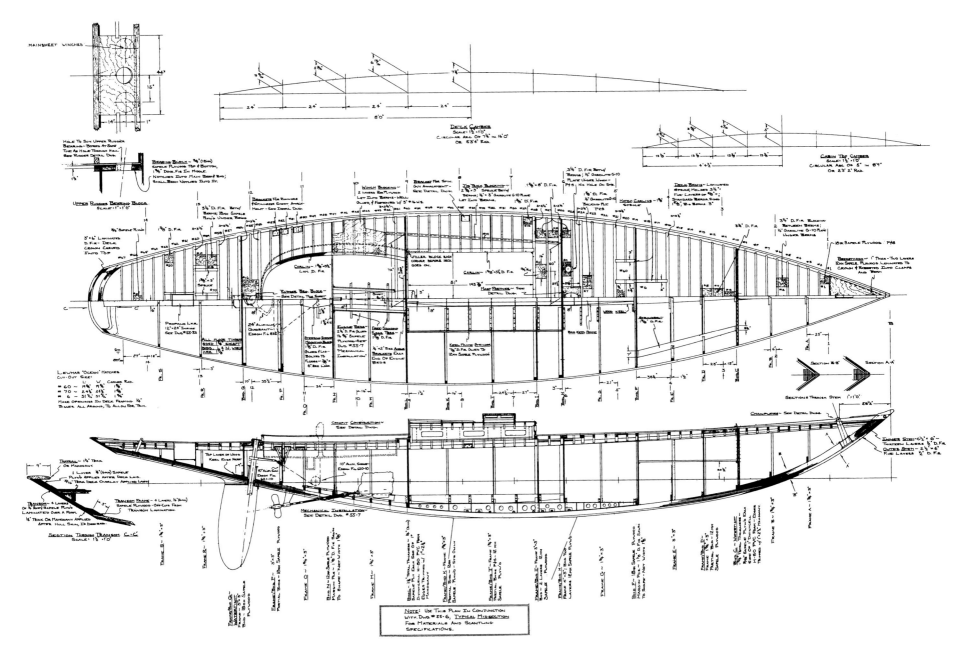

CONSTRUCTION PLAN

Glue plays a big role in this hull. The backbone is made in layers of $7/8''$ mahogany topped by a layer of $3/4''$ plywood all glued together. The stem is glued up from Douglas-fir, and the deck beams and sheer clamps are epoxy-glued from spruce. The five layers of wood and single layer of fiberglass that form the hull planking are also epoxied together, as are the three layers of wood that make up the deck. The hulls were built upside down over their bulkheads and their permanent, laminated Douglas-fir frames.

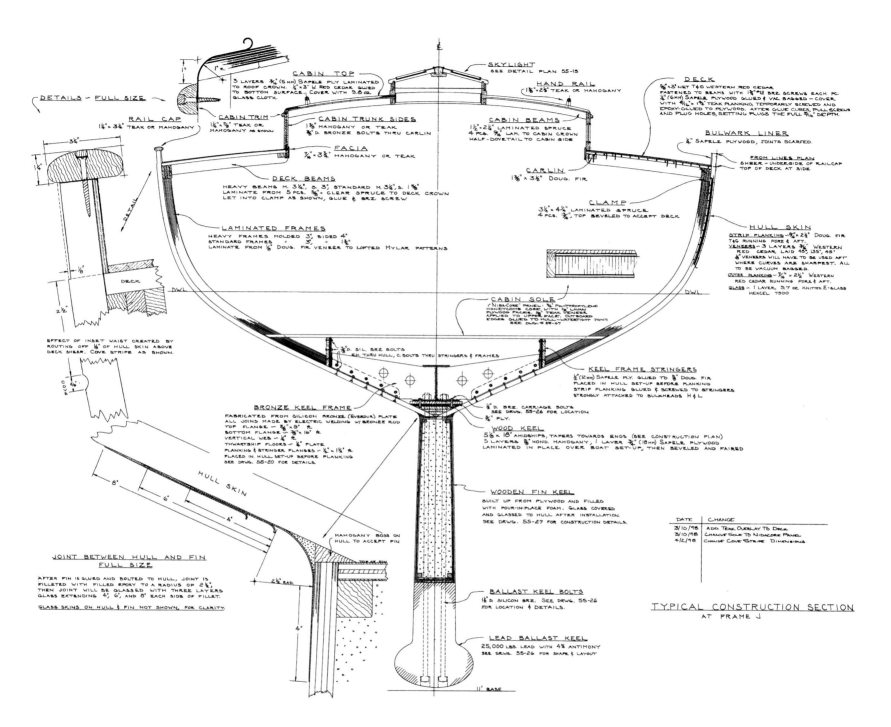

DETAILS ~ FULL SIZE

CABIN TOP
3 LAYERS 3/16" (5 MM) SAPELE PLY LAMINATED
TO ROOF CROWN. 1/8" W. RED CEDAR GLUED
TO BOTTOM SURFACE. COVER WITH 9.8 OZ.
GLASS CLOTH.

SKYLIGHT
SEE DETAIL PLAN 55-15

HAND RAIL
1 3/8" × 2 1/8" TEAK OR MAHOGANY

DECK
3/8" × 3" NET T&G WESTERN RED CEDAR
FASTENED TO BEAMS WITH 1 3/8" #12 BRZ SCREWS EACH PC.
1/4" (6MM) SAPELE PLYWOOD GLUED & VAC. BAGGED ~ COVER
WITH 5/16" × 1 3/8" TEAK PLANKING, TEMPORARILY SCREWED AND
EPOXY-GLUED TO PLYWOOD. AFTER GLUE CURES, PULL SCREWS
AND PLUG HOLES, SETTING PLUGS THE FULL 5/16" DEPTH.

RAIL CAP
1 1/8" × 3 1/4" TEAK OR MAHOGANY

CABIN TRIM
1 1/8" × 7/8" TEAK OR
MAHOGANY AS SHOWN

CABIN TRUNK SIDES
1 3/8" MAHOGANY OR TEAK
3/8" D. BRONZE BOLTS THRU CARLIN

CABIN BEAMS
1 1/2" × 2 1/8" LAMINATED SPRUCE
4 PCS. 9/16" LAM. TO CABIN CROWN
HALF-DOVETAIL TO CABIN SIDE

BULWARK LINER
1/4" SAPELE PLYWOOD, JOINTS SCARFED.

FROM LINES PLAN
SHEER ~ UNDERSIDE OF RAILCAP
TOP OF DECK AT SIDE

FACIA
7/8" × 3 3/4" MAHOGANY OR TEAK

DECK BEAMS
HEAVY BEAMS M. 3 1/2", S. 3", STANDARD M. 3 1/2", S. 1 5/8"
LAMINATE FROM 5 PCS. 5/8"+ CLEAR SPRUCE TO DECK CROWN
LET INTO CLAMP AS SHOWN, GLUE & BRZ. SCREW

CARLIN
1 3/8" × 3 1/2" DOUG. FIR

CLAMP
3 1/2" × 4 1/2" LAMINATED SPRUCE
4 PCS. 7/8", TOP BEVELED TO ACCEPT DECK

LAMINATED FRAMES
HEAVY FRAMES MOLDED 3 1/2", SIDED 4"
STANDARD FRAMES " 3", " 1 3/8"
LAMINATE FROM 1/8" DOUG. FIR VENEER TO LOFTED MYLAR PATTERNS

HULL SKIN
STRIP PLANKING ~ 3/8" × 2 1/8" DOUG. FIR
T&G RUNNING FORE & AFT.
VENEERS ~ 3 LAYERS 3/32" WESTERN
RED CEDAR LAID 45°, 135°, 45°
1/8" VENEERS WILL HAVE TO BE USED AFT
WHERE CURVES ARE SHARPEST. ALL
TO BE VACUUM BAGGED.
OUTER PLANKING ~ 7/16" × 2 1/8" WESTERN
RED CEDAR RUNNING FORE & AFT.
GLASS ~ 1 LAYER, 5.7 OZ. KNITTED E-GLASS
HEXCEL 7500

DETAIL

DECK

EFFECT OF INSET WAIST CREATED BY
ROUTING OFF 1/8" OF HULL SKIN ABOVE
DECK SHEER. COVE STRIPE AS SHOWN.

DWL

CABIN SOLE
1" NIBACORE PANEL 3/4" POLYPROPYLENE
HONEYCOMB CORE, WITH 1/8" LAUAN
PLYWOOD FACES. 3/4" TEAK VENEER
APPLIED TO UPPER FACE. OUTBOARD
EDGES GLUED TO HULL~WATERTIGHT JOINT
SEE DWG. 55 #6-67

3/8" D. SIL. BRZ. BOLTS
E.H. THRU HULL, C. BOLTS THRU STRINGERS & FRAMES

DWL

KEEL FRAME STRINGERS
1/2" (12 MM) SAPELE PLY. GLUED TO 5/8" DOUG. FIR
PLACED IN HULL SET-UP BEFORE PLANKING
STRIP PLANKING GLUED & SCREWED TO STRINGERS
STRONGLY ATTACHED TO BULKHEADS H & L

1/2" D. BRZ. CARRIAGE BOLTS
SEE DRWG. 55-26 FOR LOCATION

3/4" PLY.

BRONZE KEEL FRAME
FABRICATED FROM SILICON BRONZE (EVERDUR) PLATE
ALL JOINS MADE BY ELECTRIC WELDING W/ BRONZE ROD
TOP FLANGE ~ 5/8" × 9" ft.
BOTTOM FLANGE ~ 3/8" × 16" ft.
VERTICAL WEB ~ 1/4" ft.
THWARTSHIP FLOORS ~ 1/4" ft.
PLANKING & STRINGER FLANGES ~ 1/4" × 1 1/2" ft.
PLACED IN HULL SET-UP BEFORE PLANKING
SEE DRWG. 55-20 FOR DETAILS.

WOOD KEEL
5 5/8" × 18" AMIDSHIPS, TAPERS TOWARDS ENDS (SEE CONSTRUCTION PLAN)
5 LAYERS 7/8" HOND. MAHOGANY, 1 LAYER 3/4" (18 MM) SAPELE PLYWOOD
LAMINATED IN PLACE OVER BOAT SET-UP, THEN BEVELED AND FAIRED

HULL SKIN

WOODEN FIN KEEL
BUILT UP FROM PLYWOOD AND FILLED
WITH POUR-IN-PLACE FOAM. GLASS COVERED
AND GLASSED TO HULL AFTER INSTALLATION.
SEE DRWG. 55-27 FOR CONSTRUCTION DETAILS.

MAHOGANY BOSS ON
HULL TO ACCEPT FIN

JOINT BETWEEN HULL AND FIN
FULL SIZE

AFTER FIN IS GLUED AND BOLTED TO HULL, JOINT IS
FILLETED WITH FILLED EPOXY TO A RADIUS OF 2 1/2",
THEN JOINT WILL BE GLASSED WITH THREE LAYERS
GLASS EXTENDING 4", 6", AND 8" EACH SIDE OF FILLET.

GLASS SKINS ON HULL & FIN NOT SHOWN, FOR CLARITY.

2 1/2" RAD.

BALLAST KEEL BOLTS
1 1/2" D. SILICON BRZ. SEE DRWG. 55-26
FOR LOCATION & DETAILS.

LEAD BALLAST KEEL
25,000 LBS. LEAD WITH 4% ANTIMONY
SEE DRWG. 55-26 FOR SHAPE & LAYOUT

11' BASE

DATE	CHANGE
3/10/98	ADD TEAK OVERLAY TO DECK
3/10/98	CHANGE SOLE TO NIDACORE PANEL
4/2/98	CHANGE COVE STRIPE DIMENSIONS.

TYPICAL CONSTRUCTION SECTION
AT FRAME J

TYPICAL CONSTRUCTION SECTION

Since the footprint of the fin keel on the hull is so narrow and small, the method of connecting it has to be carefully thought out. This drawing provides those details. The fin is basically a foam-filled, plywood-sided box through which the eleven 1½" diameter keel bolts pass. At their lower ends the bolts are recessed into the 25,000-pound lead ballast casting, while at their upper ends they pass through the bottom flange of the welded-bronze keel frame where they are secured with nuts. Additional details are shown here as well—the fin keel-to-hull fairing, and the inset waist, the railcaps, and the trunk cabin being examples.

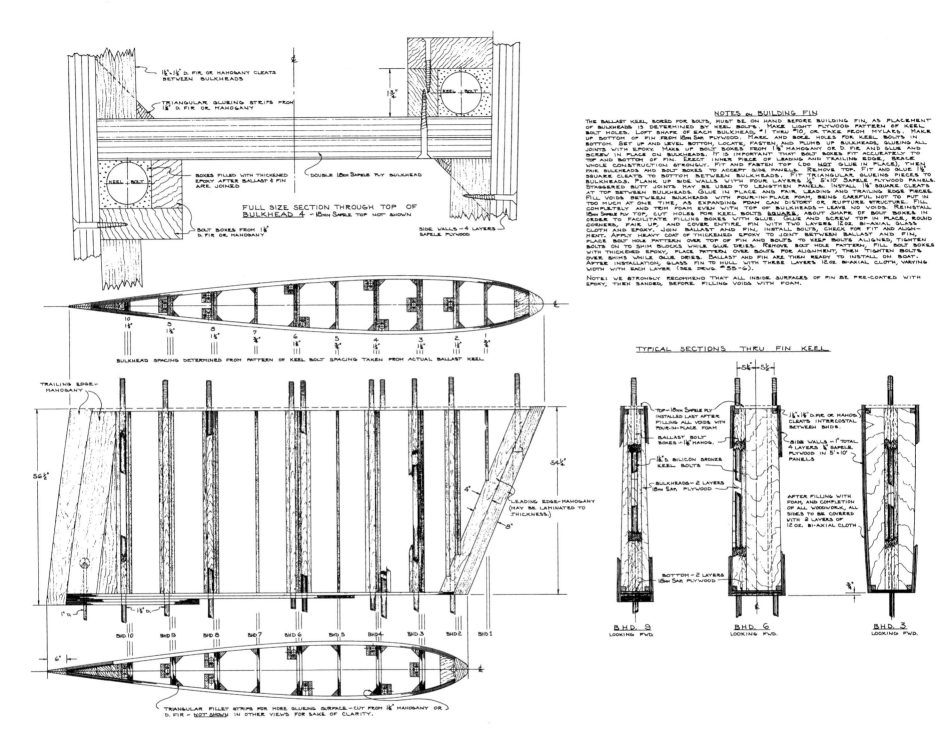

FULL SIZE SECTION THROUGH TOP OF
BULKHEAD 4 – 18mm SAPELE TOP NOT SHOWN

NOTES ON BUILDING FIN

THE BALLAST KEEL, BORED FOR BOLTS, MUST BE ON HAND BEFORE BUILDING FIN, AS PLACEMENT OF BULKHEADS IS DETERMINED BY KEEL BOLTS. MAKE LIGHT PLYWOOD PATTERN OF KEEL BOLT HOLES. LOFT SHAPE OF EACH BULKHEAD, #1 THRU #10, OR TAKE FROM MYLARS. MAKE UP BOTTOM OF FIN FROM 18mm SAPELE PLYWOOD. MARK AND BORE HOLES FOR KEEL BOLTS IN BOTTOM. SET UP AND LEVEL BOTTOM, LOCATE, FASTEN AND PLUMB UP BULKHEADS, GLUEING ALL JOINTS WITH EPOXY. MAKE UP BOLT BOXES FROM 1⅛" MAHOGANY OR D. FIR AND GLUE AND SCREW IN PLACE ON BULKHEADS. IT IS IMPORTANT THAT BOLT BOXES FIT ACCURATELY TO TOP AND BOTTOM OF FIN. ERECT INNER PIECE OF LEADING AND TRAILING EDGE, BRACE WHOLE CONSTRUCTION STRONGLY. FIT AND FASTEN TOP (DO NOT GLUE IN PLACE), THEN FAIR BULKHEADS AND BOLT BOXES TO ACCEPT SIDE PANELS. REMOVE TOP. FIT AND GLUE 1½ SQUARE CLEATS TO BOTTOM BETWEEN BULKHEADS. FIT TRIANGULAR GLUEING PIECES TO BULKHEADS. PLANK UP SIDE WALLS WITH FOUR LAYERS ¼" 5'×10' SAPELE PLYWOOD PANELS. STAGGERED BUTT JOINTS MAY BE USED TO LENGTHEN PANELS. INSTALL 1½" SQUARE CLEATS AT TOP BETWEEN BULKHEADS. GLUE IN PLACE AND FAIR LEADING AND TRAILING EDGE PIECES. FILL VOIDS BETWEEN BULKHEADS WITH POUR-IN-PLACE FOAM, BEING CAREFUL NOT TO PUT IN TOO MUCH AT ONE TIME, AS EXPANDING FOAM CAN DISTORT OR RUPTURE STRUCTURE. FILL COMPLETELY AND TRIM FOAM EVEN WITH TOP OF BULKHEADS – LEAVE NO VOIDS. REINSTALL 18mm SAPELE PLY TOP, CUT HOLES FOR KEEL BOLTS SQUARE, ABOUT SHAPE OF BOLT BOXES IN ORDER TO FACILITATE FILLING BOXES WITH GLUE. GLUE AND SCREW TOP IN PLACE, ROUND CORNERS, FAIR UP, AND COVER ENTIRE FIN WITH TWO LAYERS 12oz. BI-AXIAL GLASS CLOTH AND EPOXY. JOIN BALLAST AND FIN, INSTALL BOLTS, CHECK FOR FIT AND ALIGN- MENT. APPLY HEAVY COAT OF THICKENED EPOXY TO JOINT BETWEEN BALLAST AND FIN. PLACE BOLT HOLE PATTERN OVER TOP OF FIN TO KEEP BOLTS ALIGNED, TIGHTEN BOLTS ON TO SHIM BLOCKS WHILE GLUE DRIES. REMOVE BOLT HOLE PATTERN, FILL BOLT BOXES WITH THICKENED EPOXY, PLACE PATTERN OVER BOLTS FOR ALIGNMENT, THEN TIGHTEN BOLTS OVER SHIMS WHILE GLUE DRIES. BALLAST AND FIN ARE THEN READY TO INSTALL ON BOAT. AFTER INSTALLATION, GLASS FIN TO HULL WITH THREE LAYERS 12oz. BI-AXIAL CLOTH, VARYING WIDTH WITH EACH LAYER (SEE DRWG. #52-6).

NOTE: WE STRONGLY RECOMMEND THAT ALL INSIDE SURFACES OF FIN BE PRE-COATED WITH EPOXY, THEN SANDED, BEFORE FILLING VOIDS WITH FOAM.

TYPICAL SECTIONS THRU FIN KEEL

BHD. 9
LOOKING FWD.

BHD. 6
LOOKING FWD.

BHD. 3
LOOKING FWD.

FIN KEEL CONSTRUCTION

This teardrop-shaped plywood box serves as a spacer between the hull and the lead ballast keel. It is built around ten plywood bulkheads and a leading and trailing edge that give shape to the ends. Joel built this unit step by step in his mind then carefully described the building process in 30 lines of hand-lettered text entitled "Notes on Building Fin."

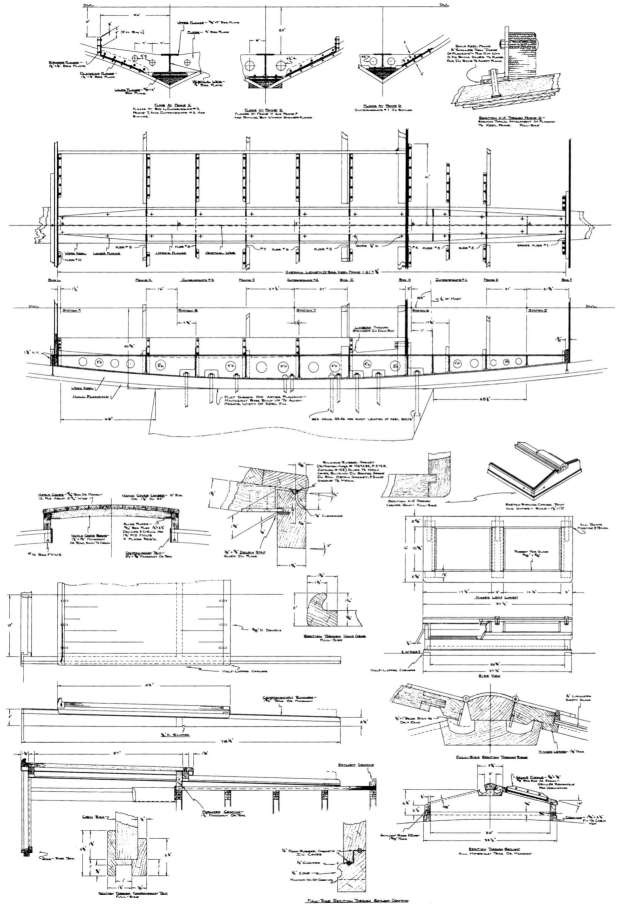

BRONZE KEEL FRAME

This welded bronze unit is what holds the fin keel securely to the hull, and spreads out the load so that all members stay together during normal use and can survive without damage if the yacht accidentally drives onto a ledge. The keel frame is hoisted atop the hull frames soon after they are set up, and bolts securely to them. Its ends attach to structural bulkheads and its sides run outboard to the two laminated stringers that form the sides of this robust box-like keel frame. When everything is fair the first layer of hull planking ($\frac{9}{16}''$ Douglas-fir strips) is put down and then bolted to the keel frame as detailed on this drawing.

COMPANIONWAY AND SKYLIGHT DETAILS

This plan, as well as a number of others including three of those above, were drawn by Bob Stephens who worked closely with Joel and gradually took over Brooklin Boat Yard's designing as Joel's health deteriorated. Like Joel, Bob can build anything he can draw, and comes at designing from a builder's perspective. Near the end of his life Joel told me how pleased he was to have Bob assume the role of designer—a pleasure equal to his feelings about his son Steve having taken over the yard's operation. Joel left this world well satisfied that Brooklin Boat Yard was in good hands that would continue designing and building strong, durable, fast, and beautiful boats.

Joel White Design List

DESIGN NO.	YEAR	LOA	TYPE	NAME	CLIENT	BUILDER
0	1954	34'0"	Tunnel-sterned powerboat	power cruiser	Martin Quigley	Newbert & Wallace
1	1962	34'0"	Power cruiser	*Kishti*	Anthony Michel	Brooklin Boat Yard
2	1963	9'6"	V-bottomed plywood skiff	*Martha's* Tender	E.B. White et al.	Brooklin Boat Yard et al.
3	1969	35'3"	Cruising sloop	*Cachalot*	Peter Sturtevant	Brooklin Boat Yard
4	1975	34'0"	Tugboat (steel)	*Mussel*	Russ Devereux	Devereux
5	1975	34'0"	Power cruiser	*High Time*	Peg Hunt	Brooklin Boat Yard
6	1976	9'0"	Sailing dinghy	dinghy	Peter Black	Brooklin Boat Yard
7	1976	8'4"	Pram	*Stormsvala*	Alex Forbes	not built
8	1977	60'0"	Scallop dragger	*Nicole*	John Jones	Wallace
9	1978	14'0"	Peapod	peapod	Ted Leonard & WB	Brooklin Boat Yard et al.
10	1979	42'0"	Power cruiser	*Lady Jeanne*	Joe & Jeanne Merkel	Brooklin Boat Yard
11	1980	36'0"	Cruising ketch	*Alisande*	H.K. Faulkner	Brooklin Boat Yard
12	1980	41'0"	Lobsterboat (fiberglass)	lobsterboat	Duffy & Duffy	Duffy & Duffy
13	1980	12'8"	Sailing dinghy	Catspaw dinghy	Ben Emory & WB	Brooklin Boat Yard et al.
14	1981	20'0"	Sliding-seat rowing shell	*Bangor Packet*	Ted Leonard	Brooklin Boat Yard et al.
15	1981	50'1"	Power cruiser	*Maine Idea*	A.S. Martin	Brooklin Boat Yard
16	1981	23'0"	Sliding-seat rowing shell	*Gerry Wherry*	Dave Bradley	Brooklin Boat Yard
17	1982	32'0"	Cruising cutter	*Mimi Rose*	Bill Page	Swift/Page
18	1983	20'0"	V-bottomed daysailer	sloop	Todd Cheney	not built
19	1983	7'7"	Sailing pram	Nutshell Pram	Sarah Bray & WB	Brooklin Boat Yard et al.
20	1983	10'4"	Sailing dinghy	dinghy	WB School	WoodenBoat School
21	1983	35'0"	Cruising cutter	*Forthright*	John Carson	Swift
22	1984	16'0"	Double-ended pulling boat	Shearwater	White & WB	Brooklin Boat Yard et al.
23	1984	9'6"	Sailing pram	Nutshell Pram	Frank Walker & WB	Brooklin Boat Yard et al.
24	1984	24'0"	Cruising sloop (fiberglass)	Bridges Point 24	Wade Dow	Bridges Point Boat Yard
25	1984	33'0"	Cruising sloop	*Keloose*	Gerry Peer	Covey Island Boat Works
26	1985	12'0"	Sailing dinghy	*Just a Mite*	Bill Page	Rockport Apprenticeshop
27	1985	36'0"	Power cruiser	power cruiser	Tom Welch	not built
28	1985	32'5"	Power cruiser	*Lark*	Tom Welch	Swift

Design No.	Year	LOA	Type	Name	Client	Builder
29	1986	29'4"	Double-ended cruising sloop	*Circle*	Glenn Baldwin	Baldwin
30	1986	22'0"	Double-ended daysailer	Fox Island class	Geoff Heath	Heath et al.
31	1987	15'0"	Catboat	Marsh Cat	Sam Holdsworth	Brooklin Boat Yard et al.
32	1988	20'0"	Garvey	*Marika*	Mosquita Indians	WoodenBoat School
33	1988	30'11"	Power dory	*Venita*	Mosquita Indians	WoodenBoat School
34	1988	83'0"	Sardine carrier (conversion)	*Pauline*	Ken & Ellen Barnes	Barnes et al.
35	1989	16'0"	Keel/centerboard daysailer	Haven 12½	Sam Neel & WB	various
36	1989	32'0"	Admiral's barge	water taxi	unknown	not built
37	1989	43'0"	Cruising cutter	*Sweet Olive*	H.K. Faulkner	Brooklin Boat Yard
38	1989	11'2"	Sailing dinghy	Shellback	Joel White	Brooklin Boat Yard et al.
39	1989	32'0"	Cruising sloop	sloop	Allan Stern	not built
40	1990	12'10"	Sailing dinghy	Pooduck Skiff	WB & Dick Hawes	Brooklin Boat Yard et al.
41	1990	46'0"	Fast powerboat	Eggemoggin 45	A.G.A. Correa	not built
42	1990	20'10"	Outboard runabout	*Snapshot*	Ben Mendlowitz	not built
43	1990	15'0"	Guideboat	guideboat	Eric Dow	not built
44	1991	18'0"	Electric launch	launch	Henry Davis	not built
45	1991	19'0"	Outboard runabout	runabout	Slick Craft	Norton et al.
46	1991	26'0"	Cruising ketch	ketch	Charles Butcher	not built
47	1992	23'0"	Double-ended daysailer	*Lala*	Tom McGuane	Norton et al.
48	1992	44'0"	Cruising ketch	ketch	Woodson Woods	not built
49	1993	74'0"	Fast cruising ketch	*Dragonera*	Bruce Stevens	Brooklin Boat Yard
50	1994	62'2"	Fast cruising sloop	sloop	Kim & Sue Bottles	not built
51	1994	42'1"	Cabin launch	*Everglades*	Mike & Ann Matheson	Matheson
52	1995	20'3"	Cabin daysailer	Flatfish	WB & Joe Youcha	Youcha et al.
53H	1995	31'1"	Cabin ketch (CH-31)	*Grace*	Frank Henry, Sr.	Brooklin Boat Yard
53S	1995	32'3"	Cabin sloop (CH-31)	*Linda*	Allan Stern	Brooklin Boat Yard
53G	1997	32'0"	Cabin sloop (CH-31)	*The Mantlepiece*	James Geier	Brooklin Boat Yard
53D	1997	31'2"	Cabin sloop (CH-31)	*Pudding*	George Denny	Brooklin Boat Yard
55	1995	76'8"	W-Class sloops	*Wild Horses* & *White Wings*	Donald Tofias	BBY & Rockport Marine

Boats Built by Brooklin Boat Yard

Year	LOA	Name	Client	Designer	Type	Material
1962	34'0"	*Miss Caroline*	MacDonald	MacDonald	Lobsterboat	W
1963	34'0"	*Kishti*	Michel	White	Power cruiser	W
1964	30'0"	*Manana*	Nealy	Hamlin	Cruising sloop	WS
1965	36'7"	*Daisy*	Nichols	Alden	Cruising cutter	W
1966	39'0"	*Surfing Seal*	Williamson	Gilmer & Williamson	Cruising ketch	WS
1967	32'5"	*Amita*	Thatcher	Hamlin	Cruising yawl	WS
1967	20'0"	*Martha*	White	Crocker	Cruising sloop	W
1967	9'6"	*Martha*'s Tender	White	White	V-bottom tender	PW
1968	34'0"	*Mary H.*	Heanssler	Webbers Cove	Lobsterboat	FG
1969	34'3"	*James Adger*	Neel	Hamlin	Cruising ketch	PW
1969	18'7"	*Brilliant*	Mystic Seaport	Herreshoff	Yacht tender	W
1969	18'7"	*Clearwater*	Clearwater	Herreshoff	Tender	W
1970	35'3"	*Cachalot*	Sturtevant	White	Cruising sloop	WS
1971	36'0"	*Nasket II*	Grindle	Crocker & White	Cruising ketch	WS
1972	36'0"	*Nannook*	Holbrook	Newman & White	Power cruiser	FG
1973	37'0"	*Jericho Queen*	Thompson	Repco	Lobsterboat	FG
1973	36'0"	*Lulu*	Gove	Newman & White	Lobsterboat	FG
1974	36'0"	*Myrna & Sandra*	Gove	Stanley & White	Lobsterboat	FG
1974	42'5"	*Dovekie*	Bancroft	McIntosh & White	Cruising ketch	W
1975	36'0"	*Kristy Leigh*	Hutchinson	Stanley & White	Lobsterboat	FG
1975	37'0"	*Interport*	Interport Pilots	Repco & Wallstrom	Pilot boat	FG
1975	36'0"	*Thetis*	CMP	Stanley & White	Patrol boat	FG
1976	34'0"	*High Time*	Hunt	White	Power cruiser	W
1976	36'0"	*Dream On*	Sherman	Stanley & White	Lobsterboat	FG
1976	9'0"	Sailing dinghy	Black	White	Lapstrake dinghy	W
1976	37'0"	*Mary Noreen*	Greenlaw	Repco & White	Lobsterboat	FG
1977	40'0"	*Marie C III*	Clifford	Webbers Cove & White	Lobsterboat	FG
1977	44'0"	*Shirley & Freeman*	Robbins	Stanley & White	Lobsterboat	FG
1978	40'0"	*Leeway*	Hollingsworth	Webbers Cove & White	Power cruiser	FG
1978	14'0"	(Peapod)	Leonard	White	Peapod	W
1979	30'0"	*Kimberly T*	White	Holland & White	Lobsterboat	FG
1979	30'0"	*Tansy*	Garseau	Holland & White	Open launch	FG
1979	37'0"	*Connemara Bay*	O'Hara	Repco & White	Lobsterboat	FG
1980	42'0"	*Lady Jeanne*	Merkel	White	Power cruiser	W
1980	32'0"	*Mary Elizabeth*	Hutchinson	Holland & White	Lobsterboat	FG
1980	12'8"	Catspaw dinghy	Emory	Herreshoff & White	Sailing dinghy	W
1981	36'0"	*Alisande*	Faulkner	Hand & White	Cruising ketch	W
1981	20'0"	*Bangor Packet*	Leonard	White	Sliding-seat rowing shell	WC
1982	23'0"	*Gerry Wherry*	Bradley	White	Sliding-seat rowing shell	WC
1982	50'1"	*Maine Idea*	Martin	White	Power cruiser	W
1983	7'7"	*Sarah's Swallow*	Bray	White	Nutshell Pram	WL
1983	38'6"	*Lucy Bell*	Sellers	Brewer & Wallstrom	Friendship sloop	W

Year	LOA	Name	Client	Designer	Type	Material
1983	7'7"	*Nutshell*	Mayher	White	Nutshell Pram	WL
1983	7'7"	*Restless*	White	White	Nutshell Pram	WL
1984	7'7"	Nutshell Pram	Wilson	White	Nutshell Pram	WL
1984	16'0"	Castine Class, 2 boats	Eaton	Eaton	Daysailing sloops	W
1984	9'6"	Nutshell Pram	Walker	White	Nutshell Pram	WL
1984	16'0"	Shearwater	White	White	Double-ended pulling boat	WL
1985	29'10"	*Trouble*	Varney	Hamlin	Cruising cutter	WS
1986	26'0"	Runabout hulls, 2 boats	Matheson	Hacker	Runabouts	W
1986	16'0"	*Petrel*	Neel	Herreshoff & White	Haven 12½ sloop	W
1986	45'0"	*Vintage*	Mitchell	Culler	Scow schooner	W
1987	24'0"	*Ellisha*	White	White	Bridges Point 24 sloop	FG
1987	24'0"	*Quarter Moon*	Edgerton	Long & White	Ketch	WC
1988	15'5"	Tugboat	Cannell	Culler	Harbor tug	W
1988	16'0"	*Bluebird*	Clagget	Herresoff & White	Haven 12½ sloop	W
1988	24'0"	*Caution*	Myers	White	Bridges Point 24 sloop	FG
1988	15'0"	*Homer*	Holdsworth	White	Marsh Cat	WC
1989	11'2"	Shellback	White	White	Shellback dinghy	WL
1990	52'6"	*Vortex*	White	Reimers	Swede 55 sloop	WC
1990	12'8"	Catspaw	Rogers	Herreshoff & White	Catspaw Dinghy	W
1990	12'10"	*Lamb*	Hawes	White	Pooduck skiff	WL
1991	43'0"	*Sweet Olive*	Faulkner	White	Cruising cutter	W
1992	55'6"	*Aurora*	Sheldon	Tripp	Racing sloop	CP
1993	47'11"	*Lucayo*	Wick	Marshall	Cruising sloop	WC
1994	74'0"	*Dragonera*	Stevens	White	Fast cruising ketch	WC
1994	59'3"	*Rosie B*	Solton	Sprague & Stephens	Tugboat cruiser	WC
1995	32'3"	*High Cotton*	Gill	Herreshoff	Buzzards Bay-25 sloop	WC
1995	32'3"	*Pride*	Duncan	Herreshoff	Buzzards Bay-25 sloop	WC
1996	32'3"	*Tomahawk*	Wharton	Herreshoff	Buzzards Bay-25 sloop	WC
1996	31'1"	*Grace*	Henry	White	Center Harbor-31 ketch	WC
1996	32'3"	*Linda*	Stern	White	Center Harbor-31 sloop	WC
1997	32'0"	*The Mantlepiece*	Geier	White	Center Harbor-31 sloop	WC
1997	31'2"	*Pudding*	Denny	White	Center Harbor-31 sloop	WC
1997	22'8"	*Tango*	Coombs	White & Stephens	Outboard runabout	PW
1998	76'8"	*Wild Horses*	Tofias	White	W-Class sloop	WC
1999	39'4"	*Va Pensiaro*	Weber	Stephens	Center Harbor-39 sloop	WC
1999	35'0"	*Kells*	McShane	White & Stephens	Center Harbor-35 sloop	WC
1999	10'11"	Dinghy	Grishman	Stephens	Dinghy	WS
2000	69'10"	*Sonny*	Phelps	Empacher	Cruising sloop	WC
2001	35'4"	*Tendress*	Manheimer	Stephens	Babson Island-35 sloop	WC
2001	46'7"	*Lena*	Schotte	Stephens	Racing sloop	WC
2001	44'11"	*Zingara*	Lawson	Peterson/Waring	Cruising yawl	WC

Key: W = WOOD (PLANK ON FRAME); WC = WOOD (COLD MOLDED); WL = WOOD (LAPSTRAKE PLYWOOD); WS = WOOD (STRIP-PLANKED);
PW = SHEET PLYWOOD; CP = COMPOSITE; FG = FIBERGLASS (BARE HULLS PRODUCED IN OTHER SHOPS)